"Here you'll find answers to questions you never knew you had—not just about miracles, but about what can happen to you if you dare to say yes to the Love behind them."

—Patrick Coffin, author and radio host
Catholic Answers Live

"Anyone picking up this book will be moved by these manifestations of the love of God reaching into human lives with healing power. Take up and read! You will enjoy!"

—Patti Gallagher Mansfield
Catholic Charismatic Renewal

"At a time when the world has deluded itself into thinking that science has all the answers, this book reminds us that God has answers of his own."

—Matthew Kelly, *New York Times* bestselling
author of *Rediscover Catholicism* and
founder of DynamicCatholic.com

"It is possible to be holy in the modern world, and the miraculous lives described by Patricia Treece will serve as both your model and inspiration in your life of faith!"

—Msgr. Richard Soseman,
Congregation for the Clergy, Vatican City

Nothing Short of a Miracle

Patricia Treece

Nothing Short of a Miracle

God's Healing Power in Modern Saints

SOPHIA INSTITUTE PRESS

Manchester, New Hampshire

Nothing Short of a Miracle was first published as an Image book in 1988 by Doubleday, a division of Bantam Doubleday, Dell Publishing Group, Inc., New York. Our Sunday Visitor, Huntington, Indiana, published a second edition in 1994. This 2013 updated edition by Sophia Institute Press adds recent cures and several chapters of completely new material on very recent saints and their authenticated miracles.

Sophia Institute Press

Box 5284, Manchester, NH 03108

1-800-888-9344

www.SophiaInstitute.com

Sophia Institute Press® is a registered trademark of Sophia Institute.

Library of Congress Cataloging-in-Publication Data

Treece, Patricia.
    Nothing short of a miracle : God's healing power in modern saints / Patricia Treece.
        pages cm
    Originally published: New York : Image Books, 1988.
    Includes bibliographical references.
    ISBN 978-1-933184-58-6 (pbk. : alk. paper) 1. Christian saints—Cult.
    2. Spiritual healing—Catholic Church. I. Title.
    BX2325.T73 2013
    231.7'3—dc23

                                                    2013016141

First printing

This book is for
JESUS:
Even Your greatest saints only mirror You dimly.
Jesus, may we love You as they do.
And may You gather us all, writer and readers,
into Your healing and life-giving arms.

Contents

Prologue

"Nothing Short of a Miracle Can Help This Kid"

March 14, 1921

Yawning openly on this gray afternoon, a young nurse makes a last round of her newborn charges in New York City's Columbus Hospital Extension on 163rd Street. In the final moments of an unusually busy shift, the weary nurse's thoughts are already far from babies as she bends over the whimpering Smith infant at whose midday birth she assisted two hours earlier.

Instantly wide awake, Mae Redmond gasps, "Oh God! Oh God!" for infant Smith's face is like charred wood, cheeks and lips blackened and burnt. Pus exudes from both tiny nostrils. Worst, where eyes should be are only two grotesque edemic swellings.

Horrified, Mae must struggle not to pass out as her mind grasps for how this can be. No one has handled the newborn after his normal delivery since she herself weighed and measured him and put in the eye drops prescribed by law.

The drops! Suddenly her panic lunges in a definite direction. She staggers across the nursery and picks up the bottle of 1-percent silver-nitrate solution used in the newborn's eyes. What she reads on the label makes her shriek hysterically again and again, "Doctor! Oh God! Get a doctor!"

Into infant Peter Smith's eyes the rushed nurse has deftly dropped, carefully pulling back each lid to get it all in, not 1-percent silver-nitrate solution, but 50-percent silver-nitrate solution. Even 5-percent to 25-percent solution is used only on unwanted human tissue—tumors, for instance—because it eats away flesh as effectively as electric cauterizing tools. Fifty-percent solution will gradually bore a hole in a solid piece of wood. And it has already been at work on the soft human tissue of infant Peter's eyes for two hours.

Dr. John G. Grimley is the first physician to hear the nurse's shrill cries. Looking at the badly burnt face and the bottle label, the suddenly ashen-faced doctor can only shake his head helplessly. A few minutes later he is reporting to an anguished Mother Teresa Bacigalupo, Superior of the Missionary Sisters of the Sacred Heart who own and run Columbus Hospital, that the nurse has accidentally destroyed a newborn's sight.

Desperately, the deadly bottle in hand, Mae meanwhile runs to find Dr. Paul W. Casson. But Casson cannot help the baby either. In fact the second doctor to see the infant will later recall that the sight of the tiny charred face and the 50-percent label knocks him speechless and breathless—at a loss for what to do. It is obvious to his experienced eye that the deadly solution has penetrated every layer of facial skin. And by now in those eye sockets there can be nothing left to treat. All Casson can do is put in a call that Dr. Michael J. Horan, who delivered Margaret Smith of a "perfect son" less than three hours ago, should return immediately to the hospital.

As he is telephoning, Mother Bacigalupo scurries anxiously into the nursery, interrupting him to plead he do something to save the baby's sight. Casson can only explain no human remedy can restore destroyed tissue. "Nothing short of a miracle," he ends, "can help this kid."

Her whole body bowed with sorrow, the nun says resolutely in Italian-accented English, "Then we will pray."

"God! Do!" the doctor urges, his face as stricken as her own. When Dr. Horan arrives, Casson meets him in the hall and tries to break it gently, saying only that "a slightly stronger solution of silver nitrate" has been used for the Smith infant's eyes.

Dr. Horan exclaims at once, "*Anything* stronger than 1-percent solution and that's a blind baby." A minute later as he bends over the crib, the eyes which are now beginning to exude pus like the nose are so swollen he cannot open them. Three doctors have already seen the baby, and except for ordering cold compresses to reduce inflammation, they can do nothing for him. Horan sends for an eye specialist and waits, a nervous wreck, Casson notes. The eye specialist Dr. Kearney's expertise merely confirms the other men's medical knowledge of the properties of nitrate. As if the situation cannot be worse, Horan bears the additional burden of knowing Mrs. Smith's first baby, a girl, lived only five days. How to tell her and her husband that *if* their second baby lives, he will be totally blind? He will also be terribly disfigured, since, when a burn goes through all the layers of skin, the body cannot repair itself with new skin, but only with scar tissue.

That afternoon and evening as the spiritual daughters of Frances Cabrini, foundress of the hospital and their religious order, go off duty, they gather one by one in the chapel. All the long night they remain there begging Mother Cabrini, dead only three years, to obtain from the bountiful heart of Jesus the healing of the Smiths' whimpering infant. Mae is with them, praying her heart out too.

At nine o'clock the next morning, when Kearney and Horan arrive at the nursery, to their astonishment they find baby Peter's eyelids much less swollen and pussy. Gently the eye specialist opens the eyelids, his stomach tightening as he prepares to see the ravages on the delicate eye tissue of the deadly acid.

Instead, looking back at him with the vague, slightly unfocused gaze of the one-day-old are two perfect eyes.

Kearney and Horan are staggered, as are Casson and Grimley when they arrive. Mae, who shudders to recall how she held back the baby's eyelids to make sure the drops went in, can only sob with delirious gratitude.

Amid the smiles and backslappings someone points out something else inexplicable: the horribly charred skin is healing to smooth infant satin, instead of blistering and contracting.

But no smiles are so broad as the nuns'. They knew Mother Cabrini's sanctity personally. Now that she has proven it they exult. Her prayers have obtained this "impossible" cure from the Lord.

Then another tragedy looms. Almost immediately after the miracle, the baby comes down with pneumonia. His jubilant doctors plunge back into fear once more, for infant Peter's temperature, in this pre-antibiotic era, is so high at 107, it appears he will die. This time the summoned Mother Bacigalupo practically laughs at the anxious doctors as she says, "Mother Cabrini did not restore his vision for him to die of pneumonia." But again the Sisters spend the night in prayer. By morning, another miracle: fever down, pneumonia gone.

⁘

In 1938 Mother Cabrini is beatified by the Catholic Church, Several miracles are cited as signs from God in favor of this step, one being the healing of Peter Smith. Seventeen years old, he attends the ceremonies in St. Peter's, Rome, where onlookers notice his striking and expressive eyes that need no glasses and his smooth-skinned face. Only those who know to look carefully for them make out the two tiny scars where deadly nitrate solution once burned a furrow down his cheeks.

All the way to his death in 2002, Fr. Peter Smith will love to talk about Mother Cabrini, whose prayers to God when he was an infant, as he put it, "show the age of miracles has not passed."[1]

---

[1] Learn more about Fr. Smith in chapter 19.

Introduction

Friends in High Places

This book is about cures like Peter Smith's. Cures which are given members of our human family not by medical skill, but by God. Further, this book is about physical healings given by God in answer to the prayer of saints. Cures will include those in which a living saint turns to God in prayer as well as cures in which, at the time of the healing, the saint prays with the perfected prayer power of those who see God face-to-face.

In filling this gap in the literature of Christian healing, it is my intent to show our human family's "wholest" people, the saints, not only as God's frequent instruments of healing, but as fully real people who need to *receive* God's healing as well. To avoid a deadly repetitiousness in doing this, I vary the emphasis and depth of my inquiry, probing one saint's own remarkable cure at more length, another's spirituality of healing to greater depth, and still another's life journey in somewhat more detail. To make the humanness of saints more accessible, I have favored those who lived, worked, and vacationed in North American areas the reader may well know personally, including adding a new chapter on Fulton Sheen, the TV priest. I also spotlight figures well known to the entire world, such as Padre Pio, and, in two of the book's other new chapters, Pope John Paul II and Mother Teresa of Calcutta. Finally, for immediacy, the well-authenticated healings—inexplicable except by using the word *miracle*—that make up the bulk of this book probably took place in your lifetime; that is, in the twentieth and twenty-first centuries (with a few clusters of nineteenth-century exceptions). The sampling of saints I present are from the same era, except where I am making the point that a saint dead far longer may still be an agent of

God's grace and healing today. Thus, America's first native-born saint, Elizabeth Ann Seton,[2] graces these pages, although she and her businessman husband danced at a ball given for George Washington. She does so because the healings attributed to her prayers that are detailed here took place in the twentieth century, with two of the three recipients alive and active in the twenty-first.

⁓

God loves us, so however unworthy any of us feel, we can go directly to Him in prayer for our own healing. Great cures have occurred this simply. I think of a clergyman with a heart so bad he had to rest all week if he gave one Sunday sermon. Told he was about to die by his doctor, he asked God for a new heart to use in the Lord's service. A few days later—without medical intervention—he celebrated his new life in God by climbing a mountain. Still, the very fact that people who pray in all faiths pray for others' healing, not just their own, and when ill, ask friends, relatives, clergy, and prayer partners to pray for them, reveals that it is natural to human spirituality to participate, as receiver and giver, in intercessory prayer.

God sent Jesus, His only-begotten Son, to redeem humanity. Among Jesus' works was prayer for the sick, who were healed. The Redeemer's healings still continue. Best-selling spiritual author Marian Father Michael Gaitley has told of his father's cancer healing through an encounter with Jesus, Divine Mercy.[3] Non-Catholic acclaimed fiction author and Duke University professor Reynolds Price reported his interacting with Jesus in a mystical experience. Battling a spinal tumor, Price was not expected to live. But Jesus indicated he would, and he did.[4] But the

---

[2] The period of her spiritual maturity and works—until her early death by today's standards at forty-seven—is the first quarter of the nineteenth century, but she was born in 1774. It is a bonus that Elizabeth's lonely, neglected childhood; her husband's failed business; her years of economic struggle as the single mother of five; her teens' worrying and sometimes humiliating escapades; as well as her gift for friendship, her sheer grit and lovableness also make her a compelling figure for our time.

[3] In his Fall 2011 *Marian Helper* column (p. 4) as Fr. Joseph MIC, the honorary title Fr. Gaitley assumed as director of the Association of Marian Helpers at the Marian Fathers' National Shrine of Divine Mercy.

[4] The experience, in Price's 1994 autobiographical *A Whole New Life* did not obtain a complete cure; Price lived productively but as a paraplegic

Lord has never reserved healing for Himself. During His earthly ministry, He sent out seventy-two apostles to heal, not through their own holiness but empowered by His. And this continues, non-saints down the ages praying for healing in the name of Jesus and God responding with miracles. Thus anyone, not just the holy, can practice intercessory prayer for healing.

But it is also a natural gesture in human spirituality to turn to the holiest members of our human family when one needs someone to pray for—that is, to intercede for—oneself or others. In Christianity, once Jesus ascended, people turned, as humanity still does, to those closest to the Lord—who predicted at the Last Supper they would do His works, and even greater wonders.

In the New Testament book of Acts, for instance, is the account of Peter saying to a man crippled from birth who was begging in his usual place at one of the doors to the Jerusalem Temple, "I have neither silver nor gold, but what I have I give you. In the name of Jesus Christ the Nazarean, walk!" Instantly the man was healed.

Of the astonished crowd that gathered Peter asked, "Why does this surprise you? Why do you stare at us[5] as if we had made this man walk by some power or holiness of our own?" Then he explained that God healed to glorify the name of Jesus, in which the petition was made. Peter wanted it clear, as does every saint, that Jesus is the only God-man. He alone is the Redeemer-intercessor who pleads for us, as Paul figuratively puts it in Romans, at the right hand of the Father. All Christian intercession, from your prayer today for a family member to St. Peter's cure of the lame beggar two thousand years ago, travels "through" Christ whether His name is mentioned explicitly or not.

The crowd, however, knew instinctively that God also cured because of Peter's holiness. This holiness Peter, measuring himself against the purity and perfection of Jesus, could emphatically deny—and did. Still the people who sought him out to intercede for their healing believed God listened with special attention when Jesus' fisherman friend prayed. They believed this for a very good reason: his prayers were

---

until dying of a heart attack in 2011. In the 1987 edition of the book in your hands find Jesus' TB healing of beloved author Presbyterian Catherine Marshall (d. 1983).

[5] Typically of a saint, he acts as if his companion is involved in the cure.

answered by cures. Acts also tells of some individuals who tried to work miracles in Jesus' name and failed.[6]

Scripture uses phrases like "the miracles he worked" (Acts 8:6) of the apostle Philip, or "he healed him" (Acts 28:8) of Paul. In the same vein people speak of the "healings of" modern "miracle workers." Even more jarring are statements such as "I prayed to St. So-and-so and was cured." *All* these phrases obscure reality.

A miracle by definition is always *God's* wondrous work, the man or woman who prays being only a humble petitioner. If pressed the woman exulting over her cure after "praying to St. So-and-so" will clarify she knows she got the healing from God and that the saint's role was as a prayer intercessor. She'd be aghast if you confronted her that what she *said* made it sound as if the saint were God since she "prayed to" him. What she meant, she'd insist, possibly adding with irritation that every-body knows this—because she is truly unaware that many, especially non-Catholics, do not—was that she begged the saint's prayers. Or she might put it that she wanted the saint to pray *with* her to God. In her offending phrase she was actually using *pray* like the far older use of the word as "I pray thee, good sir, to help me."

Understanding then that both Scripture and people often obscure what's going on by the way they talk, a good example of the *reality* of a saint as God's holy instrument is St. Anthony Claret (d. 1870), at one time missionary bishop of Cuba. Working during another period in Catalonia, Spain, Claret found himself in a situation similar to that of many areas today. Opposing civil-war factions kept seizing the town of Viladrau. By the time the place had changed hands with enormous carnage thirteen times, the medical men had all fled. Claret says in his autobiography, "Thus I had to become not only the spiritual but also the bodily physician of the people...."

While he consulted medical books and dispensed simple advice, the canonized saint, founder of the Claretians, also admits:

> During my stay in Viladrau all the sick of the town, as well as those who were brought there from other places, were cured. As word of this spread, in whatever town I went to, people would

---

[6] See Acts 19:13-16.

bring me a large number of sick persons suffering from all kinds of illness. There were so many sick and so many different illnesses, and I was so busy hearing confessions, that I didn't have time for prescribing physical remedies. I told the people, instead, that I would commend them to God, and in the meantime I would make the sign of the Cross over them, saying, [quoting Mark 16:18, where Jesus gives the signs that will mark those who believe in Him] "*Super aegros manus imponent et bene habebunt.*"[7]

Regarding results, the saint says only, "After I did this, they said that they were cured." Actually physicians testified to remarkable events such as the sudden cure of "a horrible wound in the side, exposing several ribs."

The saint's explanation for the cures is typical of the holy:

I am of the opinion that these people were cured through the faith and trust with which they came, and that Our Lord rewarded their faith with both bodily and spiritual health, for I would also exhort them to make a good confession of their sins, and they did. Furthermore, I believe that the Lord did all this not because of any merits of mine—I don't have any—but to show the importance of the Word of God that I was preaching…. Our Lord God was calling their attention to His Word by means of these bodily healings. And indeed people came in droves, listened fervently to the Word of God, and made general confessions in their own towns, or even in others, because often it was impossible to hear the confessions of the many who wanted to confess.

My God, how good you are! You use the very weaknesses of the body to cure those of the soul. You make use of this miserable sinner to heal both bodies and souls.

Then he sums up every saint's attitude and the reality of healings even through saints: "Yes, Lord, health was yours and you were giving it."

If down the ages God's gifts of miraculous healings are especially associated with those we call saints, this is natural. When a Peter or an Anthony Claret (who began as a manufacturer) is converted, jettisons

---

[7] "They lay hands upon the sick, and the sick get well."

everything that stands in the way, and runs after God with every ounce of life in him, he becomes so empty of ego he is an open conduit for healing; for Jesus promised that he, the Father, and the Holy Spirit would dwell in those who love God with a whole heart and live out that love by treating each individual as the child of God he is. As Claret said, where God is, there is healing.

Equally true, if contradictory, I could say the saint does not get more answers to prayer because she is holier than you or I. She gets more answers because she is more open to, believes more in, God's goodness. This lively faith or trust permits miracles. And it opens the one praying to God even further so that she, too, may become herself a miracle, i.e., a marvelous work, a saint.

A few saints with healing gifts are called to be right out there with them. In the chapter on St. John Bosco, you will see this saint, clearly guided by God, openly bartering healings for the huge needs of his apostolate. I say God's guidance is clear because everything promised was delivered and no cure even slightly dented Bosco's immense humility. Complimented on his vast achievements for the young, this miracle worker lowered his head in embarrassment and murmured, "It is all the work of His hands" and shrugged off personal praise with a sincere "Me? I always needed everybody's help!"

Far more frequently, saints with the gift of healing use techniques that focus attention away from themselves and toward other possible carriers of God's grace. One way to know the truly holy is that, praising the Lord for the cure, they'll be referring, as instrumental, to a dead saint's prayers; the spiritual power of one of the sacraments, such as a good confession; the good works and/or faith of the recipient; the power of the Mass; or the prayers of a spiritual group.

Saints with true healing gifts also often hide—whether this is instinctive or deliberate I can't say—behind the use of sacramentals. After Jesus appeared to homemaker Bl. Anna Maria Taigi (d. 1837) and told her she would have the power to heal in one hand, she always cited the Gospel admonition to anoint the ill with oil. The ball of oil-soaked cotton in her hand diverted attention effectively. Other saints use holy water or a crucifix. The most humorous—yes, saints can be very funny—cover-up is probably St. André Bessette's. This French-Canadian saint credited St. Joseph's prayer intercession for all healings.

He also at times adopted such a brusque, downright cranky attitude when God was giving some extraordinary cure through André's hands that the shaken recipient was only too ready to agree that, whatever did it, it couldn't be any sanctity of André's.

So there are many variants of style with this gift, but one constant: every saint's insistence healing is God's work, not the saint's.

Not all saints have the gift of healing during their lives. God still gives—even to saints—his specific gifts as he wills. Still all saints are healers. By the very definition of mental health, which is the ability to give and receive love, the holy are the most psychologically whole members of our human race and exert a magnetic pull on people of goodwill.

"Everyone just loved to be with him."

"We all wanted to be near her."

Studying the lives of saints for this and other books right up to twenty-first-century holy like Focolare foundress Chiara Lubich (d. 2008), I repeatedly found or heard from living witnesses such phrases from those who knew them. Why? Because in spite of human foibles, even occasional blunders, the holy exude a love that calms, that comforts, that gives new energy and life—in short, that heals. Consider St. John Bosco's experience whenever he ran into his mentor, educator of priests and apostle to condemned prisoners St. Joseph Cafasso (d. 1860). Bosco might be "so exhausted as to be hardly able to breathe, but ..." if he happened to meet Don[8] Cafasso he immediately felt ... his spirits revive and new "strength in his body ..."

An English psychiatrist claimed that mystic author-artist Caryll Houselander (1901-1954) "loved back to life" both neurotics and full psychotics.

If statements like these seem a lot to swallow, here's physical evidence: a physician sampled a group's white blood counts before and after showing them a documentary on Mother Teresa of Calcutta. The white counts, indicator of the body's resistance to infection, showed positive changes from just media contact with a saint.

---

[8] *Don* is the Italian title for priests.

Except in a limited portion of Protestantism that insists there have been no miracles since the opening days of Christianity, all Christians agree that holy people who "come in the name of the Lord" to pray for the sick, with or without laying on of hands, continue the tradition begun when Sts. Peter and Paul healed to glorify Jesus' name. When the healer-saint dies and people still ask his prayers, the fact that cures continue, sometimes by the hundreds or several thousands, shows that death does not end prayer power. As Scripture says of the holy Elijah, "In his lifetime he performed wonders, and in death his works were marvellous" (Ecclus. 48:14, Jerusalem Bible).

I believe the cures involving saints, living or dead, carry at least three other messages for our human family as well. First, through the wondrous cures, God seems to say we come to our fullest development as human beings, as the saints did, when we see our relationship with God not just as one-on-one, turning our backs on everyone else, but as a call to love each other — at least to the point of prayer — in and for Him. Secondly, the desire to be spiritually self-sufficient, never to ask another's prayer, is a form of pride as surely as the individual who only prays for self is an egotist. Finally, even genuine wonder workers fall from grace with a thud when they begin appropriating to self the credit for cures that belongs to God. With these reflections, let us consider again the healing of Peter Smith.

When the doctor encouraged a nun to pray for the infant, he humbly acknowledged his medical skill could not do everything. When the nun got other nuns to join her in prayer, she acknowledged she was not all powerful as an intercessor. And when the whole group praying their hearts out still humbly turned to the holiest person they knew, their dead leader, Mother Cabrini, they, too, admitted their need. Cabrini, knowing God's goodness no longer by faith or even human experience but face-to-face, must have turned even more trustingly to God. While only the baby received a physical cure, all who prayed were graced, not least by protection from pride in "the miracle my prayers worked."

By answering prayer in which the living join hands with the dead as intercessors, God reminds us of the reality of eternal life and reveals how thin is the veil between this life and the next. Far from gone beyond our reach, the holy in death, as in life, are at God's disposal as instruments of His grace. Great intercessor St. André Bessette told worried friends not long before he died, "What I can do for you now is nothing to what I'll be able to do for you when I'm in Heaven." St. Thérèse of Lisieux planned to "go on working for souls until the end of time." I have given ample evidence of that in another book (see footnote 9). Christians know that even though His human life span was cut off two thousand years ago, it is still possible to become intimate friends with Jesus. It is also possible, many know by experience, to become close friends with the holy dead. Sometimes the friendship is initiated by the saint, who returns to this world for a moment to carry out some design of God's. St. John Bosco returned to bring healing to a dying young woman who saw him clearly in 1918, thirty years after his death. She described his curly hair and engaging smile faithfully although she never saw a picture of the dead saint until *after* her instantaneous cure. Dead Mother Frances Schervier came to Brooklyn, New York, in December 1974, a visit that left behind a truck driver's total cure from terminal colon cancer. The man did not even know his wife had been asking the dead Franciscan sister's prayers until he told his spouse that "this lady" had appeared to him and he was shown a picture of the saint. The cure became Schervier's beatification miracle. This book contains Padre Pio's 2002 visit to a dying child in a coma, the miracle accepted for Pio's canonization. Returns of the holy acting as God's messengers are, in fact, so numerous, I have filled an entire book with them.[9]

Friendship with a dead saint is more often—undoubtedly nudged by the Holy Spirit—initiated by the living. Venerable Solanus Casey (d. 1957), the Capuchin Irish-American healer-saint, began a friendship with Thérèse Martin that brought him a physical healing after reading her autobiography. This was about a decade before her canonization as St. Thérèse of Lisieux. Many of us non-saints could tell of our friendships with dead saints, whether people who were friends or relatives or individuals known, like the beatified and canonized saints, only in God.

The possibility of friendship with the saints in Heaven, as with Jesus, means to Christians that we are never without another human being to

---

[9] *Messengers: After-Death Appearances of Saints and Mystics* or the condensed paperback version retitled *Apparitions of Modern Saints: Appearances of Thérèse of Lisieux, Padre Pio, Don Bosco, and Others.* I wrote *Messengers* to console the grieving. These acts of God must be differentiated from human-initiated efforts to contact the dead. Results, in the latter cases, may not be trustworthy or even of God.

pray for our healing, however isolated we may be from other believers. Not only that but we may be sure when we appeal to a saint for prayer that we indeed have a friend in high places, one who rests, like the apostle John, against the very heart of Jesus.

But all this business of my asking my friend to pray for me and her praying to St. Frances Cabrini that Frances will pray—well, it's cumbersome to the point of ludicrousness and downright inefficient, say critics.

Undoubtedly.

But wasn't Jesus' sending out the seventy-two to heal inefficient and unnecessary? Jesus healed the centurion's servant from afar. Certainly the Redeemer had the power to see every ill in Palestine and heal everyone who was cured by the seventy-two with a lot less fuss. All we can say is efficiency does not seem His highest priority. Apparently He preferred to have seventy-two disciples learn to give God's healing, and He wanted even more people to learn to receive God's healing through their fellow flawed, inadequate human beings. In the case of His saints, God certainly does not need them either to work miracles; but anyone studying the lives of the holy can only conclude that it seems to be God's good pleasure to give His greatest miracles to the world through their hands.

How He gives miracles of healing through His saints is explained by saying that the saint prays and intercedes for others, as Scripture requests.[10] But to see a saint's prayer as persuading God to override His will is to misunderstand. The essence of sanctity is to will precisely what—and only what—God wills. The best we can do is admit that the precise mechanics of God's use of His most developed human creatures to carry His healing gifts is one more mystery of His grace.

Some people fear that any honor given saints somehow takes away glory from God. This book offers irrefutable evidence, I believe, that, however you or I feel about honoring saints, God honors them by the miracles He works in answer to requests for their prayers. If there are no visible miracles occurring through the prayer of a saint during the

---

[10] "I desire"—the words are Paul's—"therefore, first of all, that supplications, prayers, intercessions, and thanksgivings be made for all men" (1 Tim. 2:1, Douay-Rheims).

person's lifetime, where there is true holiness God wishes recognized by Beatification, and possibly after that Canonization, miracle cures will follow the individual's death.

All in Heaven are saints. The Church celebrates them yearly on the feast of All Saints. But alone the saint who is officially titled "Blessed" or "Saint" is held up to Catholics, limited interested groups or world over respectively, and to all interested people, as a worthy role model. Call such a person "a living page from the Gospel." Or put it that here is a Christlike person at the apex of human development—one whose union with God gives prodigious prayer power. While certainly not implying any worthiness to be worshipped—that would be blasphemy and utterly condemned by the Church—being officially designated "Blessed" or "Saint" (beatified or canonized, respectively) entitles the individual to *honor* as a *spiritual*[11] giant. It also designates the person as a reliable prayer intercessor.

Obviously such judgments require the ultimate in human prudence. A supernatural institution as well as a flawed, human one, the Church reserves the final word for God. Let me explain.

To avoid error, the earthly Church first conducts an investigation, called a Cause, of the candidate, who at this point is titled Servant of God. The Cause begins with the local bishop's formal inquiry. If that finds real sanctity, the materials are forwarded to the Vatican's Congregation for the Causes of Saints for continued investigation. The whole process may take decades or be much briefer, depending upon how many years are needed to go over a life with a fine-tooth comb. A Cause—those of Divine Mercy proponent, Polish mystic St. Faustina Kowalska (d. 1938) and Australian foundress St. Mary MacKillop (d. 1909) come to mind—may be set aside for years, then taken up again when some point is resolved (often through new data surfacing). Or the Cause may be one of the many that fail, set aside permanently due to unanswered questions or negative findings. What is looked for is not, however, perfection; as this book will show, even these heroes of our

---

[11] Even Christians distinguished for great service to the Church or the gospel may not be considered for these titles unless they died with "a proven reputation for holiness"; that is, for *spiritual* greatness (Pope Benedict XVI's Message of April 27, 2006, to Cardinal José Saraiva Martins, C.M.F., Prefect of the Congregation for the Causes of Saints).

human family retain individual crotchets and little failings. In fact, it can be argued that, without these, holy individuals would lose their humility and dependence on God's mercy.

Still, what must be found for sainthood is not just ordinary human goodness, but *heroic* virtue, such as Don Bosco secretly providing a home for a down-on-his-luck man who had tried to assassinate him, because Christ says to do good to those who do you evil. Or Mary MacKillop rushing to the aid of a man whose lie years earlier had gotten her fired, at a time she was a single schoolteacher and the sole support of her birth family of ten. Not always so dramatic, heroic charity may take seemingly insignificant form, such as the future St. Thérèse of Lisieux's many small—but by no means easy—acts of love, like choosing to spend time with a fellow Carmelite nun usually shunned because she drove everyone nuts. In healers like Fr. Solanus Casey or Fr. Francis Seelos, heroic charity is seen in complete self-giving, practically around the clock, year after year, to others' healing and growth.

To gather evidence of heroic virtue, testimonies under oath are taken in the principal places the person lived, with adjunct hearings in other places as needed. No quick scrutiny, these filled over thirty thousand pages on Don Bosco, who lived to age seventy-two. In addition, the words (including written) and deeds of the individual are carefully examined, and a study of the life drawing on all these resources is prepared by a competent scholar.

In regard to the looked-for virtues, a wild youth such as that of playboy aristocrat, soldier-explorer Bl. Charles de Foucauld (d. 1916) or Roaring Twenties American newspaperwoman, Servant of God Dorothy Day (d. 1980), means nothing if followed by true holiness. Dorothy's early life included love affairs, an abortion, a quickie loveless marriage in order to get a trip to Europe, and a child born out of wedlock. Her life after entering the Catholic Church was a model of sexual purity and given wholly to serving God by serving a lot of difficult people—the mentally ill, alcoholics, and others who were often hard to love—in Houses of Hospitality she and a mentor founded for the down-and-out.[12]

[12] She also courageously took unpopular political positions based on her faith, such as pacifism.

If a Cause withstands all inquiry, a decree of heroic virtue is pro-claimed, and the individual is formally titled "Venerable," literally one worthy of veneration. From here to beatification (except in the case of martyrs, individuals willing to die for their faith, its own powerful sign from God), the whole process has been based for centuries on the confident assumption God will pick up the Cause if He wants it to con-tinue. As Msgr. Slawomir Oder of Rome (you'll meet him in chapter 1) explains, "When the Lord deems it opportune" He will send a "sign in an unmistakable way and we will know with certainty the moment has come." The Monsignor is referring to a canonization, but the same is true before beatification.

How does God sign which people He wants held up to the world as model Christians and prayer intercessors? His signal fires with rare exceptions (two examples shortly) consist of physical healings like that of Peter Smith, cures explicable only in reference to God. These must occur, as Peter's did, in direct response to people's prayer requests for the saint's intercession. Such "miracles constitute divine confirmation" of the Church's judgment on a life, according to Pope Benedict XVI.

The whole traditional process can be summed up: no miracle, no beatification. Following beatification, no new miracle, no canonization. Very rarely—Pope John Paul II[13] did this in 1982 and Francis I[14] in 2013—popes exercise papal prerogative to decree an exception to the procedure or to the requirements. But 99 percent of the time as of 2013 this is how the process of saint making works.

Over the often long years of a Cause, the sheer bulk of God-given prayer answers forms a compelling testimony of an individual's sancti-ty.[15] Twenty-four extraordinary cures from the first nine years after his death were selected out of many others to send to Rome in 1966 on behalf of Fr. Solanus Casey of Detroit. In the case of Br. André Bessette

---

[13] Petitioned by the Polish and German bishops for Maximilian Kolbe to also be honored for his holy death, after Kolbe had been beatified for his holy life with two authenticated miracles, John Paul agreed to canonize the Auschwitz martyr in that category. Martyrdom is considered sign enough and requires no miracle.

[14] With the positive vote of the cardinals and archbishops of the Congre-gation for the Causes of Saints, Francis decreed Bl. John XXIII might be canonized without a miracle.

[15] Some publications supporting Causes include an entire page of letters thanking God and the saint for favors monthly.

of Montreal forty cures from the fourteen-year period ending in 1958 were sent to Rome. (Solanus and André had healing charisms in life. There were equal outpourings of cures after the deaths of today canonized cloistered nun Thérèse of Lisieux and Maronite-rite hermit Charbel Makhlouf, neither of whom had healing charisms.)

But bulk is not enough: it is cures authenticated to meet the seven criteria for an authentic Church-named miracle set down for the Church by Cardinal Prospero Lambertini[16] that makes a saint eligible for beatification and later canonization.

The seven criteria are:

1. The disease must be serious and impossible (or at least very difficult) to cure by human means.

2. The disease must not be in a stage at which it is liable to disappear shortly by itself.

3. Either no medical treatment must have been given, or it must be certain that the treatment given has no reference to the cure.

4. The cure must be instantaneous.

5. The cure must be complete.

6. The cure must be permanent.

7. The cure must not be preceded by any crisis of a sort which would make it possible the cure was wholly or partially natural.

The daunting task of weighing any proposed case against the criteria is done by medical men whose expertise on the disease in question, not their religious conviction—or lack thereof—is the important point. There are no religious tests for this work. The physicians who treated the cured individual must be willing to provide all the medical records and acknowledge that the cure exceeded what treatments, if any, could ever have achieved. One doctor who refused snorted, "What! Say that if she had died I killed her but since she has a spectacular cure mine is not the credit!" But it is other medical men, with no personal involvement in the case, who make the decision.[17] If a healing, however stu-

---

[16] Later Pope Benedict XIV (1675-1758).

[17] As of 2008 there were sixty-two doctors of varied specialties on the

pendous, does not meet all seven criteria, the Church, *while not denying that it may be, even at times undoubtedly is, supernatural in origin*, withholds the formal title "miracle" to avoid the slightest taint of promoting spurious miracles.

To give an idea of how stringently these standards are applied, I put before you from another of my books the rejected cure of Gerard Baillie, a child whose blindness from atrophy of his optic nerves and both retinas was instantaneously healed.[18] Gerard sees in spite of physiologically being "unable to see since the atrophy remains." While this is a miracle to doctors as well as to us ordinary observers, the cure was rejected as a *formal* miracle because it is not "complete": technically the disease (bilateral chorioretinitis and double optic atrophy) still exists. Another miracle cure where the disease is technically still there is the case of Alice Topping, a Protestant Englishwoman who saw Padre Pio after his death and since then walks, even jumps and hops, unaided, although her spine damage makes even walking "impossible" without crutches or other aid.[19]

In this book, then, whenever I refer to a cure as accepted for a saint's beatification or canonization miracle, you will know this healing has met the seven rigorous criteria under the most searching medical inquiry. I also freely use the word *miracle* in well-authenticated cures like Gerard's or Alice's that are merely humanly impossible.

In the careful process that seeks God's say regarding beatifying or canonizing someone, there are more steps. Next the medically verified miracle is looked at by theologians for their judgment that the inexplicable healing is due to supernatural factors, including that it is specifically a divine response to the prayer intercession of the sainthood candidate in question. A last stop for the miracle and its Cause is a special commission of cardinals and archbishops. Medical men and theologians have spoken. Now these representatives of the Church take a

---

    medical commission of the Congregation for the Causes of Saints. At the diocesan level, too, the cure has been scrutinized through interrogation of the recipient, involved physicians, and witnesses under the leadership of a non-involved physician appointed by the bishop.

[18] This took place at Lourdes, a French healing shrine established by appearances of Jesus' Mother to a young girl, today St. Bernadette Soubirous (d. 1879). See more detail in my book *The Sanctified Body*.

[19] Detailed in my book *Messengers/Apparitions*. Pio's Cause did not even bother to submit Alice's healing for formal miracle status.

gander. After their go-ahead, everything settles on the desk of the pope. Only after this—green-lighted by science and theology and approved by leaders of the Church, including the pope himself, who indeed has the final word—does the Church, with a papal announcement, joyously proclaim a formal miracle and a formal saint.

Every physical illness has emotional, intellectual, and spiritual factors. Likewise, healing can begin in the human person's soul, emotions, or intellect, not just in the body. Thoughtful readers may wonder if even healings meeting the seven criteria or at least lesser cures received after appeal to a living or dead saint's prayers are not examples of the placebo effect.

An individual expects to be cured through a given saint, an intellectual conviction that generates positive emotions such as hope and confidence, in turn stimulating the body's physical systems so that healing ensues with nothing supernatural involved. Undoubtedly this is a good description of some so-called lesser cures; if belief in a saint's help can succeed where medicine couldn't, this is nothing to look down on: it reflects how important it is that in healing, the whole person, soul included, be treated, and it points out how much greater are the resources for facing life's hazards of those who have a living faith, a fact acknowledged by many medical studies.[20]

Nevertheless, while there are cures in this book that could be cited as evidence that the psychosomatic dimension may be operative in wonderful ways, there are many others—take Peter Smith's for example—where such a suggestion would be ludicrous.

If one-day-old Peter Smith was influenced by anything "human," the most logical factor to cite would be the healing prayer he received. Other researchers than those just mentioned (see footnote) in places

---

[20] These include work at Duke University Medical Center, University of Louisville School of Medicine, and Fordham (a Catholic) University. See also, among a number of books, one by Larry Dossey, M.D., *Prayer Is Good Medicine* (San Francisco: HarperCollins, 1996) citing other studies. Whether following groups of the aging (three studies) or women with metastatic breast cancer, study participants who were involved in religion, prayer, or rated spirituality as "important" showed the strongest immune systems by various markers.

like Atlanta's Agnes Scott College, London's Institute for Psychobiological Research, and UCLA have used skin response meters, blood tests, blood pressure meters, and electroencephalographs to see if anything that can be measured scientifically happens to someone receiving healing prayer

Just as the physicist knows invisible particles are there because of what they do, these researchers—people of medicine and science, many non-Christians—have found that healing prayer is a real force or energy, even if invisible, *because it changes things*. Besides causing seeds to sprout faster and increasing plants' rates of growth over that of plants not prayed for, healing prayer for human beings has numerous positive effects as measured by blood-cell count, skin temperature, blood pressure—even brain waves. Prayer for self works too: The *Annals of Behavioral Medicine* reported a 2002 study that linked AIDS patients' survival to how much the patient prayed.

Further, healing prayer can achieve results across distances. A baby near death was healed when a praying saint at the other end of the country had the mother kneel by the phone while he blessed them (p. 49). This prayer energy that someone praying for healing projects, many of us Christians believe is both "natural," since anyone of goodwill, non-Christians included, can "do it," and "supernatural," since, anyone of goodwill praying for healing, we believe, taps into or opens the door for God's healing power.

Studies years ago with nurses at New York University showed individuals who merely have a healing *intent* without reference to prayer or God benefit others *if* they themselves are in good health, not tired or depressed. Less well-known studies, such as those by the C. Maxwell Cade research group in England, demonstrated that certain individuals have strong innate healing gifts—again, as long as the healer remains well-rested and without mental distress. Such gifts seem as hereditary as other, often-termed psychic abilities. Cade's electroencephalographs found evidence these natural powers can be increased to a degree by the practice of meditation exercises and techniques which increase psychological integration, compassion, and empathy.

But the book you are beginning shows convincingly that prayer energy on the level generated by the saints goes much farther than the energy of well-intentioned individuals or even gifted empathetic healers, since they are limited by the need to themselves be in excellent shape. (Distressed, fatigued, or ill, it appears, they may actually slightly worsen the condition of the individual they are, in good faith, attempting to help, a phenomenon sometimes termed "sapping.")

Saints' prayers for healing, on the other hand, do not seem impeded if the one praying is tired or sick or in tough circumstances. In fact, in Catholic tradition, fatigue, illness, problems of age, non-body distresses—every burden—can be "offered up," united to Christ's self-offering, as prayer—including for physical healing.[21] There is even a rare vocation in the Church in which certain individuals are called for much of their lives or for certain limited periods to be part of God's healing for others by suffering redemptively in union with Christ. The apostle Paul refers to this in Colossians 1:24-25. (This requires discernment by competent authority, however, to distinguish between those authentically called and those suffering religious neurosis or other forms of delusion.) Pertinent here is that the healer saints profiled in this work, to the end of their days, grew in power to transmit God's healing; there was no decline with either old age or chronic illnesses. Saints, in fact, have healed while dying, like Bl. Anna Maria Taigi, who after weeks of exhausting illness, was God's instrument to heal her confessor half an hour before she died. Saints from this book from whom healing came on their deathbeds include André Bessette, Solanus Casey, and Francis Xavier Seelos.

This power in powerlessness underlines God's role, as do instances, like Peter Smith's cure, where something like destroyed delicate eye tissue is not just healed but literally remade.

During the pontificate of John Paul II (d. 2005) well over eighteen hundred men and women were added to the saints' rolls either by beatification (1338) or canonization (482). Minus the martyrs, each beatification represents an *authenticated miracle.* Canonization represents another. John Paul raised more individuals to the altar than any previous pope because of the growing size of the Church and his concern

---

[21] See my leaflet on the subject: "Even Disabled, the Christian Is Never Useless."

that every area, and as many occupations and lifestyles as possible, should have a saint as a role model. *But he was able to do this only by God speaking through miracles* (except for that other sign, martyrdom), physical cures inexplicable by human effort, even as physical miracles became harder to find that met the Church's criteria due to intensive treatment of almost anyone seriously ill.

For years the Church required two to four authenticated healings for beatification and the same number for canonization. Pope John Paul II reduced this requirement to one before beatification, then a new one before canonization. Did he lower the number, I wondered, because miracles were drying up? My investigation discovered the pope's motive was speeding up the process of making saints in order to put relevant role models before the world more quickly.

The new norms save huge amounts of time and money, as well as work by Church personnel with better things to do. The time saved includes that having to do with Lambertini's insistence that a cure be permanent. With diseases like cancer this used to mean waiting until the miracle recipient died to prove the disease was not just in remission. If this has to be done for two to four cures before a beatification, it can put off providing a greatly needed role model for decades. (This requirement for some time was eased with cancers that pass the medical "cure" mark, but there is a current turning away from cancer miracles out of fear that even the medically accepted five-year cure is not trustworthy enough.) Moreover it has become increasingly complicated—requiring a great deal of work by expensive medical experts—to sort out medical interventions from supernatural ones, even in cases where a medical intervention has never produced a cure. Also expensive and time-consuming is the compiling of medical dossiers running five hundred to well over a thousand pages. Finding money and personnel for this makes some groups decide not to pursue a Cause at all.[22]

If the official requirement has lessened in number for important reasons, the number of cures has *not* lessened. As in the past, there remain

---

[22] Bl. Frances Schervier's order is one that told me this regarding her possible canonization. The Belgian Benedictines of Fr. Paul of Moll are a second.

a few sainthood candidates where remarkable healings seem to far exceed the number needed (the case of Bl. Francis Xavier Seelos, for instance), but this does not mean one will be easily and quickly accepted! Mary Ellen Heibel, with a kidney transplant from polycystic disease, was terminally ill with a esophageal cancer when, after appeal to Seelos's prayers, the cancer vanished. Although she died of pneumonia, her medically inexplicable case was rejected by Rome because she had not quite passed the five-year cancer-survivor mark.

Besides John Paul II, the popes since, as well as the long line of popes before them, also named saints and beati. A large number of the people named in recent decades have lived in recent times. This means God's miracles that made them formal saints took place in our day. Cures are associated also with asking the prayer intercession of those in earlier stages on the road to sainthood—Venerables and Servants of God. Even martyrs are associated with cures.[23] And what about the "old saints"; that is, those before the modern era?

In 2012 the first American Indian saint, Kateri Tekakwitha, was canonized in St. Peter's. The canonization miracle was the 2006 healing of an eleven-year-old boy, an American Indian from Washington State, cured of flesh-eating bacteria (necrotizing fasciitis) after his parents sought Kateri's prayer intercession. Their doing so was suggested by the priest who came to give the failing boy the last rites. At the canonization, healthy Jake Finkbonner received Communion from Pope Benedict XVI. In 1980 Kateri had been beatified. Present for that imposing ceremony was eleven-year-old Peter McCauley of Phoenix, Arizona. At the age of four Peter had been partially deaf in both ears when a visiting Jesuit suggested to his family they pray that Venerable Kateri ask God to heal the boy. On the last day of a novena (nine days of prayer for a certain request) for this intention, Peter McCauley was instantaneously healed. God touched these boys with healing through a woman dead over three hundred years. That's right: Bl. Kateri Tekakwitha died in 1680.

---

[23] For example, see Albert Groeneveld's short book *A Heart on Fire* on Dutch WW II martyr, joyous Carmelite Bl. Titus Brandsma or my booklet "God's Healing Power in St. Maximilian Kolbe."

I use these Kateri cures to stress that, with its many healings in-volving a comparatively few so-called modern holy, the book in your hands can be only the tiniest sampling of the miracles going on all around us through the intercession of God's saints. No single volume could contain all the healing miracles attributed to just recent saints. In fact, God's cures through some of these holy individuals need—and have—books of their own. And from the apostolic era to the present, there are at least several thousand recognized saints. While healings in relation to a saint generally peter out as newer saints take the place of older ones in public consciousness, this is not always true.

A small number of saints who actually walked with Jesus—con-sider St. Jude, St. Joseph, and Jesus' Mother, Mary, as the most promi-nent—have ongoing reputations as channels of the Lord's healing. Some saints have centuries-long associations with cures of particular conditions or types of illness, such as St. Blaise with throat difficulties.

Some shrines of canonized saints—St. John Neumann's in Philadel-phia is a good example—receive reports of healings long after these are no longer "necessary" as signs favoring a Cause.

To still-active "old saints" add that the Congregation for the Causes of Saints is currently investigating over three thousand worldwide Causes that have survived the introductory investigation handled by local bishops. Many of these are associated with cures.

To say then that God is healing at all times and among His many ways are abundant healings through his saints is a statement free of even the slightest exaggeration.

What all this means when a healing is needed for self or others is that the intercession of the saints is a huge available channel for healing, in addition to the many others, such as every one of the sacraments,[24] reg-ular "soaking prayer"[25] by someone who can commit to this, attendance

---

[24] My files include such cases as the woman whose broken bone refused to heal for months–until, without thinking of her health, she went to Confession. To her surprise, the leg healed immediately. She conjectures that something else in her had to be healed before the leg could mend. Other cases include a dying boy given Baptism, Confirmation, first Confession, and first Communion all in one day. His terminal-cancer condition immediately changed, and he recovered (p. 73).

[25] Popularized in *The Power to Heal*, by Francis MacNutt, a Catholic "healer" in good standing with the Vatican, who attributes it to Methodist

at special healing services or Masses, laying on of hands by anyone who has compassionate love to spare, including those called to ministry in this area who are genuinely[26] graced with the charism of healing, and one's own personal relationships with Jesus, the Holy Spirit, and (for non-Christians) God our Father.

Some people think you must be a certain kind of person to receive a miracle. Actually miracles go to every kind of person, from nuns living quiet, pious lives to a man who had lost his battle with alcohol. He was healed of terminal cirrhosis of the liver and pneumonia while in his death coma, a cure accepted for the beatification of Bl. Clelia Barbieri (1847-1870). They go to babies like Peter Smith, too young for faith, and to individuals "too old to hope for a cure," like Anna Maccolini, whose cure at age seventy-eight was a canonization miracle for St. John Bosco. They go to the devout and to those who must say like another man cured through Bosco during the saint's lifetime, "I don't believe in God."

While they are primarily received by Catholics, that is simply because few non-Catholics turn to a dead Catholic saint for prayer. Where a miracle was sought through the intercession of St. Elizabeth Ann Seton for a Protestant, the Protestant received a cure so extraordinary it was accepted as one of the saint's 1975 canonization miracles. Frenchwoman Jeanne-Emile de Villeneuve's 2009 beatification rested on the 1994 miracle cure of a teenage African Muslim girl from Guinea. The cure that met all the criteria for Mother Teresa of Calcutta's beatification

---

clergyman Tommy Tyson, this term refers to regularly (daily or weekly) repeated prayer of some minutes to an hour for healing. Alice Williams, my long-term prayer partner, endured ten years of fourteen surgeries, including amputation of her left leg below the knee and seven bypass grafts, all due to vascular disease. In 1976 two groups of specialists said there was nothing more that could be done, and she was sent home, not just hopeless, but in such pain that she had sixteen nerve blocks at the USC Pain Center. Bedridden at this point, she was prayed over for about an hour a week by a woman she barely knew from St. Thérèse Parish in Alhambra, California, who sat quietly in a chair by the bed. At the end of the year of soaking prayer, Alice got up and got a job. Over thirty years later she was active as a water colorist and art volunteer in Nevada public schools.

[26] See "A Word of Warning" on p. xxxvii.

(ch. 25) went to an animist woman. During his lifetime, Fr. Solanus Casey was associated with the cures of a Jewish child desperately ill with spinal meningitis and one or two rabbis, as well as a number of Protestants. So whoever you are, there is no reason to disqualify yourself from asking Catholic saints for help.

After all, no longer confined to doing good in the era and area in which he or she lived, every saint now belongs not only to the Church but to the world and to all ages.

This means they also belong to you.

⌒

But it is possible you will read this book and still feel no inclination to ask a saint's prayer intercession. Let me summarize a letter by St. Maximilian Kolbe (d. 1941) responding to someone who wondered if he should mimic Kolbe in seeking the prayers of the Virgin Mary. Kolbe assured the questioner that everyone must pray with complete freedom in such matters. One person, said the saint, will be drawn to take all requests to the Holy Spirit, another to Jesus, a third to God the Father. Another individual may often ask one of God's holy, as Kolbe did Mary, to pray for or with him or her. There is no "best" way.

Most of us, in fact, pray now one way, now another. If this book reminds readers that saints are as ready to pray for us as our other friends, it has accomplished its purpose.

A Word of Warning

Those who feel inspired to find a living saint for healing prayer will want to keep in mind that *healer* and *saint* are not necessarily synonymous. Most healers are compassionate people without being saints. And there are some morally dissolute or troubled people who are "healers." I think of one described in Francis MacNutt's book *Healing*, who used to get out of his drunken stupor just long enough to conduct healing services. Cases could also be cited of laymen or women or, more rarely (rare because most have the sense to go regularly to savvy confessors), of Catholic priests who appeared to have potential for sanctity, then fall victim to pride in "my ministry" and become clogged channels of grace, overbearing to those who assist them and projecting a sense not of service but of vanity. Worse, some flamboyant so-called miracle workers are like twentieth-century morally dissolute and demon-ridden charlatan Jim Jones of Guyana-massacre notoriety. Jones's "Christian healing services" in Oakland, California, were planted by the "holy minister" with phony ill and fake cripples who were "miraculously" healed. Jones saw himself as God, debasing followers and stripping them of goods, spiritual health, freedom, and eventually, forced to drink poisoned Kool-Aid, of life. So check up on any healer "saint" lest you get involved with a huckster after your money, or, worse, an evil person who destroys those falling under his spell.

Nothing Short of a Miracle

Chapter 1

"Make Him a Saint Now!"

Moments after Pope John Paul II's death on April 2, 2005, the chant *"Santo subito! Santo subito!"* ["Sainthood now!"] begins from the sad, but somehow exhilarated, crowd in St. Peter's Square. Through all the events that are part of burying a pope, it continues.

In response, as soon as he succeeds the pope many are calling John Paul the Great, Benedict XVI—who knows his predecessor's holiness up close and personal—waives the five-year waiting period for starting any saint-making process.

Through all this, in the south of France, Sr. Marie Simon-Pierre Normand's struggle with Parkinson's, the disease John Paul II had, is not going well. For some time before his death—close as she felt in prayer to one who could understand—watching him on television had gotten too hard. "I saw myself," she would later remember, "my own future." And that future looked like disabled, immobilized, confined in a wheelchair . . .

The start of her battle lay in the recent past. Not that long ago she had been a bustling RN maternity and neonatal nurse described as "full of life" and "dynamic"[27]—one who brought her patients a room-light-

---

[27] Sr. Marie Thomas Fabré, in a talk given May 1, 2012, at the Medicine, Bioethics, and Spirituality Conference, Worcester, Massachusetts, hosted by Healthcare Professionals for Divine Mercy and the Marian Fathers of the Immaculate Conception and published on their website: "Witness to a Miracle," *Divine Mercy News*, http://thedivinemercy.org/news/4916.

ing smile. That light had already gone out, extinguished by rigid facial muscles on her left side. Yet it had been only four years earlier when doctors had finally pinpointed the reason for the forty-year-old nurse's ever-increasing exhaustion and the pain throughout her body. Because she had been ever more tired for years, she was told she may easily have had the debilitating, degenerative, and incurable disease of the nervous system for a decade.

When Parkinson's hits an individual who is sixty or seventy, the disease often moves slowly. Sr. Simon-Pierre[28] was probably already ill in her early thirties. In younger people, Parkinson's can move very fast. After diagnosis, she did her best to carry on her work in the maternity birthing ward, including her second, neonatal, specialty, care of new-borns, often premature births, born ill or disabled in some way. Their moms—and indeed, families—needed extra support she gladly gave. But before the pope died, tremors causing trouble controlling her hand movements forced her to give up handling fragile newborns for off-the-floor work in administration. To add to her distress, although she was exhausted, sleeping was becoming increasingly difficult.

Pope Benedict's waiver to open the Cause became official on May 13. Immediately Sister's community, the Congregation of the Little Sisters of Catholic Motherhood,[29] united in asking John Paul II to get God to work a miracle for Sr. Marie Simon-Pierre. Nurses like her were just too needed to let her work be stolen by Parkinson's. Women of faith as well as of medicine, they prayed fervently with "strong hope." Even their one foreign mission in Senegal, Africa, joined in.

As if thumbing the papal nose at the little French community, rather than a cure, Sr. Marie Simon-Pierre's condition at once deteriorated markedly. June 1, the two-month anniversary of John Paul's death, she could no longer go on. The pain was unbearable. It was a struggle to

---

[28] In this order specializing in maternity care, upon entering the congregation every member honors Jesus' birth mother by taking Marie, Mary in French, as her first name. After comes a saint's name, such as Thomas or Simon-Peter (Simon-Pierre), by which members are more apt to be called among themselves. I will use sometimes the full formal name, sometimes the less formal.

[29] Congrégation des Petites Soeurs des Maternités Catholiques.

even stand. Walking, kneeling, and driving a car were terribly difficult, all hampered like face, hand, arm, and other parts on her left side by stiffening as the muscles hardened. She was left-handed, and the entire left arm now hung as if lifeless at her side. So far using a computer had helped. But now the tremors in her medically "better" right hand were so severe that writing—necessary for any professional healthcare position, even administration—was becoming impossible.

That afternoon, she dragged herself to the office of her immediate superior of the past sixteen years, Sr. Marie Thomas Fabré, a midwife serving the congregation as one of its leaders. The suffering sister asked permission to give up professional work. Sr. Thomas, not quite grasping the deterioration the last two months had brought, thought to encourage her younger charge's hope and faith, reminding Sr. Simon-Pierre that the community were sending her to the healing shrine Lourdes in August. The superior asked her to stay at her post until then. When Sr. Simon-Pierre tried to explain about her hands, Sr. Thomas told her to write the name of John Paul II. (Later she would hope she had not embarrassed[30] her, explaining, "Unconsciously, I wanted to verify that she could still write, it was not the end, and that she should not give up.") Sr. Simon-Pierre didn't want to show what her handwriting had become. It was only after being asked three times that—a woman who could no longer hold a utensil—she got hold of a pen and wrote the pope's name with her tremulous hand: the scrawl was far (there is a photo) from her once-clear handwriting. A graphologist would later describe it as the writing of someone near death.[31] As she looked at the paper, it hit Sr. Thomas just how bad Sr. Simon-Pierre's condition had become. They looked at each other and then simply sat silently for a time praying. Sr. Thomas recalls, "I remember praying and thinking at this moment that we had tried everything [medically] and that we had reached the end. 'Lord, the only thing left is a miracle!' That's how I expressed my thoughts ..."

But Sr. Simon-Pierre, surprisingly, had good news to share too. Reticent in interviews about her interior life, she has publicly admitted this much: during her illness, in spite of her desire to do God's will and live as a woman of faith, she struggled with anxiety, even terror, and fear

---

[30] Another translation says "humiliated."
[31] "Witness to a Miracle," *Divine Mercy News*.

of burdening her community, while her superior noted that her sense of self-worth was also under siege, as Parkinson's seemingly inexorable march rolled over her body like a tank. But on this day, both women confirm, Sr. Simon-Pierre told Sr. Thomas that, even as her body was tumbling headlong into this pit of deterioration, she had received a healing. She had been enabled to look squarely at the dreaded picture of herself in a wheelchair—one of the disabled rather than someone who helps them—and to accept this as, apparently, God's will for her. She knew now she could carry this cross with peace, as John Paul II had done. She even counted blessings: she was not alone; besides Sr. Thomas's support, she had full support from the community; with new hope, she even thought she somehow could nurse from the wheelchair. At any rate, she would always be a Little Sister and somehow she *would* serve. Today in the position of mother superior of the entire community, Sr. Marie Thomas elaborates: she says she believes the suffering sister's first victory, before any victory of physical healing, was the grace by which Sr. Marie Simon-Pierre "embraced her sickness and did not run away from it." The mother superior explains that disease may evolve and advance, but the person has the capability to recover interiorly. "[Even] the periods of desolation[32] can mysteriously become the beginning of inner joy," affirms the woman whose congregation's work gives her hands-on experience with these things.

Before Sr. Marie Simon-Pierre made her laborious way out of the office, her superior found herself saying, "John Paul has not said his last word."

She had no idea how true that was about to be!

∽

Since May 14, the day after Benedict's waiver and her congregation's beginning special prayers for her, Sr. Marie Simon-Pierre had always interiorly "had with me," like a song that plays over and over in one's head, a verse from John's Gospel: "Believe and you will see the glory of God" (John 11:40).[33] That gave her no conscious sense whatsoever she

---

[32] Every illness affects the whole person, body, mind and soul (see p. xxviii).
[33] Mentioned in her talk given May 1, 2012, at the Medicine, Bioethics, and Spirituality Conference, Worcester, Massachusetts, hosted by Healthcare Professionals for Divine Mercy and the Marian Fathers of

was going to be cured. In fact, at the moment she left the superior's office it seemed the important cure of soul and mind was the healing her community's prayers had obtained for the Parkinson's sufferer.

But some hours later alone in her room, somewhere between 9:30 and 9:45 p.m., she relates today, "something in my heart seemed to say, 'Take up a pen and write.'"[34] She did, writing some Scripture, and, in her words, "the pen skipped across the page." Before her eyes, her handwriting was clear, completely legible, *normal*.

Filled with excitement—still, as is actually not uncommon with those receiving miracles, she did not take in what had happened to her two months to the day and hour[35] after John Paul died of her disease. An event so momentous, simply too much to absorb, continuing her routine, she went to bed. But at 4:30 in the morning she woke. First she was in awe that she had actually slept. Mornings with the stiffness and fatigue unconquered by sleep were normally "very difficult" but not this one. She recalls, "I got up fully alive." There was no pain, stiffness, nothing. Even interiorly, she could later say of the moment that she felt "much different." Dressing without trouble, she hurried to Jesus in the tabernacle.[36] Filled with thanksgiving for the changes in her body, she spent an hour or so expressing her gratitude and joy for what she would later describe as "a bit like a rebirth." Then she went to the community chapel and joined her community for Mass. She—who for a long time had not been able to stand steadily enough to do so—volunteered to do the Scripture readings for the daily celebration, proclaiming with gusto. It was only as she received Jesus in the consecrated bread during

---

the Immaculate Conception and published on their website: "My Miraculous Cure," *Divine Mercy News*, http://thedivinemercy.org/news/story.php?NID=4917.

[34] It has been erroneously reported in many accounts that she said she heard, "Write the name John Paul II."

[35] 9:37 p.m.

[36] Catholics believe in the Real Presence of Jesus Christ (see John 6:51-56; Luke 22:19-20; Matt. 26:26-28; Mark 14:22-24) in the bread and wine once it is consecrated. Between use for Communions, some of the hosts (bread), stored in a tabernacle, form the living heart of every Catholic church, chapel, or place of prayer where a tabernacle resides.

the Mass, she says in one interview, that she was able to finally absorb beyond a shadow of doubt that she no longer had Parkinson's.

Buoyed by the "peace and joy of her Communion," Sr. Simon-Pierre, for whatever reason, still went back to her room as she did each day and took her morning medication. As always, it caused nausea and made eating so difficult that her weight over time had plummeted. At noon, she decided to stop medication and noticed she was eating that meal normally.

꩜

Sr. Marie Thomas was in the chapel that morning. Deep in prayer, she only half-consciously noticed that Sr. Marie Simon-Pierre looked different. Perhaps adrift in their own thoughts or prayers, no one else seemed to grasp the change either. If someone did notice, at least somehow nothing was said. Later that day, Sr. Thomas relates that she met Sr. Simon-Pierre, who had put in a phone call wanting to see her "right away," in a corridor. Sr. Simon-Pierre excitedly shared her cure. She produced an account she had written.

Now it is Sr. Marie Thomas's turn to not quite get it. Deeply shaken, she can't understand what is going on even with the handwritten document before her. As Simon-Pierre insists that she is healed, her stupefied superior demands, "How come you are healed?" The miracle recipient wants to rush to tell the mother superior, Mother Marie Marc. But when she further gushes she has taken no more medication, Sr. Thomas exclaims, "That will kill her!" These are, after all, professional medical women oriented to complying with medical directives.

Eventually calm returns. Shocked but believing, Sr. Marie Thomas joins the community for the Rosary. She does find, to her consternation, that at the end of the prayer period, still off kilter, she says aloud, "St. John Paul, pray for us." Other than that lapse from Church decorum (his Cause barely open, this is completely inappropriate), she settles down. In the afternoon the two sisters are able to meet. Sr. Simon-Pierre demonstrates the miracle by writing John Paul's name in handwriting her superior once knew well.

The mother superior, Marie Marc, is told the following day. She waits for Marie Simon-Pierre's visit to her neurologist. That takes place on the seventh, a regularly scheduled checkup. As she walks in, the absence of any Parkinson's symptoms is so striking, the physician exclaims, "What have you been doing? Doubling up on your Dopamine?[37]

Sister replies, on the contrary, she is taking no medication (this is now four days). When she tells the doctor what God has done through the request for John Paul's intercessory prayer, he is shocked, speechless. But his examination agrees that his suddenly former patient has no sign of Parkinson's. (He will see her again to confirm this several weeks and then several months later.)

The visit over, Mother Marie Marc consults with the neurologist herself. That evening she tells the community. Given the news (although asked to keep it among themselves), members enthusiastically switch from asking for a miracle to praising and thanking God and His praying servant, as they marvel over the cure of their "incurable."

Next the mother superior reports what to her and the other sisters is a miracle, not to the local bishop, as would be expected, but directly to the postulator[38] of John Paul II's Cause, Monsignor Slawomir Oder. A couple of months later, he actually makes two visits to them in Puyricard, France, the location of their motherhouse and of the facility where Sr. Marie Simon-Pierre has been stationed. Oder asks the local bishop, Archbishop Claude Feidt, head of the diocese of Aix-en-Provence, to investigate. Following standard procedures in such matters, Feidt sets up a special commission under Fr. Luc-Marie Lalanne. Fr. Lalanne's attitude: "The Church has deep respect for science and it ... [has] to be established that there is no explanation [for the cure] using scientific knowledge." To him purported miracles are "where science and faith [need to] meet." The thorough investigation involves an expert neurologist—not the cured woman's doctor—who sets up the questions that need answers. Those involved include other neurologists, professors of

---

[37] A medication.

[38] Title of the official, required to be based in Rome, who may be in charge of just one or of a number of Causes. In the country of the person proposed for beatification and/or canonization there are one or two local officials dubbed vice-postulators. They work only on one Cause and would normally receive reports and propose the most impressive for investigation. There are no vice-postulators for the Cause of John Paul II because he lived in Rome. So Oder handled both posts' tasks.

neurology, a neuropsychiatrist, a plain psychiatrist, and even a hand-writing expert, since handwriting is an important gauge of Parkinson's.[39] Theologians and canon lawyers also play a part.

It takes a year, during which Sr. Simon-Pierre is probed and prodded, body, mind, and soul. In the end, the verdict is favorable. Sr. Marie Si-mon-Pierre's cure becomes one of those inexplicable-by-human-efforts, doctor-seconded cures that are being sent by bishops to the postulator.

During 2007 Sr. Marie Simon-Pierre, now 46 and working quietly at the order's maternity hospital in Paris, comes into the public eye as a beatification-miracle candidate (this is rare, a new phenomenon as cures being studied are traditionally kept under wraps). Interviewed, before TV cameras, at a press conference with Archbishop Feidt she admits willingly, "I am cured. It is the work of God, through the intercession of Pope John Paul II."

Pressed by members of the press to claim the healing is a miracle, she sagely mimics a man cured by Jesus: "I was sick, and now I am cured [cf. John 9:25]. I am cured, but it is up to the Church to say whether it was a miracle or not." The mother and baby nurse ends the interview that knowing she is well, she understands she must continue working to help others find life and health, "to serve life and to serve the family."

She and the archbishop are present in Rome that year on April 2. It is the second anniversary of John Paul's death, and Pope Benedict cel-ebrates a Mass to mark the occasion. It is also, minus two months, the second anniversary of her cure. Archbishop Feidt formally delivers the findings of his commission to the Congregation for the Causes of Saints. The archbishop and nursing sister also attend ceremonies that mark this as the day when the Cause of John Paul, fast-tracked by Benedict, ends the diocesan inquiry and is formally sent, with favorable findings, to the Vatican for investigation at that level. (Even if pope and bishop of Rome, John Paul II was a member, like all who live there, of the Diocese of Rome, and Causes are begun in one's diocese.)

The next portion of the investigation will be a meticulous inquiry as to whether John Paul II practiced heroic virtue. After that, if the conclusion is favorable, the part of saint making that relies on the ut-most in human investigatory powers will take a break and wait for God

---

[39] See page 5; "Witness to a Miracle," *Divine Mercy News*.

to speak. For this, like any other, Cause to succeed, God must demonstrate divine approval. Almost always—martyrs are the common exception—this is done by miracles. Specifically there would have to be cures of illness from God in response to individuals, like the French sisters in the case of Sr. Marie Simon-Pierre, asking John Paul II's prayer intercession. Presented with a possible miracle, human investigators will again swing into action. Any potential official—that is, Church-proclaimed—miracle, approved by diocesan medical experts already, will be given rigorous scrutiny by the Congregation for the Causes of Saints' men of science—medical experts called in without reference to their religions or lack of belief. (An atheist can certify something is beyond explanation.) The investigators would hold the potential miracle up against seven scientific principles (see p. xxvi). If even one of these is not met, however astounding the cure, it will not make the grade. This could take *lots of time*, as a Cause tries to find one that can pass the tough criteria.

But not in John Paul's case. From the moments of his death, as if by instinct, people around the globe—by no means all Catholics—began turning to John Paul as a man who surely must have God's ear.

Postulator Slawomir Oder, the man in formal charge of John Paul II's Cause, in his words, was "being inundated with emails and letters … at a level of 80-100 a day." Sent directly to Rome in envelopes of every shape and size "they came," Oder stated, "from all over the world, even from nonbelievers." Their writers reported various favors, including healings many did not hesitate to dub miracles.[40] Also arriving after diocesan investigation were claims of miracles from bishops, like the one made on behalf of Sr. Marie Simon-Pierre. By 2007, from varied sources, there were many cures that looked as if they might be the real thing.

⌒

Sister Marie Simon-Pierre's case could easily have been just one in what was, so to speak, a huge pile. But Mother Marie Marc's report for some reason had caught postulator Oder's eye. Perhaps because it is Parkinson's? Perhaps because it was submitted by a mother superior rather

[40] *Orange County Register*, June 29, 2005, 2.

than a bishop or just anyone? At any rate, he had looked into it even before the local bishop did. Now, for whatever reason, her cure is one of those submitted by bishops chosen for a deeper look. Ignoring the Aix-en-Provence inquiry, as is required, Rome starts from scratch, busying a new group of expert examiners.

As this inquiry by the Congregation of the Causes of Saints' medical commission is in progress, there is a flurry of opposition to Sister's cure in the press. It goes like this: Parkinson's is incurable. If she has been cured, she must not have had Parkinson's. Since she *was* healed, she had some neurological condition that can be cured. Ignored is that her complete instantaneous cure of an advanced neurological disorder was obviously not of a kind to be ascribed to medical intervention whatever neurological disease she had—and that, more importantly, the nurse's Parkinson's diagnosis was well established.[41] A second, more reasonable complaint: no miracle should be proclaimed until Sr. Marie Simon-Pierre is dead, in case the disease returns in her old age. The postulator responds to the critics by bringing in more experts to join those studying the case to make doubly sure this healing will stand. It is not as if he cannot turn to others should they decide against it.

To sift a life can take decades. Even more true is this for individuals who have done so much, written and spoken so much and lived as long as John Paul II. But here, also, events, under Pope Benedict's loving eye, continue to move with amazing speed. Following the diocesan inquiry, formal investigation by the Vatican's Congregation for the Causes of Saints has no trouble quickly establishing—through eager, under-oath testimonies by competent witnesses, 120 of them by one estimate, from many nations—that the pope from Poland had lived to glorify God, not self, thirsting to do God's will, not his own, in a life of heroic virtue,[42] visible in both individual good deeds and overall committed service to the Church and humanity.

---

[41] Concurring in the original 2001 diagnosis were three physicians: her doctor of many years, the neurologist he sent her to, and, for confirmation, a second neurologist in Marseilles. See "Witness to a Miracle," *Divine Mercy News*.

[42] See examples of heroic virtue on p. xxiv.

In other words, John Paul II was worthy, investigators conclude, to be held up as a role model for following Christ, newest in the line stretching back to the Apostles after each saw the Risen Christ, including St. Paul, who urged, "Be imitators of me as I am of Christ" (1 Cor. 11:1). With personal joy, on December 19, 2009, Pope Benedict issued the decree of heroic virtue.

John Paul's title thus went from Servant of God, given all formal sainthood candidates, to Venerable, meaning one worthy of honor or, in the old word, veneration because of proven holiness. Now God must speak for the Cause to move to beatification.

It was time for proven miracles. That of Sr. Marie Simon-Pierre Normand—gone over with a fine-tooth comb by Rome's medical men—was the one chosen over others examined. After passing the medical commission's tests, it had been sent to a theological commission that verified, among other things, that the healing could be clearly tracked to the miracle recipient and others' asking John Paul's prayer, not, for example, sometimes his and sometimes someone else's. Then, vetted by science and theology, it passed through a third commission of cardinals and archbishops for approval by representatives of the Church and into the hands of Pope Benedict XVI, who had the final say. On January 14, 2011, Benedict formally proclaimed the French sister's cure from Parkinson's as his predecessor's official beatification miracle. With every one of the required steps accomplished, Pope Benedict, only six years after John Paul's death—something unheard of for centuries in the Church—set a date to beatify his predecessor in the huge square fronting St. Peter's, since by no means would there be room enough inside the church. He chose the Sunday after Easter, known as Divine Mercy Sunday. Not only the closest Sunday to John Paul's death anniversary, it was a feast the pope loved and brought to the universal Church by canonizing Polish visionary Faustina Kowalska.

On May 1, 2011, Sr. Marie Simon-Pierre is there seated among those who will play a part. Near the doors of the immense church, she is on the shore of a sea of a million and a half people from all over the world who have flowed into the square, the streets leading there jammed backwaters of humanity too. Near her is a section for dignitaries from many nations. As the rite progresses, in the simple but tasteful (although sisters, they are still Frenchwomen) white, dress-length uniform of her order, eyes bright behind oval glasses, she is one in a short line that processes to the outdoor canopied altar high on the steps. Her task of honor is to carry a relic[43] of the dead pope.[44]

A year later, a priest asks her on TV[45] whether she was scared doing this, reminding her of the million and a half onlookers. The sister, who has sat for the TV interview with this priest who wants people to be made aware miracles do actually happen, with her hands quietly in her lap (there is only once a glimpse she has in them a small circle of rosary beads), happy to let others do the talking for her, lights up. She responds at once, "I had the impression that I was being carried by angels, one on each side. I felt very light." She sensed, she goes on, that she was carrying to the altar all the sick who ask her congregation's prayers (a companion sister interjects that it is the cured sister who is asked a lot for her prayers). It seems from her description that the verse that rang in her head about seeing glory has been fulfilled.

Miracles affect a recipient, body, mind, and soul. The French nurse, working again today with mothers experiencing difficult pregnancies and babies born with problems, has been a person of faith at least since she gave herself as totally as she could to God when she was a teenager. When she is next asked by the inquisitive priest what, after the miracle is different in her life, she does not speak again of her restored physical abilities. She speaks instead of her experience of "great interior peace and joy. My spiritual life has been completely transformed." There is much she could say,[46] but she volunteers only one example to the TV interviewer: "Eucharistic adoration [being with Jesus in the tabernacle] is a very powerful moment in my life." And finally the nursing sister says she believes she has a greater compassion for the sick and those who suffer. She admits to receiving letters from Americans who write her for

---

[43] See note on relics on p. 221.

[44] A gift of John Paul's secretary of decades, as well as his friend and confidant, Stanislaw Dziwisz, now returned to Poland to serve as a diocesan archbishop.

[45] Fr. Benedict Groeschel, during one of his last airings as host of *Sunday Night Prime*, May 22, 2012, on EWTN.

[46] For her full testimony, see "My Miraculous Cure," *Divine Mercy News*, http://thedivinemercy.org/news/story.php?NID=4917.

prayers and, through the translator, expresses her desire to reach out to these people.

A miracle is also never just for the individual who receives it.

This act of God, permitting his beatification, served John Paul and the Catholic Church. It has also given new encouragement, says Sr. Marie Thomas Fabré, to the sisters. The eighty-some-year-old congregation founded in 1930 has always operated on the principle that every human life is precious, even one that may have to live with limitations and disabilities. In a time when many disagree that all life is worthy of defense, affirming life's value is getting harder. With the miracle, she says, "John Paul II has looked on our little community and given us the courage to continue" this part of their mission. Both Sr. Marie Thomas and Sr. Marie Simon-Pierre believe John Paul II is truly with their congregation, referring, for one thing, to the feeling each had, when they sat silently together in prayer when things looked darkest and later, when they told then mother superior Marie Marc of the miracle, that he was "in the room."

Beyond all this, to some of us it seems fitting that Sr. Marie Simon-Pierre was cured through the dead pope's compassionate prayers for someone whose condition he understood only too well, God gifting not just Marie Simon-Pierre but newly dead John Paul II, as well. After all, what does a saint like better   after God — than bringing God's help to a brother or sister in need? That he may have especially liked bringing it to a Parkinson's sufferer seems entirely reasonable.

Chapter 2

Turning Life's Tough Things
into Blessings—for Others, Too

French miracle recipient Sr. Marie Simon-Pierre Normand wafts toward the altar feeling angels have shown up to carry her at the beatification of John Paul II on May 1, 2011, in Rome. If there are any visiting angels around Floribeth Mora, watching on TV in Costa Rica, the easy assumption would be they've come to waft her to the next life.

Although a faith-filled woman still reaching out to God, the full-faced fifty-year-old—given up by medicine—does not face her impending death in peaceful surrender. Instead Floribeth's is a mixture of hope for a miracle and deep sadness because her death will leave her husband, who is trying so hard to be brave, and their children bereft.

And it has all happened so suddenly: only twenty-three days ago, after going to bed with everything normal, she woke the next morning clamped in the nightmare of an excruciating headache. Not just an ordinary bad headache, but one so painful that this owner, with her husband, of a private security business must leave her home in one of the middle-class neighborhoods of Dulce Nombre de Tres Rios (about twelve miles from Costa Rica's capital) to seek help in a hospital.

Physicians in Cartago, a nearby city, offer a quick diagnosis of severe migraine. She went home, but three days later—the pain unrelenting—she returned to the hospital.

Doctors began to take notice. Tests were done this time, and what was found was no migraine. An aneurysm on the right side of her brain was hemorrhaging. Aneurysms kill a lot of people if not discovered in time to be taken care of surgically. This one had been discovered, but Dr. Alejandro Vargas could not in good conscience propose surgery to his patient. Consulting with colleagues around Latin America and Spain, the consensus was that access to the area was too tricky, truly perilous. He would explain in 2013, "With [either] an open operation or an endovascular intervention, the risk to Floribeth would have been to die or be left with a significant neurological deficit." With the best will in the world to help her, Dr. Vargas in April 2011 could only send his patient, bleeding inside her brain, home with painkillers. Keeping her in the hospital when she was beyond medical help would have been cruel.

Looking back, the wife and mother recalls, "I returned home with the horror of imminent death. Seeing my children walking by looking at me, standing beside my bed, seeing my husband making himself strong, taking my hand and crossing himself every night, it was very sad."

Then her faith came to the fore. In spite of her inoperable aneurysm and the fact that aneurysms can "go off" fatally at any time, she insisted on participating in a religious procession. During it she had a sign, she believes, she would be healed. She has not shared the link between that and the family's decision made just afterward.

That decision was to build a shrine outside their house. It was in the form of an altar, colorfully done in the Latin[47] American style using strings of Christmas lights, candles, and flowers surrounding an image of the Madonna—and a photo of John Paul II. So basically it was a shrine at least half-dedicated to the late pope. Which has to make you wonder if the undisclosed sign during the procession had something to do with him.

The day of the pope's beatification came, and although she was in bed, she insisted on watching along with her family, who gathered about her. On her bedside table was a magazine with John Paul on the cover, arms outstretched. Floribeth recalls, "I contemplated the photo of the Holy Father with his arms extended and I fixed my eyes on him. In this moment, I heard a voice tell me, 'Get up, don't be afraid,' and I could

---

[47] This is not, however, your usual Central or South American nation, even though one border abuts Nicaragua, but one of the overall best countries in the world by many international measurements, from environmental achievements and economic status to the peaceful lifestyle that has had no army since 1949 and does not even allow sport hunting.

only say, 'Yes, I'm going to get up.'" Another unverified account adds that one of the extended arms in the photo seemed to gesture invitingly for her to leave her bed. This has happened in miracles.

In her case, we don't know that for sure. We do know Floribeth responded to the voice she heard interiorly because she goes on to say about what she was experiencing, "I was afraid to tell my husband because he was going to think I was crazy or on drugs." To the shock of her family, she did get out of bed.

She felt instantly better.

This was not self-suggestion: new medical exams revealed the aneurysm was gone.

This instantaneous healing as she faced death (while aneurysms occasionally are there without causing harm for years,[48] hers was already actively bleeding) eventually made it to Rome. How did that happen? Overjoyed and overcome—even two years later she weeps with emotion when talking about the events—she described what God had done for her through the prayer intercession of John Paul II on a blog dedicated to the late pope. Some who saw it recognized this might have the right stuff for a miracle meeting those seven scientific criteria (see p. xxvi). And because it happened the day of beatification, if it could be proved a miracle, it could meet the canonization miracle requirement of a healing through the sainthood candidate's prayer intercession that took place after, not before, beatification.

Floribeth was contacted and the local church alerted. The archbishop of her diocese agreed this cure warranted investigation. Making her claim to a miracle believable were the brain photos Dr. Vargas produced, showing the bleeding, inoperable aneurysm and then, shortly thereafter, the same area of the head aneurysm-free without medical intervention. The doctor, who had been stymied in efforts to help, stated honestly, "It's the first time I've seen anything like it."

When the local inquiry proved favorable to the miracle, Floribeth traveled, by invitation, to Rome to be given a going-over by doctors there. That hurdle passed and her records and the testimonies pertaining

---

[48] The writer's grandmother's aneurysm had still not "gone off" when she died at ninety-three, but a son's in the same inoperable area as his mother's, killed him in his forties.

to the cure forwarded by her Costa Rican diocese, the Congregation for the Causes of Saints set in motion its formal study by a medical commission. The committee of seven doctors acting for the Congregation is said to have been presided over by Dr. Patrick Polisca, who had been John Paul II's cardiologist, then Pope Benedict's, and in 2013 Pope Francis's personal physician.

When her case went to Rome but had not yet passed its inquiry, Sr. Marie Simon-Pierre Normand had been taken to a press conference by her bishop, a rare thing, perhaps necessitated, in his eyes, by a leak of information. Following the more usual custom regarding those whose inexplicable cures are being studied for possible formal miracle status, Floribeth and her family remained silent through the two years it took for the local and Roman inquiries to be completed. These, as always, included passing not just the medical study but a theological one, and finally, before going to the pope, the commission of cardinals and archbishops who represent the Church.

In June 2013, she was told her miracle was the one chosen for Bl. John Paul's canonization. Pope Francis I made the official announcement July 5. Weeping, the Costa Rican wife, mother, and businesswoman relived the events that had given her back her life, at a formal press conference in her archbishop's residence in San Jose. Her family had always been with her, and they were bulwarking Floribeth Mora now, along with her doctors and Church officials—some of whom would also testify—as she spoke.

Miracles at a holy person's burial, beatification, or canonization happen frequently. There are a number of them in this book. In this era of reduced requirement for formally proclaimed miracles, only two of God's healings received by asking a dead saint's prayers can survive the winnowing out of all the favors that come to a postulator's attention. Millions were watching the beatification. Many other cures could have occurred on May 1, 2011.

When they do occur, of course, many healing recipients won't think of reporting what happened—or would have no idea how to do so. Then there are all those—sometimes striking—cures that *are* reported out of thanksgiving to God that won't pass the seven criteria (see p. xxvii for two of those). And you may be surprised to know there are those that *could* pass but aren't submitted for mundane reasons, like a Franciscan friary pledged to poverty going with the cheaper-to-investigate miracle rather than a more spectacular one (see ch. 20).

That there are many partial or complete healings out there in the case of a few extraordinary saints like John Paul II gets a nod from Msgr. Slawomir Oder. Remember the piles of mail coming to him after he was tapped by the pope's Vicar General for the Diocese of Rome, Cardinal Camillo Ruini, to take on the job of postulator for John Paul II's Cause? Seven years later Oder told another interviewer, "The phenomenon [of miracle reports in] ... letters and testimonies continue to arrive in my office. ... Some are very interesting and significant."[49]

It is both interesting and significant that Sr. Marie Simon-Pierre's is not the only Parkinson's testimony. Two others show that if the Church for reasons many applaud is limiting the number of miracles it devotes time and money to formally investigating, God, on the other hand, is not cutting back on His works honoring Pope John Paul II. Here's a cure from that big pile of healings sent to Rome:

In December 2005, Marco Fidel Rojas began experiencing symptoms of Parkinson's. The former mayor of Huila, a town in Colombia, underwent a series of examinations that found he had both suffered a stroke and, perhaps as a result, developed the neurological disease. According to Colombian newspaper *El Tiempo*, Rojas gradually got worse. He felt he might collapse any time and did actually fall on the street at times. Once, he says, he was almost run over by a taxi.

Five years passed with continuing deterioration until in his pain on the evening of December 27, 2010, it suddenly occurred to him that during a trip to Rome, he had once met Pope John Paul II and spoken with him for a few moments after a Mass.

"I have a friend up there," Rojas told himself. "And he had Parkinson's. Why didn't I pray to him before?" (This way of putting it obscures that a cure must come from God; the saint can only be asked in prayer to intercede by praying for or with the petitioner; see p. xvi.) Then, envisioning the dead pope as if he were a live priest present to offer the prayer for God's healing by the laying on of hands, Rojas begged, "Venerable Father John Paul II: Come and heal me; put your hands on my

[49] Wlodzimierz Redzioch, "Looking for a Miracle: Postulator Awaits John Paul's Canonization (Part 2)," *Zenit*, May 8, 2012.

head." (Many scriptures show God's healing sometimes being delivered this way, primarily by Jesus[50] but also by saints. For an example of the latter, see Acts 28:8 regarding Paul.)

After this, Rojas went to bed. He slept perfectly and woke up with no symptoms of Parkinson's. The cure and that Rojas is in good health were verified, according to *El Tiempo*, by Dr. Antonio Schlesinger Piedrahita, a renowned neurologist in Colombia.

Rojas says, "Yes, John Paul II gave me the miracle of curing me; my great promise ... is to spread devotion to him wherever I can."

Rojas's cure did not take place after beatification—necessary for a canonization miracle. Nor was it submitted before Sr. Marie Simon-Pierre Normand's cure was chosen for the formal beatification miracle. Thus, as far as official miracle status from Rome, this healing can only be an also-ran. But think what it means to the man and all those close to him. Think how it may inspire and console people who learn about it. And isn't it a good example of the surprising caliber of some of the healings being attributed to John Paul's prayers that will not gain any special status?

Among those are certainly the vast number—Floribeth at the John Paul II blog a rare exception—of cures or improvements posted on the Internet. Here's one from February 15, 2013: "My mother has the same disease [as John Paul] Parkinson's and we had lost hope that she will get better and she made the novena[51] of John Paul II and she got better. She could not write, eat, bathe herself, but after she was able to do them [all] again."

⌒

In these years certainly many other types of healings than ones from Parkinson's are being shared in circles small or large, including some sent to Rome. For instance, in 2007 it was reported—not by Rome; cures under consideration in Rome are not publicized by the investigators—that a cure from cancer was also being studied as the possible beatification miracle. This involved a man from the area of Italy south

---

[50] See incidents such as Mark 6:5; 8:23ff; Luke 4:40; 13:13; Matt. 8:2-4, 14, 15, among others.

[51] Nothing magical, just nine days praying for something, often—but not necessarily—asking a saint's intercession.

of Naples. John Paul had visited Salerno, where the man and his wife lived, in 1999. The husband was diagnosed in 2004 with lung cancer that had spread to other areas of his body. Although he was being treated at his city's Riuniti Hospital, doctors did not see healing in his future. On the contrary, they considered his condition terminal. But his wife, refusing to accept losing her husband, prayed incessantly for John Paul's intercession. Early in 2005, she says the Polish pope came to her in a dream. John Paul assured her that her husband would be healed.

Soon doctors could detect no cancer. While accounts of the couple's ages and situations differ, there is unanimity about the cure, attested to by the local archbishop. With his return to perfect health, after diocesan investigation, the man's case, too, wended its way north to Rome.[52]

With all the attention on the cures God is working after John Paul II's death to honor him, something remains out of focus for most people. Even many who followed this pope's activities do not know that during his lifetime, John Paul was one of that group of holy through whom God heals physically, and in other, sometimes more subtle ways, as well.

Healing charisms are given by God. Yet looking at John Paul's life one can see how God permitted many events early on that formed his personality and spirituality in such a way that the gift seemed almost a natural overflow of his temperament. The particular gift of carrying God's physical healings to others is also somehow a part of the larger—because touching more people generally—nonphysical healings John Paul brought members of the human family. Perhaps the most important: that he demonstrated time and again that the bad things God permits[53] to happen to someone can turn into immense blessings for that person and, at least for the holy, for huge numbers of others as

---

[52] Fr. John Zuhlsdorf, "2nd John Paul II 'Miracle' Under Investigation," *Fr. Z's Blog*, November 10, 2006. Also found in the Irish magazine *The Curate's Diary* for May 2007, this report was repeated in the American publication *The 101 Times* 19, no.1 (Spring 2007). Since the Congregation for the Causes of Saints does not verify which reports it is investigating, this can only be given as having been publicly spoken of by the local archbishop.

[53] Catholic theology differentiates between those things God causes to happen and those He, perhaps sadly, permits to honor free will.

well. Much of this took place as we watched; but some happened before he was known — so offstage, if you will — and comes to us now through others' memories and scholars' and other writers' research, via media and books.

During his early life in his native Poland, Karol Wojtlya (say voy-TEE-ya), the future pope, suffered one family tragedy after another. He was only nine when he was taken out of his school classroom to learn the doting mother who had made his breakfast and sent him off to school that morning was dead. In his teens came word that his healthy older brother, a gifted young medical doctor, self-sacrificially caring for a patient, had caught her infectious disease and died of it. Karol and his remaining family member, his father, moved to Kraków for Karol's university studies, so he was separated from hometown support the day he came home to find his frail dad dead of a sudden heart attack. While there were a few relatives here and there, the family he had been born into of father, mother, and children was extinct.

That was the dread year 1941, Karol left essentially alone to survive, if he could, under Nazi, not just invasion, but deliberate terror. Like almost everyone, but young men especially, he was in constant danger of death. Near fatal moments included being hit by a Nazi truck and left for dead in the middle of a busy road at night, as he returned from pulling a double work shift in a quarry — backbreaking work keeping him from deportation to slave labor in Germany. A countrywoman seeing him hit, jumped off a tram, shielded his bloody, unconscious body, and flagged down a car. It held a German officer. This decent man, after helping her use gutter water to deal with the blood, in turn stopped another truck, ordering it to take the semicomatose youth to a hospital. Karol would always have one low shoulder, but he lived.

Another time he cowered, praying with a pounding heart, in his basement apartment, a place so tiny he would only be able to try to hide behind the opening door, while soldiers searched for young men after an uprising. Some reports say he was saved that time when a call came from an impatient officer for the searchers to move on to the next building.[54]

---

[54] Find versions of these two accounts in George Weigel, *Witness to Hope: The Biography of Pope John Paul II* (New York: Cliff Street Books, 1999), 71-72.

Between the constant insecurity of life and his losses to death, he could easily have turned into a morose, self-centered person. But from childhood, from his saintly father above all, he had learned to accept God's will and believe God meant him good, not evil. He had also learned not to waste suffering but to take his troubles and join them to Christ's as prayer for himself and for others. Belief in the potentially redemptive power of life's inevitable burdens would last his entire life.[55] All he went through awakened in him not self-pity, bitterness, or cynicism, but a great compassion for the suffering. In his life "a privileged place" demanding, he felt, a response of service would always be "occupied by" those like his lost loved ones, "the sick, the poor,[56] the 'least brethren' [Matt. 25:40, Douay-Rheims]." Years later, as an archbishop, speaking in a parish, he would urge the congregants, too, that the essence of their apostolate should be "precisely that of concern for the sick, for the suffering, for the abandoned and the needy."[57] Among "the needy," calling to his compassion even as a youth and forever after were those deprived of their dignity and fundamental rights. These marginalized in WW II included his Jewish countrymen, among them the future pope's childhood best friend, Jerzy Kluger,[58] all marked by the invaders

---

[55] "I make up in my body what is lacking in the sufferings of Christ" (Col. 1:24). Regarding the word *lacking*, a note in the Ignatius Bible explains: "Christ's sufferings were, of course, sufficient for our redemption, but all of us may add ours to his, in order that the fruits of his redemption be applied to the souls of men."

[56] Too frail to work, his father had provided for them by a military pension cancelled under the Nazis, leaving them dependent on what Karol could earn or legitimately scrounge.

[57] Czeskaw Drazek, S.J., *Caly dla Boga i ludzi; Habemus Papam* (Kraków, 1979), 167-168; quoted in Stanislaw Dziwisz; Czeslaw Drazek, S.J., Renato Buzzonetti; and Angelo Comastri, *Let Me Go to the Father's House: John Paul II's Strength in Weakness* (Boston, Pauline Books and Media, 2006), 10.

[58] The boy and his family remained in the town where Karol grew up, when he left the area to attend the university in Kraków. It was only years later they refound each other. Many of this friend's family—people Karol and his father held in great esteem they tried to demonstrate when anti-Semitism began to rear its ugly head—had perished. Find various incidents in Weigel's *Witness to Hope* (see index under "anti-Semitism" and under "Kluger"); pages 38-39 are examples. See also the book *The Pope and I* by Kluger, who died in Rome, January 2, 2012, always a close friend until the pope's death.

for annihilation. Rejecting violence, Karol reached out as an actor to affirm forbidden culture in underground theater that had to be hidden from the Nazis, and, after a time, his self-giving went even further. He took up dangerous, clandestine studies to become a priest.

⌒

As Hitler's forces marched out, Communist tyranny took over. Resisters who had survived the Nazis were now often exterminated like so many bugs by the new regime. This did not stop Fr. Karol, as a young priest, from leading first country parish and then university youth to the ultimate Communist enemies, God and the Church. On hiking, skiing, and boating trips, Uncle Lolek[59] (it was not safe to call him "Father") took youth where they could speak freely under the Communist regime that now dogged the heels of any of Christ's people. To the companions of those years he modeled a resilience and canny ability to let neither past personal injuries and sorrows nor government tyranny and debilitating hatreds of oppressors squash his joy or diminish his trust in God. His spiritually based freedom was a healing model for many.

As pope, John Paul II was almost murdered by a fanatic from Turkey (theorized as acting for the security apparatus of a Russian Communist government alarmed at this pope's ability to galvanize hearts and minds toward political freedom in Poland and other Iron Curtain countries). Visiting his imprisoned remorseless would-be assassin, the pope modeled for the world how Christ's men and women forgive even those who show no sign of repentance. Forgiveness is a healing always needed in the world.

There were the physical healings too. His compassion would well up for some person stricken with some awful illness—usually, but by no means always, a child. He would touch the person and speak a few words. The individual would be healed. At times there was not even a touch, just his prayer, later found to have been at just the time the inexplicable cure took place. They weren't all Catholics either. An American Jewish man was one whose terminal illness vanished.[60] Oc-

---

[59] A nickname from childhood.
[60] Pawel Zuchniewicz, *Miracles of John Paul II* (Toronto: Catholic Youth Studio-KSM, Inc., 2006), 19.

casionally something made the media, but most of the time, the pope managed to keep cures unknown. Anything the press did get wind of he exerted himself to quickly smother by lack of Vatican cooperation. His personal secretary knew about many cases but has said publicly that he never kept any records of the cures. "I can only say," [today Archbishop] Stanislaus Dziwisz, said on Italian television, "that the Holy Father did not want to hear about it and always said, 'God performs miracles. I simply pray. Those are divine mysteries. Let's not dwell on it.'"[61]

You'll recall in the introduction I mentioned that the healings attributed by recipients to the prayer intercession of some individual dead saints, if given in some detail, fill entire books. A year after John Paul's death, in 2006, there appeared a book by Catholic Polish journalist Pawel Zuchniewicz, who had covered many events in John Paul II's life. It compiles testimonies from media and other sources, including people responding directly to the journalist's request for this type of information and the interviews he did. Zuchniewicz called it simply *Miracles of John Paul II*. Published first in Polish, it offered cures that had taken place after Pope John Paul's death, but Zuchniewicz also used his research skills to ferret out healings that took place during John Paul's life. The testimonies crediting the Polish pope's prayer intercession triggering particular blessings from God have global stretch, from the Philippines to Mexico's Yucatan Peninsula to Russia to the United States—and, of course, the countries where John Paul II lived, Poland and Italy.

From this gripping compilation, I select one story to stand for the many cures during the pope's lifetime. If it whets your appetite, look for more in Zuchniewicz's book. Here I condense the long account rich in details that began with a family of six in Poland, harassed and homeless in 1981, because of the father's involvement with the Solidarity labor movement that was bringing the nation new hope for freedom from Russian-backed Communism. Franciszek Szechynski and his wife, Danuta, their family living in different households with people brave enough to give them shelter, did not even qualify to have her deliver

61 Ibid., 21.

their fourth child in a hospital. But courageous medical workers got them in through the ER and intended to have them out so quickly that they need never be registered. The disappearing act was made harder when baby Victoria was born with a growth by her heart. They were sent, clandestinely again, for visits to a children's hospital physician who, observing the growth just get larger, had to say there was nothing that could be done medically. She suggested emigration to Canada—to Toronto where there was a hospital specializing in such problems.

Providentially the Communist regime was encouraging men like Szechynski to take one-way tickets out of the government's hair, while in Toronto the Church had asked each parish to take in one of these Polish families. Safely settled in Toronto, the family sought the wondrous hospital. They found, instead of help, disappointment: the renowned specialists were in accord that only an operation could help Victoria; but being an infant and in her condition, it was the counsel of a number of these doctors not to attempt the extremely high-risk surgery. Trying to be consoling, medical men told her parents that if nothing were done, the baby might live three years.

John Paul II came to Toronto, and the family's hopes shot up, but things went awry and Victoria did not get his blessing. In desperation, the family wrote the pope. With an answering invitation to visit him, Danuta took Victoria to Rome. At this point the growth took up half the toddler's body. The Holy Father put his hands around the baby, adorable in her mother's arms in a white pinafore over a red-collared and cuffed garment, and kissed her. His counsel for Danuta and her family: trust God, who might want Victoria with Him.

"If he wants her to remain with you, you don't have to worry or do anything at all. Treat her the same as your other children." Victoria, whose eyes had been riveted to the pope, hugged and kissed him, as babies rarely do a stranger.

Mother and baby flew home. They were barely in the door of their house, when it seemed God did want Danuta and Franciszek's fourth child. And right now: She was roasting to the touch and her body turning colors. At the hospital the doctors confirmed the child was dying. The hospital would keep her, if desired. The parents took her home. They were resigned. At least she was dying with John Paul's blessing.

But she did not die.

A few days later she got up and ran—not her usual hunching along—but ran into another room. And she wanted something to eat.

Her flabbergasted parents took her to the hospital again. The doctors were equally struck. Tests showed the growth had dwindled to something so small it could be removed with just two procedures. Nor was it any longer malignant.

In Pawel Zuchniewicz's well-detailed ten-page account,[62] you will also enjoy two wonderful photos: Danuta holding baby Victoria with John Paul II and Victoria as a lovely young woman, with her parents and her fiancé.

For many reasons—although he had fierce critics from the start[63] to the end of his pontificate, as well—John Paul II held a big place in many hearts. Just to mention North America, there are places and undertakings named for him all over the continent. More importantly many of the huge region's priests will tell you it was he who inspired their vocation and their determined fidelity to the Church. Those priests and numerous Church intellectuals fed on the brilliant Pole's learned and spiritually profound writings, such as his philosophical works and encyclicals. But John Paul had sides other than the scholarly: certainly his intense prayer life was what many most admired. A robust man who amazed secular journalists covering his trips with his stamina, which some—like a *Los Angeles Times* writer[64]—connected to his spirituality, he always led the masses of people worldwide more with his life and personality—what he *was*—than with what he wrote. They appreciated

---

[62] Zuchniewicz, *Miracles of John Paul II*, 38-48.

[63] In the early days, for one thing, he was assumed anti-Semitic because he was Polish, thus his canonizing of Maximilian Kolbe in 1982 was seen by some as one anti-Semite celebrating another. Actually neither were anti-Semitic, such charges against Kolbe, originating in an Austrian journal, already having been refuted by a joint Jewish-Catholic inquiry before they somehow spread widely. My research raises the question whether this may have been, perhaps duping the Austrian writer, another KGB ploy to discredit pope and Church even more than an attack on Kolbe, a holy communications genius who volunteered to die for a condemned man in Auschwitz. Eventually John Paul's lack of anti-Semitism was accepted; on other issues over the long pontificate some criticism was credible, since sanctity does not give omniscience. Regarding the charges of Kolbe being anti-Semitic, see the afterword of the 2013 edition of my book *A Man for Others* (Libertyville, Illinois: Marytown Press).

[64] *Los Angeles Times* reporter Don A. Schanche, February 21, 1982.

his challenging homilies calling them to live boldly for Christ in a world of materialism, hedonism, and secularism that ignored or scoffed at "religion." Such words, as well as dramatic gestures that somehow always fit the situation, galvanized huge crowds at events around the world as he visited many nations, gathered the world's youth, one could say into his arms, in now one country, then another, or held gatherings in Rome of universal Church groups.

Many people were drawn to the physical manifestation of a strength that, whether they knew it or not, encompassed spiritual, emotional, and mental power too: his athleticism. As an adult the former goalie on a mostly Jewish boys' soccer team whether as a university professor priest, archbishop of Kraków, cardinal, or pope, inspired the young—some as an icon of fatherhood, virile and protective, but warmly accessible; others as an icon of the great leader—as his powerful body skied gracefully down mountains, took long hikes in stride, or paddled a full canoe out into the country.

Then in old age, God permitted a huge humiliation and impediment to the work of worldwide importance John Paul was carrying out so brilliantly. The trained-as-an-actor pope, who knew how to project his richly inflected voice, understood the power of facial expression and dramatic gesture, and in every way brought not technique but *technique at the service of deep self-sacrificing love for God and humanity*, lost the use of all these gifts. Those who had watched him draw the human family toward freedom—politically and, even more, interiorly—with élan and brilliance now watched him stooped and hanging on aides, that expressive face a flat mask due to Parkinson's. What ignominy, what humiliation. And then the miracle began to be noticed: he was going right on drawing the human family—many even more profoundly—by the dramatic gesture of his non-gesture, the projected richly inflected "voice" of those flattened tones. Gifts broken and trampled by illness turned into a strewing of flowers for the old pope's ascendant path to Calvary and greater holiness. "If I be lifted up," Christ had said, "I will draw all men to me" (John 12:32). Now here was John Paul II on the cross of disabling, disfiguring illness, wringing not just compassion from the world, and another healing in the form of new dignity for those whose lives looked like his, but admiration—especially, it appeared, from the young and able—for his heroic courage.

Even as the pope's once powerful body failed completely, it seemed God was blessing this stalwart friend, by permitting him as so many previous times, to turn his troubles—even his body's deterioration, final sufferings, and death—into an offering and blessings for others. Like a magnet, his impending death drew thousands to St. Peter's Square to watch and pray. Their cries "*Santo subito*" at his death set in motion events that continue. That is, if you believe the testimonies of people like Sr. Marie Pierre-Simon Normand, Floribeth Mora, Marco Fidel Rojas, and the Szechynski family. From such witnesses, God seems to still be using John Paul II to do good to others. Through canonization, the Church even proposes the amazing Pole as a man who will pray for you and who, potentially, could become your role model for letting God turn the hard things of your own life into growth and blessings—for yourself and for others, too.

Chapter 3

Just a Red-Blooded American
Male and Miracle Worker

Sixteen-month-old Elizabeth Fanning lies listlessly in her mother's arms. Anxiously, drawn-faced Mrs. Fanning coaxes her child to take even a spoonful of the liver soup recommended by doctors. But although Elizabeth's swollen belly and twiglike limbs make her look like a starvation victim, the lethargic baby has no interest in food of any kind. Little Betsy, as her parents call her, has a fatal disease in 1940: the blood cancer known as leukemia. What makes her case especially tragic is that the illness may be the result of new medical technology. Born in August 1938, Elizabeth appeared normal. But, three or four days later, a thick red growth appeared on her cheek, while a red birthmark marred the child's neck. To stop the growth and prevent the spread of the unsightly birthmark, a series of radium treatments were given. The cheek growth disappeared, and the birthmark's spread was halted. But after this "success" the child simply stopped growing normally. She seemed lifeless. Even her hair drooped and grew no more.

A specialist's deadly diagnosis was only confirmed by a trip from the Fannings' Dearborn, Michigan, home to Minnesota's renowned Mayo Clinic. The baby's spleen should be removed, all doctors consulted agree, but the Mayo physicians in Rochester warn that the baby is already too weak to live through such an operation.

The rich nutrition of liver soup may buy a little time, but the doctors all warn Mrs. Fanning there can be but one outcome to childhood leukemia.[65] The mother must prepare herself that she may simply find

---

[65] Happily, no longer the case.

the child dead in her crib at any time. So sure is Elizabeth's death that her doctors in Dearborn waive any further fees.

Then Mrs. Fanning's aunt, who belongs to a spiritual group affiliated with St. Bonaventure's Franciscan Capuchin monastery in Detroit suggests little Betsy be taken to a lively, seventy-year-old priest there called Fr. Solanus Casey.

"He's a saint, and he heals people all the time," Mr. and Mrs. Fanning are told. With no earthly possibility for their dying daughter's recovery, the Fannings drive to Detroit. They carry the child, who at a year and a half cannot walk, up to the door of St. Bonaventure's.

The Franciscan who greets them so warmly wears the Capuchin brown robe, its pointed hood thrown back on his skinny shoulders. In spite of his untrimmed white beard, the old priest has the shining face of a happy child, his blue eyes as innocent as their baby's.

As he listens to their personal tragedy, Fr. Solanus's face radiates loving compassion. In spite of the many other sufferers waiting to speak with him, the Fannings sense that he is totally —and peacefully—at their disposal. The only thing, he assures them, that can stop the power of God at work in our lives is our own doubt and fear. He urges the parents to make concrete acts that will foster their confidence in God's goodness. Let them try to overcome their sadness and anxiety, which "frustrates God's merciful designs." He even recommends they thank God *now* for what He will do in the future, *whatever that may be*. This kind of confidence in God "puts Him on the spot," he explains with a grin. He tells them of some healings he has witnessed, cases just as "hopeless" as their daughter's. The Fannings enroll Betsy in the Capuchin Order's Seraphic Mass Association[66] to benefit from hundreds of Mass prayers with a donation to the missions. Each also makes a personal promise to God of a spiritual nature. (Samples: an infrequent Protestant churchgoer commits to go every Sunday; a Catholic who goes to Communion weekly commits to go twice weekly; spiritual reading is promised, in one case from the Bible, in another from the work of a saint.)

Now, in his unusually high-pitched yet whisper-soft voice (the leftover, it is believed, of childhood diphtheria, which killed two of his sisters), Fr. Solanus talks to listless Elizabeth for a few minutes. Then he

---

[66] At present called Capuchin Mission Association.

says matter-of-factly, "You're going to be all right, Elizabeth." Ignoring her skeletal appendages and distended stomach, he hands her a piece of candy as if the child *he* sees is well.

Elizabeth Fanning has been leukemic almost her entire short life. She has never done the things babies do, any more than she has ever attained the rosy looks of normal babyhood. But as her parents begin the drive home to Dearborn, Elizabeth has a new alertness. For the first time in her life, she watches everything with interest. She smiles. She sits up.

Her parents are startled, almost shocked, but are so happy at the sudden, inexplicable change that they stop at a restaurant "to celebrate." Mrs. Fanning says: "The place was crowded—and Betsy—who only an hour before had been lying in my arms as limp as a rag doll— immediately became the "life of the party." She waved to the people about us, jumping up and down. She was full of life."

Soon she was walking. In the late 1960s, when Betsy's mother was interviewed by James Patrick Derum for his book on Fr. Solanus, *The Porter of Saint Bonaventure's,* Mrs. Fanning recalled: "When I brought her back to the doctors, they were incredulous. She looked so different—healthy, lively, and her once wispy, lifeless hair was now curly."

"That's not Betsy!" they exclaimed.

But it was. While childhood leukemia remained a fatal disease for many years after 1940, little Betsy Fanning simply didn't have it anymore after visiting Fr. Solanus Casey.

⌒

"You'll be all right," the Capuchin priest had said simply. Betsy was no isolated instance of his prophecy proving correct. For half a century, Fr. Solanus's gift of healing was so great that, beginning in November 1923, when he was stationed at Our Lady Queen of Angels Monastery in Harlem, New York, his superiors asked him to keep a notebook of prayer requests and answers. Always obedient, he tried. But "the holy priest," as people referred to him even in his first priestly assignment at Sacred Heart Monastery in Yonkers, New York, in 1904, had so many demands for prayers, it proved impossible to record them all, even in his eighteen- or nineteen-hour days. This became clear after his death, when scores of people were interviewed regarding physical cures and other favors they said they received after Fr. Solanus had enrolled them in the Seraphic Mass Association, the organization that combined mutual prayer support, including prayers and remembrances at Mass by all the Capuchins, with aid to the missions. Even the six thousand notes from just his twenty-one years at St. Bonaventure's must be only a fraction of the Detroit total, since only a few of the cures that interviewers found in that city had been recorded.

About one in ten of these notes has a follow-up entry. Many of the healed either never took the trouble to come back and report or Fr. Solanus never got around to entering their statements. Known cures, whether logged or not, include everything from cancer to heart disease, from deafness to diabetes, from polio to bone disease, from broken backs to infertility. A few samples from the log, which include a follow-up, are given pretty much verbatim but without addresses:

March 8, 1925—Mrs. Stella Sherwin, 47, from McKeesport, Pa., suffering from gall stones when, on Feb. 10, her daughter, living in Detroit, enrolled her in S.M.A. and sent her the certificate. The time of her cure corresponded with that of the issuance of the certificate.

July 26, 1926—Russell Jay, 17,... 49 inches tall is enrolled ... (non-Catholic). Asks Fr. Solanus to "make me grow."

Jan. 2, 1927—Today Russell Jay reported he grew 4½ inches—1st change in 12 years—Now developing normally.

Oct. 12, 1931—Mrs. Mary E. Reynolds, 59, of Clinton, Ont. 17 years with epileptic seizures. Enrolled about July 25th. Has not had a shadow of an attack since. Deo Gr.[67]

Dec. 9, 1932—Doraine Innes, 8, of Montreal. At 4 had meningitis of brain—then paralysis and curvature of spine and cross-eyed. Enrolled in 1930. Since day of enrollment has been able to walk without crutches.

August 8, 1935—Floyd McSweyn, now 24, of Merrill, Mich. In May 1933, fell 18 feet to cement floor, received to all reckoning

---

[67] This Latin phrase for "Thanks be to God" is found over and over in the ledger.

fatal skull fracture. His mother tells us today that Fr.[68] assured her "the boy will be better inside of five hours." [He was] blind and dumb and totally paralyzed at time mother phoned. ... Completely and permanently recovered—save hearing in one ear.

Dec. 29, 1937—John Charles Kulbacki, 6, blind since 3 weeks old; was enrolled in S.M.A. 6 weeks ago. On Xmas Day when at "Crib" here in Church, was almost frightened as he exclaimed—pointing to the lighted "crib": "Look, Mama." Deo Gr.

Nov. 19, 1938—Thanks—Marlene, 6, was inward bleeder [note: hemophiliac] before she came ... A year ago was prayed for and enrolled—had 5 hemorrhages day before—has never bled since. Deo Gr.

Oct. 27, 1943—Patrick McCarthy, 44,... lip cancer. Threatened starvation. Nov. 9 Dr. Wm. Koch ... hardly able to speak from emotion at the wonderful improvement [in McCarthy]. ...

Jan. 7, 1945—Robert Hamilton, 44, enrolled last Wed. expecting brain tumor operation on Friday. Drs. who had x-rayed his head were astounded at finding no tumor.

Modesty wouldn't have prevented recording any cures.

"If people were cured before his very eyes," according to a Capuchin quoted by Derum, Fr. Solanus's eyes "would fill with tears, and he would seem utterly amazed at the power of the Mass ... [in his mind] their cure had no connection with him...."

Few dreamed that the thousands of physical cures, changes of heart, and other graces God gave through Fr. Solanus Casey, like a great tree from a tiny seed, had all grown from one act of blind trust in God made by the young Casey as a seminarian.

Born in Prescott, Wisconsin, on November 25, 1870, Bernard Casey, Jr., as Solanus was christened, was the sixth of sixteen handsome, sturdy, well-liked children born to Irish immigrants. His mother's brother a Wisconsin priest, his father's brother a Boston judge, the Caseys were an

---

[68] In his detachment he writes of himself in the third person as having made this prediction. Because of the altered brain states associated with sanctity, he may actually have been unaware that he said such things.

intelligent family of prosperous farmers. They raised their large brood in an atmosphere combining care and firm discipline with Irish folk songs, daily family prayer and spiritual reading, and good American and Irish literature read aloud by the father on cozy family evenings.

If Barney grew up caring and well balanced, he felt it was because he had an idyllic childhood, whether as part of the baseball team made up of nine Casey brothers or reveling in the beautiful Wisconsin fields and waterways. At eighteen, after two years of a happy relationship, he proposed marriage to a girl a year younger whose mother promptly sent the intended bride away to boarding school. He kept dating, but his main energy seems to have veered away from marriage. After diverse jobs, including prison guard (typically he made friends with various prisoners), the devout young man made up his mind he was called to serve God as a priest. At twenty-six he entered the local diocesan seminary but failed there, because it was run by Germans in German and Latin. As they showed him the door, the seminary heads encouraged Barney to enter a religious order instead. Making a novena for guidance, he heard an unforgettable voice direct, "Go to Detroit" and found himself in a Capuchin seminary where the courses were again taught in German and Latin.

Because of his spirituality, the Capuchins were not about to let him go — in fact, one superior predicted even then that Casey would be an American Curé d'Ars — but neither did they want a priest who hadn't mastered all the theological nuances taught in their academic courses. Solanus, as they had renamed him, was asked in 1901 to sign a statement, the crucial segment of which translates from German as: "Since I do not know whether as a result of my meager talents and defective studies I am fit to assume the many-sided duties and serious responsibilities of the priesthood, I hereby declare that I do not want to become a priest if my legitimate superiors consider me unqualified."

Had pride or self-will reared its head, Solanus's whole future ministry would have been aborted. As it was, however hurt and baffled the intelligent and hardworking young man may have felt — something he never discussed — he made a heroic act of trust in God, who, he believed with all his heart, had brought him to this German immigrant-founded institution.

He signed.

To his great joy, he was ordained in 1904, but to his humiliation he was made a priest simplex, that is, a priest who could say Mass, but "doesn't know enough" to hear confessions or preach. Again, enormous temptation to despair, to anger, to self-pity, to depression, to every kind of negative response. Instead Solanus, in his thirty-fourth year, made the response of a person at least close to holiness: he accepted what would be a lifelong humiliation and prayed week after week, month after month, until he could actually thank God for apparently making him so ineffectual a priest that his superiors were hard put to find anything for him to do except manage the altar boys and answer the door as a porter.

A fellow Capuchin who knew him has remarked that it was through his ever more spiritualized and finally joy-filled response to this humiliation that Solanus Casey became holy. As the years passed, it also became clear that the apparent blight on Solanus's life of being a simplex priest was actually part of God's wonderful design, for it was through the Capuchin's assignments as porter in New York, Detroit, and Indiana that God carried out the immense ministry he entrusted to the man judged "too dumb"[69] to be a full priest.

Although his whole ministry grew out of Casey's heroic surrender to God's designs, the young Capuchin was not born a saint, but a red-blooded American with normal human feelings and weaknesses. He had a rebel streak and tendencies to independence and individualism that had to be sublimated to living in community. Capuchin Michael H. Crosby, in his study *Thank God Ahead of Time: The Life and Spirituality of Solanus Casey*, also notes that throughout his life the emotional Casey would "battle with feelings that could easily get expressed in anger, intolerance and excessive concern over little things." A kind of perfectionism had to be softened to keep him from excessive rigidity or anxious scrupulosity. An impulsive person who tended to act first, think later, with his idealism, emotionalism, and perfectionism, he had a tendency when young to criticize others, if only to himself. Yet, as is so often the case with this type of personality, he himself was sensitive to criticism and liked compliments.

Since he was always a well-liked, well-adjusted, "people" person, one can see that these human frailties were not extreme; still they had to

[69] Biographer Michael Crosby estimates Casey's IQ at 135.

be worked through—a matter of years, not one or two good resolutions—for Solanus to find that union with God and charity toward all from which miracles spring. Single-minded and perseveringly in love with God, Solanus grew ever more aware that, however "together" or even holy he appeared to others, he had his own imperfections and needed never-ending healing himself.

It was this knowledge of himself as one who needs conversion that gave Solanus compassion for others. His awareness of his human status as a sinner kept him safely anchored in humility, while his experience of God's grace in his weakness continually deepened his trust in God so that by his later years Solanus was "uniquely unshaken by doubt, anxiety, or fear," says Crosby.

Similarly Fr. Solanus's innate compassion for the ill was reinforced by his own physical sufferings. Already back in the Milwaukee diocesan seminary, he suffered from chronic quinsy, that is, abscesses of the tonsils and surrounding area, which not only made him feverish much of the time but caused pain and swelling in his throat so that each word became a strained croak.

In his early thirties he was in great anxiety over trouble with his eyes. He found healing when he took action against his fear of losing his sight by trying to be thankful to God and positive that whatever was occurring would be to his benefit if he let God work. Next he says: "I had completely lost the hearing in my left ear and the same condition was rapidly threatening the other side."

Returning from an ear specialist with a throbbing earache after a very painful treatment, with the prospect of becoming deaf, he decided he needed someone else to pray for him. He turned to a woman he had never met but whom he felt he could count on as a friend in Heaven after reading her biography. He made her "a mental proposition": she should pray for his healing and he would reread her book. The healing through Thérèse Martin, today canonized as St. Thérèse of Lisieux, increased in Solanus the absolute trust in God Thérèse recommended. So did a brush with death around 1920, when he survived gangrene. By 1940, when he was seventy, a chronic health problem was ulcerated eczema or psoriasis on his legs which caused open, oozing sores and hospitalized him periodically. Spiritually, his health was so good, however, that he was believed, by the majority of those who knew him, to be a saint.

Because of this psychospiritual wholeness, the skin problems, which would later advance to skin cancer and a streptococcus skin infection causing terrible itching and pain, did not preoccupy him. Even intense pain did not turn him inward: instead it increased his empathy for others in pain. But, by age seventy-six, while he desired to go on until he "died in his tracks" with his service to people of every creed, color, or condition, his superiors decided to officially retire him as the only way to prolong his life.

Still, even at eighty, between bouts with his skin diseases, his energy was astounding. Unless sick, he always ran up the monastery stairs to his room on the second floor. He played tennis and volleyball with young men and, if he fell, leapt up like a youngster and went on playing. If there weren't any games going on, the skinny octogenarian went jogging "to keep in trim."

Saints abound in paradox, and Solanus's care for exercise and healthful diet is part of a paradoxical attitude toward his health: he wanted to keep fit, but even when he was very sick or in great pain "the thought of saving himself" by not making himself available to people who bombarded him by phone, letter, or in person "would never have entered his head," because, more than he wanted anything else, he wanted to give himself to God through service to suffering humanity.

More and more, even in illness, he said from his depths, "How wonderful are all God's designs for those who have confidence." In 1949, hospitalized with legs like "raw meat," blood circulation loss was feared. Doctors stood by to amputate both legs, while every three minutes a nurse checked the seventy-nine-year-old's circulation. Fr. Blase Gitzen, interviewed by fellow Capuchin Michael H. Crosby for Crosby's biography of the holy American, recalls that Solanus's condition was so serious that his hospitalization was kept secret to spare him the people who followed him everywhere. Still, when Fr. Blase visited Solanus in a Fort Wayne, Indiana, hospital:

> To my utter surprise, despite a big DO NOT DISTURB sign on the door, I found fifteen people in the room ... Some had come from as far away as Detroit. How they found him, I'll never know. But here he was, propped up in bed, with a white canopy over his legs, amiably chatting with his visitors. And sure enough, every

three minutes, a disapproving nurse came in to check the pulse in his legs.

His attitude toward his illness was one of such lack of concern, that I was curious whether he knew how seriously ill he had been and brought up the subject on the way home from the hospital. Yes, he knew that his legs might have to be amputated, but he had the attitude: "If they came off, it was alright; if not, that was alright, too." He showed absolutely no shock, surprise, worry or upset....

He later remarked he felt his soul profited greatly from the month he spent in the hospital. His attitude was the same during his next hospitalization, in 1950—he cooperated fully with his doctors but left the outcome unworriedly to God.

When Solanus was young he had prayed for his own healing. In these later years he seems to have experienced in physical misery another way he could give himself to what he called "my two great loves, the poor and the sick." That was to make of his sufferings a kind of prayer in union with Jesus in the form of reparatory suffering along the lines of Paul's: "I make up in my own body what is lacking in the sufferings of Christ" (cf. Col. 1:24). Offering his illness, he sought healing for others but only self-giving in every possible form for himself. Thus he could say to a spiritual son who visited him during his last hospitalization and asked, "Where do you hurt?": "My whole body hurts. Thanks be to God. Thanks be to God." Then he explained, "I'm offering my sufferings that all might be one. Oh, if I could only live to see the conversion of the whole world!"

There was no self-glorifying in such remarks. Solanus, who had as a young man liked to hear himself praised, was long past caring what anyone but God thought of him. Even years earlier he had seen clearly that God graciously lets those who seek to serve Him participate in His divine activity; for that one can be grateful; to be proud would be silly. To a fellow porter, Br. Leo Wollenweber,[70] he wrote, "How can we ever be grateful as we ought to be for such a vocation!"

At the same time he did not believe he had a glamour job. Listening to people's troubles of every kind for nine or ten hours a day, he once

---

[70] Later vice-postulator of Solanus's Cause until Wollenweber's death in 2012, the much-loved Br. Leo authored a biography of his old comrade.

admitted to Br. Leo, could be unbearably monotonous. But even when the complaints against life and their fellow man were "petty, selfish, and drearily like those voiced by scores" of others, those he received for Christ's sake felt only love radiating from this priest who, with gentleness and compassion toward their weakness, tried to move them just a bit closer to God and their fellow man.

No inhuman ascetic, when he could he catnapped, even sliding to the floor to curl up under his desk. It also helped to get away and play his violin—however badly—to Jesus in the empty chapel.

Humor was another outlet. It twinkled in his reply to the young fellow who came in griping that Fr. Solanus blessed his car and on the way home it was totaled. "Ah, and look at you. Not a scratch!"

To whoever came—and he had callers of every kind—Solanus could humbly admit he did not have all the answers to the mysteries of illness and other suffering.

"I don't understand why children have to suffer," he said simply.

But he was willing to share the things he felt he did know. Above all, he told his callers, "God cares for you; only fear and distrust on your part can thwart his good designs." Let petitioners do something generous for God, within their own faith tradition, certain that this always calls forth a loving response from God.

Above all, let each individual express confidence in God by "thanking him ahead of time" for whatever He is going to do for you. This was not slot-machine religion: the thanks did not guarantee the outcome of your choosing but was a statement of confidence that whatever God did would be "healing," *even if* a particular condition is going to be the means of passing over to the next life. In this vein, when Solanus's prophetic gift let him know someone would die, he still seemed able to "heal," in the sense of achieving a wonderful change in the person's outlook on death.

Paradoxically, while Solanus took no credit for healings or graces, to help those who came to him, as well as out of his love affair with God, the American Capuchin was a mighty prayer. Besides his many regular hours of prayer with the community, he loved to slip into the chapel whenever he had a break. There he would beseech God for his petitioners, full of joy and confidence in God's loving response. At times, other Franciscans would find him lost in prayer before the tabernacle in the middle of the night. And because he was human, sometimes they found him on the floor there fast asleep.

Fr. Solanus also fasted to obtain graces for the sick. One man, who was to drive him someplace one day, recalls another Capuchin telling him behind Solanus's back that the old priest was weak from fasting for someone. Would the driver swing by his home en route and his wife have a meal ready? "Out of politeness, he'll eat." The ruse worked, for Solanus was never one to let anyone know of his fasts any more than he ever talked of those long middle-of-the-night prayers.

In 1957, just a few months away from his eighty-seventh birthday, new, very painful skin eruptions were diagnosed as severe erysipelas. From the Greek for "red skin," this is an acute streptococcus-caused disease of both the skin and the subcutaneous tissue.

Hospitalized, he was rapt in God much of the time, nurses noted, in spite of the fiery red scales which erupted all over his body. His face shining, he would muse, "The love of God is *everything*." Yet, in the way of authentic mystics, he remained down to earth and good humored.

"How 'bout a blessing, Father?" a young nun asked breezily.

"Sure, I'll take one," he teased, knowing she wanted his. Yet when she mourned aloud at having to cause pain in his poor raw hands by removing an intravenous needle, he comforted: "Don't feel bad. Think of our Lord's hands."

Needles, tubes, and everything else, like the excruciating disease sucking his life away, he used as just another offering to God. To a spiritual son he confided, "I looked on my whole life as giving, and I want to give until there is nothing left of me to give."

His friend says: "I looked at him there on his deathbed, clothed only in a little hospital gown, a rosary in one hand and a little relic in the other, and felt like crying out, 'My God, there is scarcely anything left of him to give.'"[71]

But the friend was wrong. As the next chapter shows, even in this final illness Fr. Solanus was a giver, while after death freshly uncovered healings from his lifetime would merge with new cures to testify that the dead saint's ministry was far from over.

---

[71] This testimony by Fr. Gerald Walker, O.F.M. Cap., dated April 14, 1980, found in Fr. Marion Roessler's "Written Reports Concerning Fr. Solanus Casey," is quoted in *Thank God Ahead of Time*.

Chapter 4

The Best-Loved Man in Detroit

Detroit, Michigan, 1957

Thirty-eight-year-old Gladys Feighan is overjoyed, on a visit to St. John (sic) Hospital from her home in Utica, New York, to learn that Fr. Solanus Casey, "the best-loved man in Detroit," is a patient there. It has been a dream of hers for years to get to Fr. Solanus, revered by so many as a living saint; but for some time his Capuchin Franciscan superiors at St. Bonaventure's Monastery have made it hard for anyone to see the ailing eighty-six-year-old priest. Before that, when he was "retired" to a Capuchin house in Huntington, Indiana, she had actually prepared to make a trip there, but both her physician and her pastor advised against travel because of her pregnancy.

Terrified to lose another baby, she had listened to them. And lost another child, she reflects sorrowfully.

Mrs. Feighan is a sufferer from the Rh blood factor.[72] Like most women with this problem, her first pregnancy was normal. But since her first child, she has had one miscarriage and two babies born dead.

An acquaintance with a similar history made that trip to Indiana and has three more living children to show for it.

Now Gladys sees the brown hooded robe of a Capuchin in the corridor. Running after it, she begs the brother who is looking out for Fr. Solanus if she can please see the ill man "for just a few minutes." Br. Gabriel can make no promises. Frail old Fr. Solanus has been brought in by ambulance, very sick with a skin infection, maybe dying. And people have no consideration. A woman who asked to see him for a minute

---

[72] Today rarely a problem, due to medical advances.

stayed over half an hour.... The more Brother talks, the lower Gladys's face falls. But in the end, he says he'll go ask.

What he doesn't tell Mrs. Feighan is that to ask is an empty formality with Fr. Solanus: in his fifty-three years as a Capuchin priest, he has never said no to seeing anyone, whether it was the middle of the night, the middle of his meal, or the 150th person of a day. The man has absolutely no instinct for self-preservation. Because of his great devotion to his vow of obedience, he accepts the restrictions placed on him by superiors who know the mobs coming, phoning, and writing for his prayers day after day, year after year, have taken the last drops of the holy old friar's strength. But he has been heard to groan to himself, "Oh, why must they keep me from seeing the people?" To give himself to God by giving himself to others until there is nothing left is the one desire of his Christlike heart.

Soon Gladys is in his room. Let her tell it as she related the experience for the book *The Porter of Saint Bonaventure's*:

When I entered ... Father Solanus was sitting at a little table. He welcomed me, asking me to sit down. "What is your name?" he asked.

"Mrs. Feighan."

"No—your given name?"

"Gladys."

"What, Gladys, do you want from God?"

"I want a baby. Another baby."

"A baby! For a woman to want a baby—how blessed. To hold God's own creation in your own hands."

I told him about my Rh factor; that I was well toward my middle thirties; that I feared it wouldn't be long before I might be too old to bear children.

"I do so want another child," I told him. "Perhaps I am selfish."

"No," he answered me, "you are not selfish. For a woman to want children is normal and blessed. Motherhood entails so many responsibilities—bringing up a child as it should be brought up is doing God's work. One doesn't always meet women who want children."

[Gladys expressed concern about her children who had died before they could be baptized.]

"That's not for you to concern yourself about," he answered. "Just have confidence in our dear Lord's infinite love."

Father Solanus's mind seemed above earthly things. He was ecstatic—so much so that I could hardly ask him a question. After answering my first few questions, he did nearly all the talking. His words to me were of God's infinite love for us, and of how we should place all our confidence in that divine, all-embracing love. As he spoke, he was trembling with emotion. Finally he said, "Kneel down, and I will bless you, and your husband and all your family."

The other Capuchin was there, and a Sister of St. Joseph [who was] one of the hospital sisters, and they knelt too.

Then he said to me, "You will have another child, Gladys. Your Blessed Mother will give you another child. You must believe this with all your heart and soul. You must believe this so strongly that before your baby is born you will get down on your knees and thank the Blessed Mother [for her intercession]. Because once you ask her, and thank her, there's nothing she can do but go to her own Son and ask Him to grant your prayer that you have a baby."

Tears were in his eyes.

When I reached home, I was shaken for a couple of days but uplifted. I felt confident, happy.

Not long after, on July 31, 1957, the mystic Franciscan, conscious to the last, died peacefully. He was buried in the small Franciscan graveyard next to St. Bonaventure's.[73] There, several years later, Gladys came with her children. She had become pregnant in 1962. Her doctors feared another dead child. But she was jubilant and confident. That confidence was rewarded —with twins.

Thank God Ahead of Time quotes another mother with a similar tale. Bernadette Nowak also had borne one child, then lost three due to the factor. When she became pregnant in December 1956, she wrote Fr.

---

[73] In 1987 the body was exhumed (a required step in the process toward canonization, to protect from theft or veneration of the wrong remains) and reburied inside the new addition to St. Bonaventure's Monastery Church.

Solanus, who replied urging her to name the child right away after two of God's saints and enroll in the Capuchins' Mass association. He would certainly pray for her "good intention." When he died, the following summer, the pregnant Mrs. Nowak was one of thousands who filed past his coffin. When she approached the casket, the baby, who had been very still for days, suddenly began to leap inside her. Her whole dress moved, to her embarrassment.

Anthony Joseph was born not long after with the cord wrapped twice around his neck and with a knot in it. But Mrs. Nowak wasn't worried. She had felt Fr. Solanus's comforting presence throughout the fast and easy delivery. And indeed her son was fine.

Others had similar tales of graces received. The mother of Capuchin missionary Bishop Cuthbert Gumbinger told her son in 1959 that she attributed her recovery from a heart attack to the intercession of Solanus. Bishop Gumbinger was no doubter: Fr. Solanus had appeared to him in a dream and immediately afterward obtained several things the missionary needed.

Gladys Redfern was another grateful individual. In 1964 three examinations and x-rays showing a tumor in her breast, she entered Highland Park General Hospital in Detroit for surgery May 22, the following morning. In her prayers she was asking Father Solanus's intercession that the lump might prove benign. That night the doctor stopped by her room and made his last examination before the operation. The lump was gone.

Besides the new cures, people talked of healings from Father Solanus's lifetime, many newly surfaced. A few samples:

Six-week-old Cynthia Evison was not expected to live through the night in March 1954 when her mother telephoned Fr. Solanus. As she sobbed out the doctor's verdict that the baby's wildly erratic heart would not make it through the night, Fr. Solanus insisted, "You'll bring your baby home from the hospital in a few days. I'll go down to the chapel right now and pray for her."

The next morning, when the doctor bent over Cynthia to examine her, he gave such a cry that a nurse, thinking the baby was dead, rushed to his side. But it was joy, not dismay. Little Cynthia's heart was beating normally. Mrs. Evison, after Fr. Solanus's death, could point to a child who was "the picture of health."

Cynthia's was not the only cure received by a distraught mother over the phone. One day the priest received a telephone call that baby Kathleen Ann Wolfe was close to death from early celiac disease, a condition causing the infant, unable to digest gluten, to suffer malnutrition and such life-threatening symptoms as constant diarrhea. Could the baby, Mrs. Wolfe asked, be brought cross-country to receive Solanus's blessing?

"Now, now," the priest consoled, "that's not necessary." He had the sorrowful mother kneel by the phone holding the infant while he blessed them. Then he advised Mrs. Wolfe to use the money it would have cost her to travel to "do something for a poor family."

Kathleen Ann recovered.

Because of his special love for the poor, Fr. Solanus loved to help out at the Capuchins' soup kitchen whenever his callers gave him a free hour. Capuchin author Michael H. Crosby reports the two following incidents: Ray McDonough was a soup kitchen volunteer whose daughter Rita gave birth to a little girl with a clubfoot. Ray asked Fr. Solanus to visit the baby. The Franciscan did. Holding the little foot in one hand, he blessed it in the name of the Trinity. On the next viewing, the same doctor who had pointed out the clubfoot to the mother scratched his head and said that the foot was perfect. Baby Carol grew up to become a mother herself without ever having any foot trouble.

Arthur Rutledge, who worked for the fire department, was another soup kitchen volunteer. He was being rolled into the operating room in a Detroit hospital one day when Fr. Solanus happened by.

"Hey, Art, what's up?"

Art explained he had a tumor.

"Where is it?"

"In my abdomen—my stomach."

Solanus put his hand on the area.

"Have the doctors give you a last check before they operate," he said a minute later before continuing down the hall.

Art did. The tumor was gone.

When he was "retired" to Indiana, Fr. Solanus also gave a helping hand to Fr. Elmer Stoffel, with whom he helped care for the Capuchins' beehives. One day around 1950 Fr. Elmer was stung by several bees. When Solanus saw his confrere on the ground rolling in pain, he immediately blessed him. Elmer at that time was blind to Solanus's holiness and, in fact, disliked him so much that he sent many a barbed comment the healer's way. Yet, to his chagrin, he had to admit that the second he was blessed, the pain vanished.

⁓

William King of Detroit, the son of a Protestant clergyman, had serious eye trouble. His Catholic boss at the Grand Trunk Railway suggested he see Fr. Solanus. King demurred until his doctor said one of his eyes would have to be removed to try to save the sight in the other one. So dim was his vision that his wife had to lead him into the porter's office. Fr. Solanus urged the couple, since they wanted a favor from God, to do something for Him in return. He suggested they begin attending their Protestant church every Sunday instead of just whenever they felt like it. King's eyes were cured.

So were many other sick or weak eyes—like those of John J. Regan of the *Detroit News*. In 1929 hot casting lead (used in newspaper production) blew up in his face. When Mrs. Regan got to Harper Hospital, she saw her husband's chart and the diagnosis "permanently blinded." She passed out. Coming to, she rushed to Fr. Solanus, who promised her John would see. Back she ran to the physician who had just operated on her husband. He assured her gravely that was impossible: the best her husband could hope for would be to tell light from dark. Two weeks later, when John Regan's eyes were unbandaged and he said, "I see you," to the physician, the man declared it a miracle. Regan's vision tested excellent.

As the 1940s opened, real-estate man Luke Leonard saw himself as "an alcoholic bum." Living in a seedy hotel, he decided one day he was getting nowhere "tapering off." Without any hope of success, he mustered the courage to quit cold turkey.

At once he plunged into the nightmare of delirium tremens, hallucinating monsters and trembling uncontrollably. Walking the streets hour after hour, he bought a soft drink, only to find he shook too badly to get it to his mouth unaided.

Low-voiced Fr. Solanus usually saw everyone in one room, but he took Leonard behind closed doors and let him pour out his fear, self-loathing, and near despair. Two or three times another friar peered in, saying, "Fr. Solanus, others are waiting, some from out of town."

"Ask them to wait a little longer," and the white-bearded priest went on listening.

Finally Leonard ran down. Fr. Solanus leaned toward him. "When did you get over your sickness?"

"You mean my drunk, Father?" Leonard replied, doubly astounded. In that era alcoholism was not considered an illness, nor could anyone consider Luke Leonard free of addiction. Then Fr. Solanus laughed, a laugh Leonard says was "gentle and encouraging."

A few minutes later the drinker was back on the street, but now he felt, he says, "strengthened and with a free, elevated spirit."

He never took another drink.

Another individual who gained new inner strength from the saintly Capuchin was Mildred Boyea of Dearborn, Michigan. In the manner of some overbearing obstetricians of that era, hers informed her angrily near the end of her first pregnancy that she had eclampsia, also called toxemia of pregnancy, which causes high blood pressure, convulsions, coma—and death. He figured to lose the child, he told her as if this were somehow her fault, and would be lucky not to lose her, too. In an emotional tailspin, the young wife ordered straight to bed went instead to Fr. Solanus, who promised his prayers.

"Have faith."

"I haven't got that kind of faith," she answered honestly. "You must," he insisted. Then he told her she would have "a beautiful baby" and she herself would be "all right."

That night, unexpectedly, she gave birth without the predicted tragedy. The old doctor groused, "I've heard about the guardian angels you damn Catholics have hanging over you, but you had more than angels last night." His patient agreed; next to her guardian angel, she believed, stood a praying saint.

In 1957, when Fr. Solanus was on his deathbed, a hospital cleaning woman approached the younger of his two priest brothers, Msgr. Edward Casey. She wanted to know how Fr. Solanus was.

"Pretty well."

"I'm praying for him," the woman said fervently. "I owe him so much." Then she told Msgr. Casey about the accident that threw scalding water into her face. The worst pain of her terrible burns had been that people found the sight of her repulsive because of her disfigurement. By the time she went to see Fr. Solanus at St. Bonaventure's, she never left her home without hiding under a heavy veil. The old priest did not blanch when she lifted it. Instead, blessing her, he compassionately placed his hand on the very grotesqueness that others shunned. "After that," the charwoman confided, "it almost entirely disappeared."

After Fr. Solanus's death, some of his lay friends got the Capuchins' permission to form the Father Solanus Guild. To them, Fr. Solanus's life was a model for followers of Christ. To make that life known and promote his Cause, they collected both his writings — mainly letters — and testimonies about him from those he converted, counseled, and/or healed. In the twenty-first century, the Guild stocks biographies and other materials to help others know Fr. Solanus. It also continues to accept prayer requests for his intercession. The Guild's own publication, like a visit with him, gives spiritual inspiration through Fr. Solanus's words and reports healings and favors people are still ascribing to the humble Capuchin's prayers.

As early as 1966, reports of twenty-four important cures after his death were sent to Rome, although his Cause was not formally opened until 1982. It will be God's perfect timing for one of the ongoing after-death healings to meet the stringent criteria (see p. xxvi) permitting Solanus's beatification. His heroic virtues have been recognized by the title Venerable since 1995. Meantime, the following sampling of reported cures testifies that Fr. Solanus after death is still as compassionate and willing to bring others' needs to God as he was when he gently greeted the troubled and sick in places like New York and Detroit.

An Illinois woman writes: "When I was five months pregnant, I was hospitalized for an undiagnosed illness. For two to three weeks I had bouts of fever with extremely elevated heart rates. When no cure could be found, my aunt enrolled me in the Father Solanus Guild *without my knowing it.*[74] The fever suddenly broke that very same day and did not return." The letter next tells how the baby she bore was healed from the undeveloped-lungs syndrome that can menace infant lives.

Someone's son, who has had a heart attack five years earlier, suffers cardiac arrest. His mother begs Fr. Solanus's prayers. Twenty-four days later, the son is back at work. Best, tests show no damage to the heart.

---

[74] Italics this writer's.

A December 2008 report from England is another heart healing. "You [The Capuchins] kindly promised prayers for my heart ... [They] were heard in a most unexpected way. When I saw the cardiology surgeon before Christmas, I was told that my enlarged heart was now normal size. It was hard to take in as I had never been told that this was possible."

In 2009 Fr. Solanus's prayers are sought that no one be hurt during work on a rickety old barn. The eighteen-year-old helper of the person praying suddenly plunges eight feet through an upper floor to land on rocks, just laughs, and walks away! Thanks in 2011 include gratitude for the end of a bed-wetting problem and a healing from uterine cancer. A woman who has twenty-four inches of intestine removed credits Solanus's intercession that nothing is malignant.

A person disabled for over twenty years but able to function independently becomes ashamed to go out because of drooling from a shaking mouth/chin. To the doctor's surprise, after a month's persistent prayers for Fr. Solanus's intercession, the unsightly symptom vanishes.

A young husband sends his thanks. His wife had been in a Connecticut hospital where extensive tests reviewed by three doctors revealed lymphoma tumors in the kidney and pelvis. The man added his wife to those seeking the dead Capuchin's intercessory prayers. Exploratory surgery found no malignancy—and no tumors. The letter ends, "I honestly think that Fr. Solanus's intercession resulted in a clean bill of health."

From New York, a 2006 report: "A chest x-ray revealed something suspicious on one lung. A CT scan was ordered. Cancer was suspected so a PET scan followed. Turning to Solanus' prayers, the patient four days later received good news: all negative, probably just a scar from childhood pneumonia."

A woman has been seriously diabetic since childhood. This type of insulin-dependent diabetes,[75] is a chronically life-threatening disease with a host of potentially fatal complications. For such an individual to try to bear a child is extremely risky. Determined to do so, this wife has only short-term miscarriages and the heartbreak of a full-term stillborn child to show for her risks. Yet she tries again. Her mother writes the

---

[75] Called juvenile, as opposed to adult-onset diabetes. The latter is often so mild it can be controlled by diet alone.

Guild that even spending six months of the "difficult pregnancy" in the hospital, her daughter still must let the baby be taken prematurely by Caesarean.

The grandmother can see through a window the nurses and doctors surrounding the newborn, who, she says, "appeared lifeless."

"Is the baby's condition critical?" she begs a scurrying nurse, only to be put off with insensitive remarks that imply: What can you expect in such a situation? Thinking of the previous stillbirth, the grandmother agonizes, "Oh, please, God, not again! Fr. Solanus, please pray for her." Even when she is told to go home, on the way she repeats, "Please, God; Fr. Solanus, please pray for her." She admits she has no idea—for at the time she knows little of him and nothing of his special concern for mothers and babies—why she feels led to ask Fr. Solanus's prayers. Today, however, she is sure Solanus's request to God is the main reason for her "miracle" granddaughter, who survived a good deal of time in intensive care and is neither, as had been predicted, retarded nor diabetic.

From New England, the grateful parent of a fifteen-year-old boy writes:

> My son, age 15, was diagnosed as having lymphoma [cancer of the lymph-node system]. Two biopsies were done. The surgeon told us that he was quite sure the biopsies would be malignant and that we should not even consider that they would be benign. We were devastated, but we told the surgeon that we believed in miracles. We asked for the intercession of Fr. Solanus.
>
> Praise be to God, the biopsies were benign and the surgeon was amazed. My son had further testing with an oncologist and all was fine. I thank Fr. Solanus for his intercession and I praise the Holy Name of God. Fr. Solanus's intercession must be so powerful before the throne of God.
>
> Amen.

Chapter 5

"No Comparable Case in Medical Literature"

Catholic immigrants poured into America in the nineteenth century. Low on the economic and social totem poles, the newcomer's spiritual poverty was often greater: with no knowledge of English, in far too many cases the immigrant could not understand a sermon, be counseled in Confession, or read a Catholic periodical. On his deathbed he had little hope for recognizable words of priestly comfort. To answer these needs, heroic priests and nuns left their homelands, many times never to see their families again.

An intelligent, quietly good-tempered young seminarian from Bohemia,[76] short, stocky, big-eyed John Neumann heard the call from God, he thought, to missionary life. The wrenching part was telling his supportive, pious family, who were already preparing new clothes for his first Mass and happily contemplating his years of service in their little town.

Two brief anecdotes courtesy of Redemptorist Michael J. Curley's biography[77] of Neumann describe the parents who molded this sturdy lad.

An industrious small businessman with a tiny home factory of three or four employees where stockings were loomed, Philip Neumann once discovered a thief was quietly stealing from him. When he confronted the fellow in the act with witnesses, instead of sending for the police, he asked, "How can you go on offending God like this?"

"I'm so poor," pleaded the thief.

[76] His father came from Bavaria, in today's West Germany; his mother was Czechoslovakian. Bohemia is inside today's Czech Republic on the west side. People of the area are still called Bohemians.
[77] *Bishop John Neumann C.SS.R.: Fourth Bishop of Philadelphia.*

"But if you'd only let me know, I'd *give* you what you need," Neumann declared. Then he made the witnesses promise to say nothing about the matter, added a bit more to his robber's take, and dismissed the man with a reminder that whenever he was in need he should come for Neumann's help.

Agnes Neumann, who cheerfully bribed whichever one of her six children was handy to attend daily Mass with her, was known for her charitable tongue. If by chance someone began to blacken the character of another, she would stop the trend of the conversation by saying, "Oh, what use is this talk about another's sins? We, too, have our weaknesses, and God is so patient with us!" Visitors who refused to take the hint were not invited again. The deep spirituality of such parents set young John free to be a missionary.

But even with his family's unselfishness, young Neumann was beset with bureaucratic difficulties when he actually tried to leave for America. Checks for many months both at home and from America grinding away at his idealism, the young linguist (he already had under his belt German, Czech, Greek, Italian, Spanish, Latin, French, and English) proved himself a true son of his parents when it came to doing God's will whatever the cost. When others backed out he made the trip alone, paying his own way. Worse, he was unordained, all ordinations having been postponed indefinitely in his home diocese, and no bishop had agreed to receive him for Ordination in the United States. That strength of character and courageous reliance on God was typical of Neumann, who would become a saint by simply putting one foot in front of the other wherever God pointed the way, no matter what the obstacles.

Arrived in New York City in May 1836, the young man found all obstacles suddenly melted away: he was greeted with open arms for his knowledge of languages and ordained at the old St. Patrick's Cathedral on Mott Street within a month.

After serving his fellow immigrants in such places as upper New York State, Pittsburgh, and Baltimore, John Neumann was proposed as bishop of Philadelphia, a town which had burned a church, convent, and forty homes in anti-Catholic riots just eight years earlier.

Humble and self-effacing, Neumann, who had joined the Redemptorist religious congregation to find support for a deep interior life, appealed to everyone—his religious superiors, American bishops, even various houses of nuns to help him "escape" becoming a bishop. But when the pope ordered him to accept the job, he quietly proved a real father to his people and an innovator: his was the first diocesan school system and the first diocesan Forty Hours' Devotion to the Eucharist. He not only welcomed various other religious orders to his diocese but, at the pope's urging, founded an order of sisters as well. A prodigious worker, in spite of economic depression and the prevailing prejudice against anything Catholic, he built and staffed schools, churches, convents, orphanages, and other charitable institutions. Above all, he was the good shepherd: children running to him for a shy smile and the candy ever present for them in his shabby coat pocket; the poor encouraged to count on his openhearted charity whatever his own financial worries; and the suffering sure of a supportive word. To offer those words, he taught himself new languages (it is said he could get by in eleven), at least well enough to meet the needs of his multilingual flock, whether Gaelic-speaking coal miners or the Italians for whom he founded the first national parish conducted all in their native tongue.

This workaholic (he made a vow never to waste time and kept it) was still an ardent lover of God, who, besides his ongoing prayer life, tried to set aside a whole day each month to be alone with the Lord.

You understand the man's soul when you see him, smiling benignly, lost in the crowd at the dedication of one of the new churches, while his associates bask in glory, heading the ceremonies in the bishop's place up on the altar. No wonder wise people looked beyond Neumann's unprepossessing manner to whisper that their soft-spoken bishop was surely a saint. Still, if his prayers healed anyone during his lifetime, it is a well-kept secret. Indeed the only miracle recorded of his life is how one man could so totally pour himself out in love of God and service to the human family.

Worn out at only forty-eight, he collapsed on the street and died.

What he himself had judged a life that fell short in many ways, others saw differently. Mrs. Mary Allen, who had written her friend the archbishop of Baltimore her conviction of Neumann's sanctity, now wrote in another letter, "We miss our bishop very much; we go to his tomb to pray...." From the day of the funeral, January 9, 1860, cures were attributed to the bishop's intercession, one of the first being that of a child who had never been able to stand.

Only four years after Neumann's death, Father Luhrmann, rector of St. Peter's Church in Philadelphia, where the bishop is buried, asked a mother superior for an additional sister to teach at his new primary school for boys.

Mother Caroline responded she had no sister to spare but Sr. Anselma, who couldn't teach any longer because she was almost stone deaf.

Somehow priest and mother superior, faced with 120 to 140 little boys, conceived the idea that Neumann, who had begun so many schools, would intercede. They told poor Sr. Anselma to take on the boys and that the bishop, who was such a promoter of Catholic education and friend of children, would help her.

The tomb of the bishop was just outside the school. On her way in each morning, Sr. Anselma knelt at the grave and said three to five Our Fathers and Hail Marys, depending upon how close the hour to starting time, asking the good bishop to see her through. Then she marched into class.

After a while her boys were so well taught and managed that sixty little girls were added, bringing the class up to two hundred children at its maximum.

Those who went there and those who dropped in unanimously agree that "perfect order and tranquility ruled in that school at all times." In fact the other teaching sisters referred to it as "a model school."

How was this possible?

Once the classroom door closed behind her, Sr. Anselma could hear as well as any pupil. She fielded questions, heard recitations, and had no trouble catching little Mary Feeny whispering to Billy Murphy in the last row.

Once the tired schoolmistress locked the schoolroom door at day's end, however, anyone who wanted to talk to her had to scream. She was once more deaf. Apparently she had taken the injunction a bit too literally: instead of asking Bishop Neumann's prayers for healing her ears, she had asked only to be able to teach. And that was exactly what she got.

On October 25, 1891, an Episcopalian friend visited Mary Catherine Monroe, a widow whose malignant uterine tumors were inoperable. At that time, the emaciated former schoolteacher was so feeble she could scarcely walk across her boardinghouse room. Only fifty years old, the Catholic convert was completely occupied in preparations for a happy death.

The visitor knew her deep spirituality and had come to ask a favor.

"My sister in New York is dying," she explained. "I've heard miracles can be obtained by praying at your Bishop Neumann's tomb. I want to go there and pray, but I don't know how one acts in a Catholic place. Won't you, please, come with me?"

Mary Catherine had to smile. A dying woman like herself would never be able to make it to the basement tomb in St. Peter's, she explained, in spite of her complete willingness to pray for her visitor's sister.

Mrs. Clayton, the visitor, was not quite as oblivious to her friend's condition as she seemed. At once, she reported she had already arranged for three other women to join them. For Mary Catherine's pointers on Catholic tomb etiquette—and one imagines her presence there in prayer—the healthy foursome would simply carry the devout convert wherever necessary.

"How can I refuse?"

Hauled in, however ungracefully, to the bishop's tomb, Mary Catherine led the four stalwart Protestants in fervent prayer for Mrs. Clayton's dying sister. She never dreamed, she explained later, of being so presumptuous as to pray for herself. Doctors had said she must die, and she had simply accepted the verdict as God's will.

So she was shocked when a gentle voice which she alone heard instructed, "Now pray for yourself." In response, the cancer victim said the briefest possible prayer. Immediately a "strange thrill" passed through her body, and she thought she was dying. Then she knew she was, in fact, healed.

The figure of skin and bones others had so laboriously lugged down the basement steps now zipped up those stairs, walked back to her boardinghouse, refusing every offer of a ride or assistance, and charged up the three flights to her room. She was vibrantly healthy from that day until she died, a decade later, still cancer free.

As for Mrs. Clayton's dying sister, she got off her deathbed too—and lived another five years.

Another cure whose details were collected by Fr. Joseph Wissel, the postulator of Neumann's Cause, was that of Mrs. Sarah McKeough of the Manayunk section of Philadelphia. Mrs. McKeough had tumors in her breast. Two surgeries had not helped. With a new operation scheduled, she made a novena, each day praying at the bishop's tomb.

The final day of the novena was the day for surgery. In fact she went straight from St. Peter's to the surgeon's. Putting her to sleep with ether, Dr. Gross, the surgeon, was using her case as part of his course on surgery. A number of medical students watched as he marked the very visible protuberance of the tumor site with a pencil. He would cut on the lines he had just drawn. Making a few remarks to the class, he turned and picked up his scalpel, then bent to make the incision. He stopped, because the little mound of malignant flesh was gone. Palpating and probing to no avail, the suddenly flustered professor-surgeon muttered, "Is it possible I could have been deceived [in thinking there was a tumor here]?"

But the class had seen the mound. Their professor was no hallucinator: in the seconds it takes a man who has done this hundreds of times to select his scalpel from the tray of ready instruments, a tumor had withered, died, and vanished without a trace.

Interestingly, the patient soon woke up, said, "Don't touch me—I'm cured," leapt up, and went home.

The flabbergasted physician wrote her two or three weeks later, requesting she come in for an examination. He found nothing. She explained about her novena and how the tumor had disappeared on its last day after her final prayer for Bishop Neumann's intercession. One has to feel for the poor physician, who could only reply, "Well, Mrs. McKeough, that may be, but I don't believe it."

To give one last example of the flood of cures that many saw as God's way of pushing the Cause of his good servant John, there is the case of Sr. Carlotta, who was born Margaret Murphy. A strong and healthy young woman of twenty-one when she entered the Order of St. Joseph, a year later she began to experience pains in her left side. After five years of this misery, an operation removed diseased ovaries. Sister returned to teaching, but the surgeon had left some wire by mistake inside her, and this caused a new problem. A second surgery to correct this physician error led to a worse one: a ligament of her leg was cut beyond repair. Now the young nun could not walk, even on crutches. A third operation botched things even more.

A fighter, Sr. Carlotta made eight novenas and, after the last, was partially cured, only to slip on a stair six months later. The bad fall that resulted landed her in a wheelchair.

In August 1898, when she made her perpetual vows, the officiating bishop recommended a novena to Bishop Neumann. He urged that Sr. Carlotta's whole religious community make it with her and promised he would join them in prayer for the nine days. Her relatives also petitioned the holy bishop, making a daily visit to say the novena prayers at his tomb.

On the ninth day, Sr. Carlotta went to Communion as helpless as ever, rolling up to receive the Eucharist in her wheelchair. Immediately upon swallowing the Host, a strange feeling coursed through her body. She jumped out of the wheelchair. She was cured.

The next day, when the community doctor dropped by to see Sr. Carlotta, the mother superior greeted him.

"Before you go see the dear child," she said, "tell me in confidence just what you think about her case."

Gravely, the physician volunteered his medical analysis that Sr. Carlotta could not live much longer.

"I see. Thank you, Doctor." Mother looked very thoughtful. Then she summoned Sr. Carlotta.

The doctor could only stammer that he had never been more surprised in his life and that this was a true miracle.

⌒

Along with the more important testimonies under oath to the bishop's heroic practice of charity, faith, hope, and other virtues, cures like these were eventually presented to Rome as signs from God in favor of John Neumann's holiness. Three were selected, after rigorous inquiry, as the official beatification and canonization miracles.

The earliest of the trio took place in Sassuolo, a town near Milan in northern Italy, in May of 1923. Attending a Catholic boarding school there, the Institute of St. Joseph, Eva Benassi was only eleven when she began having headaches and abdominal pain and seemed drowsy much of the time. Dr. Louis Barbante treated her, but she only got worse. Eventually a diagnosis was made. The poor child had acute diffused tubercular peritonitis. By the time this was understood, she was beyond medical help. In the advanced state of the disease now, Eva became weaker and weaker. On a Monday a priest prepared her for death, because the doctor had told her father that his daughter would most likely not live through the coming night.

Sr. Elizabeth Romoli, a teacher at St. Joseph's Institute, visited Eva between eight and nine that evening. The nun explained how her own father had recovered from an illness through the intercession of Bishop Neumann. Praying for the saint's intercession, Sr. Elizabeth touched the young girl's swollen stomach with a picture of the bishop. She also inspired the Benassi family to join her and other nuns in seeking Neumann's intercession. Sometime during what should have been the night of her death, Eva was completely healed.

Examined by the physician who thought he would be writing out her death certificate that morning, Eva Benassi was in excellent health. After a long investigation of the cure, nine physicians appointed by the Sacred Congregation of Rites agreed that Eva had indeed suffered acute diffused peritonitis. Her healing, they proclaimed, was instantaneous, perfectly complete, medically inexplicable, and permanent.

In the final examination of her case, which took place in December 1960, thirty-seven years after her cure, Eva, forty-eight years old and the mother of two children, still enjoyed perfect health.

⁓

The second healing that went through the rigorous investigatory process to be named an official miracle was that of J. Kent Lenahan, Jr., of Villanova, Pennsylvania.

On the evening of July 8, 1949, Lenahan, a frisky nineteen-year-old, was standing on the running board of a moving car. When the driver suddenly lost control, the swerving vehicle crushed the young man against a utility pole.

Taken to Bryn Mawr Hospital, Lenahan had injuries that gave no hope for recovery: besides minor things like his broken collarbone, his skull was crushed, a fractured rib thrust through one lung, an eye hung over his cheekbone, and he was bleeding copiously from his mouth, nose, and ears. His temperature was 107, his pulse 160. The best news, considering the pain of such injuries, was that he was comatose.

Physicians informed his parents that there was no possibility of recovery. Medical treatment was abandoned. But Kent's mother refused to abandon hope. Although she'd been warned it was just a matter of hours until her son's death, she raced out to the Dominican nuns of Camden, who began a novena to then Venerable John Neumann; she and her husband went themselves to the saint's shrine and prayed. Then they took a piece of Neumann's cassock belonging to one of their neighbors to the hospital. Praying fervently, they touched the bit of cloth to Kent. Just after those prayers, their dying son's temperature dropped inexplicably from 107 to 100 degrees.

Five weeks later the "hopeless" youth left the hospital—walking without aid.

A few years later, working as a band leader and music teacher, Lenahan was asked about his healing. His explanation: "They couldn't explain what happened, so I guess it was the Man upstairs."

⌒

Before the canonization, the Church also accepted as a true miracle the healing of Michael Flanigan. Michael was five years old when he fell down the stairs, injuring his right leg, which remained swollen over the right tibia and caused him pain in the following months. Walking with a limp, that October (1962) he entered Misericordia Hospital in Philadelphia for treatment. While doctors suspected cancer, the biopsy revealed no malignancy. Dr. C. Jules Rominger treated Michael with antibiotics and immobilization in a long leg cast. He went home somewhat better, but in January 1963 the leg began to swell and to be tender and painful. From February 7 to March 9, he was again hospitalized, the diagnosis still osteomyelitis of the right tibia. Home again, in June the entire leg was swollen, tender, and a strange bluish red, sending him once again to Misericordia. This time, following further x-rays and biopsy, the news was grim: Michael had Ewing's sarcoma, a lethal bone cancer which at that time was considered hopeless once spread beyond the initial area. In Michael's case, the disease had metastasized and was in both lungs and his jaw, as well as the tibia.

Told their son had no chance of recovery,[78] the Flanigans, like so many parents before them, took Michael to Bishop Neumann's shrine in St. Peter's. This was in the early fall of 1963.

Following several visits by the West Philadelphia family and many prayers, by October all cancer had vanished from the child's jaws and lungs. By Christmas that year, when Michael should have been dead or dying, according to every known medical history of metastasized Ewing's sarcoma, there was no trace of the deadly disease anywhere in his body. Nor would the cancer ever return.

Investigators naturally asked what role might the medical treatment Michael received have played in his cure. He was treated with both radiation and with chemotherapy, using Vincristine, a derivative of the periwinkle plant *Vinca rosea*. The radiation initially reduced but did not destroy the tumor masses. Chemotherapy, given between August and October, resulted in a healthy decline in the white blood count and a marked regression of the lung nodules but had to be discontinued on October 2 because of severe side effects.

The lung nodules began to grow again and were radiated again, whereupon they regressed. Expectation would have been that eventually the tumor growth would have outstripped the body's ability to take either radiation, which itself is fatal beyond a point, and/or chemotherapy, also toxic. Death would follow.

Dr. Rominger wrote me regarding his patient's recovery from metastasized Ewing's sarcoma: "There is NO comparable case to this [one] in world medical literature." In other words, others in the same stage of the disease, given the same treatment, simply did not recover.

Another physician, a member of the panel of medical doctors investigating the cure, stated Michael's chance of survival after treatment "was practically zero." Years later the same doctor, emphatic that he has no belief in miracles, insists treatment must somehow have saved the boy. Still the investigatory panel, including this cancer specialist, found at the time that, in spite of medical treatment, the healing of Michael Flanigan could be termed "miraculous" with complete propriety.

[78] For this rare and very serious cancer, almost exclusively attacking those ages ten to twenty, primarily white males, the outlook is much rosier in the twenty-first century, when almost two-thirds of those diagnosed will survive.

The Flanigan youngster's near-lethal bout with cancer was the end of any medical problems. Still even those cured by miracles do not live forever. Like his friend in Heaven for whom Flanigan, as an adult, told an interviewer he "felt an almost personal closeness," Michael Flanigan, the married father of two, died young of a sudden, massive heart attack.

Chapter 6

Miracles in Philadelphia

John Neumann became the first male American citizen to be canonized, on June 19, 1977. For the members of his Redemptorist Order, who staff the shrine where the saint is buried in Philadelphia, his new status meant not only rejoicing, but a sigh of relief. No longer would they have to run down medical attestations and watch changes of address for individuals claiming the dead bishop's intercession had gained them a miracle. But if the tedium of investigating cures for qualification as official miracles was over, the cures were not.

Decades later bulletins published by this great center for prayer still at times publish letters from those gratitude prompts to detail a healing the recipient attributes to St. John Neumann's prayers. The priests who serve there are still approached by visitors who enthusiastically report healings for which they are now making a thank-you "visit." The late Fr. Charles Fehrenbach, for instance, many times shared with the author extraordinary cures from his personal log. Like the logbook kept by Fr. Solanus Casey, these are often abbreviated accounts, but they and the occasional bulletin reports make it clear that a lot of people—some of them from faraway countries—believe St. John Neumann's prayers are still triggering healing of everything from simple deafness to advanced cancer. This chapter will give the reader some idea of the variety and magnitude of the healings still being reported to the Philadelphia shrine.

The quoted material that follows is taken either from Fr. Fehrenbach's log, from shrine bulletins, or from letters reporting cures.[79] In

---

[79] Some of those cured through this saint have also been interviewed by the author.

most cases either I or someone from the shrine has condensed the account, since my purpose here is to suggest something of the scope of the saint's after-death apostolate as a bearer of God's healing, not to give as many details as possible of individual healings. Because of this I have also left identification undetailed, using only first names or none.

◦

After prayers for St. John's intercession, a child underwater more than three minutes and thought drowned is completely well without any sign of brain damage.

An eighty-year-old widow of Nashua, New Hampshire, writes her thanks. She explains, "I've had arthritis about twelve years and was contemplating having an artificial hip put in." Regularly asking the saint's prayers, she reports that after six months she's "walking as straight as could be, without the help of a cane and no more pain."

An Episcopalian priest, at that time aide to General John Collins (a Redemptorist priest serving as Chief of Chaplains for the U.S. Air Force) visits the shrine to pray for his wife, who has just been diagnosed as having multiple sclerosis. At the time of the visit, she is suffering intensely and has no control of some organs. Within a week after the husband prays at the shrine asking God for relief for his wife, she returns to the hospital. There further tests suddenly discover she does not have MS, but a tumor on the spine. Removing it restores her to perfect health. Doctors say that had one more week elapsed, she would have been crippled for life.

Also grateful are the parents of premature Joseph Francis. The two-pound, two-ounce baby had a massive cerebral hemorrhage at birth. A shunt to the stomach was done, but then spinal meningitis was discovered. Because it was thought the child would not live, the shunt was removed. Two weeks later, as he still lived, a second shunt was done. At this time the prognosis for the baby's future was epilepsy or cerebral palsy. Following two seizures from the spinal meningitis, it was believed the baby's phenobarbital medication would be necessary for life. At the age of a year, he is doing fine *sans* phenobarbital, a fact his parents attribute to the saint's intercession.

Pictured in the spring 1986 bulletin is another little boy. Before birth his spleen had pushed its way through a hole in his diaphragm, preventing proper lung functioning. The grandmother holding "normal, healthy" young Scott Daniel credits the saint's intercession with successful surgery. Of course Neumann would no doubt smile that a good grandmother's prayers equal any saint's.

A man from Villas, New Jersey, where miracle recipient Michael Flanigan lives at that time, writes about his wife's amazing cure from psoriasis. After a week of treatment during which St. John Neumann has been asked for his prayers, the woman's doctor exclaims, "I feel like God." Other dermatologists, called in to see the wonderful results, say, "Miracle!"

From New York comes a healing that shows how often the intercession of a saint is but part of the overall picture in a healing. I quote the condensed account directly from a 1981 bulletin:

> [The individual], 18 years old, was baptized, confirmed, anointed and enrolled in the scapular on July 6. Next day he made his First Communion. That same night, started novena to Mary and St. John Neumann. Prayer was that if he was not cured of the terminal cancer he had, God would give him the grace to suffer willingly and accept His will....
>
> Next morning the pain was completely gone; he ate and drank for first time in months without becoming sick, and the lump on his hip was gone. Every day since then he has been riding his bike, hiking, jogging, and no signs of the cancer have returned. The doctors don't know what to make of it!

A woman comes to the shrine in April 1985 from her home in Blackwood, New Jersey. In his log, Father Fehrenbach, as usual, carefully notes her full name, address, and phone number, then jots just the highlights of the healing. In this case, highlights are enough to leave the reader with complete understanding of why Annette is grateful to God and St. John Neumann. Just a month earlier, in March, she has been diagnosed with stage 4 lymphoma. Stage 4 is about as bad as deadly lymphoma can get. The bedridden cancer victim turns to God and asks the saint's help. Without any medical aid, the disease, which might easily in stage 4 be fatal even *after* aggressive treatment by radiation and chemotherapy, simply disappears. Father's note ends as do so many: "Doctors cannot explain the cure."

A twenty-three-year-old man has severe hepatitis. Bedridden for eight months, he loses thirty pounds and has signs of early cirrhosis of the liver. He will need a liver transplant. After two months of prayer asking St. John's intercession, his jaundice is gone, he has gained back twenty pounds, elevated liver enzymes count is returning to normal, and his surprised doctor exclaims, "You probably won't need that liver transplant!"

A fourteen-year-old boy is in Children's Hospital with a malignant tumor on the back of his neck. Doctors believe the cancer has spread through his entire body.

"Am I going to die? I'm afraid," the youth cries out as they prepare him for further exploratory surgery. Fr. Fehrenbach, contacted by the parents the day the boy enters the hospital, has those at the shrine praying. Two days later he learns the boy is no longer hospitalized. Those presurgery tests found no cancer anywhere, so doctors have sent the boy home.

Also grateful are the family of healthy triplets whose grandmother writes in 2008 when the girls are one. Their mother had been told she had a pregnancy complication called TTT (twin-to-twin transfer) which would kill the triplets in the womb. The family sought Neumann's prayers to God. Two weeks later the letter exults "the TTT had totally disappeared!!!" adding "the doctor could not explain the disappearance."

A senior citizen testifies: "Five years ago I thought I was doomed to a life of darkness because of retinal hemorrhages in both eyes. I could not see an object placed right before me. I had exhausted medical attempts in Philadelphia, Pittsburgh, and elsewhere." After asking Neumann's prayer help, she says: "I am enjoying my golden years abundantly, reading, attending travelogues with my husband and, with his help, taking care of the housework and gardening. With a heart full of gratitude, I am faithfully devoted to St. John Neumann."

Another Shrine priest puts this notice in a 2005 bulletin:

The wife of a labor leader here in Philly had a brain cancer the size of a grapefruit. She suffered a stroke at the same time. Her chances in surgery were estimated at 10 percent. Friends and union members joined in prayer here at the Shrine. A date for the risky surgery was set for a Thursday. Wednesday evening, at a special Mass for his wife and the medical team, a note was passed to the worried husband. A final pre-surgery test was just completed to determine how much of the bone to remove to get at the tumor. There was <u>no sign of the tumor</u>. It was gone. This weekend the family headed to the Jersey Shore.

A second spouse is grateful. Her husband, a medical doctor in Cebu, Philippines, she writes, suffered

liver cirrhosis. He was continually being treated for ascites [fluid accumulation in the abdomen] until July 4, 1980, when he was confined in a hospital. His abdomen became more and more enlarged but he was skin and bones, weighing 128 pounds. He started gaining weight and his waist reduced from 97 cms. to 79 cms. He has no more fluid in his abdomen and the doctor thinks that recovery was due to the miraculous intervention of beloved St. John Neumann.

How did it happen? Well, last May the relatives of my husband and I made a pilgrimage to the Shrine in Philadelphia, purposely to request the miraculous healing of my husband. Praise the Lord! We had our miracle!

Another letter is from Brooklyn, New York:

On Saturday, April 8, 1986, I first noticed a large lump on my neck, two or three fingers' breadth from the collarbone. It was surprisingly big and ugly. Doctor suspected malignancy. Even if benign, it would be extremely difficult to remove because of its depth. On Monday, April 14, I went to Philadelphia by train and visited the Shrine of St. John Neumann. I spent several hours in the church ... hoping that the lump would go away then and there. But it didn't.

I felt more than halfway certain the cancer would prove fatal and I spent my time praying more for a good death than for a cure. I had an appointment with the doctor at 2:00 the following afternoon. Crossing the street in front of his office a moment before 2 o'clock, I prayed again for the saint's intercession....

When I opened my shirt, the doctor said, "The tumor has disappeared!"

Someone writes in gratitude that a friend's brain tumor, removed after prayer for the saint's intercession, has left "no impairments. She is perfectly well again."

While complete cures are frequent, other people are grateful for partial cures or improvements. For instance, someone from Maryland reports: "Eighteen years ago I had surgery of the intestine … because I suffered from fistula, abscess and a long-standing inflammatory process. The surgery left me with diarrhea every day of my life and a difficult and stressful problem of control. Since my visits to the Shrine, I have improved considerably and I want to express my gratitude…."

A child who is only twenty-one months old has serious diabetes. In a coma for ten days and with the very lethal complication of intracranial pressure, he is not expected to live. If he does, say physicians, he will be unable to walk and otherwise without "any quality of life." On the feast day of St. John Neumann, the parents visit the shrine on their way to the intensive care unit where the toddler lies unconscious. After their prayers that the saint—who was always so kind to children—will intercede with God, they go on to the hospital. There they find the dying child awake and out of his coma. In 1986, when he is eight years old, his mother reports that "he is almost completely recovered," although he still has "some diabetes and some signs of brain damage."

If a saint's shrine is a place where one is confronted by the fact that miracles take place all around us, a shrine is also a place where the mysteries of suffering and death are very much in view. At the Neumann shrine, as at every place where the saints are vehicles of God's healing, not everyone is healed. The Redemptorist fathers are extremely open about this fact. While St. John Neumann prayer intercession is associated with many spectacular healings of children, sometimes even for children God's gift is not physical cure but something longer-lasting. Take a twenty-first-century five-year-old who died of her recurring bouts of cancer. She whispered to her parents of her happiness that being sick had brought her into eucharistic Communion with Jesus, as early as age three.[80] "I'll be able to die with Him," she explained.

---

[80] Catholic children generally are not given Communion until they are about seven, permitting a period of preparation—which this child obviously did not need; the possibility of such spiritual precociousness is recognized by the Church in her children saints.

The bulletin also reports the occasional case in which it seems there has been a permanent miraculous recovery and actually, after a period of restored health, the former condition returns and the individual dies.

One of those instances is found in a 1980s bulletin — the case of a little boy who had seemed to be cured of cancer of the spine with paralysis that left doctors doubting that he would ever walk again, if he lived. Walking, running, playing, the child enjoyed several years of life, then died. Publishing this heartbreaking news, the Redemptorist fathers can only say truthfully, "God's ways are not our ways," and promise the family their continued prayers.

That those prayers may make a significant difference in dealing with the tragedy of losing a child I find unintentionally indicated in Fr. Fehrenbach's notes, where he scribbles to himself about the marvelous hope and faith he found in the parents of another tiny cancer victim who died.

Many people who contact the shrine are deliriously grateful for changed diagnoses after asking St. John Neumann's prayers. Four samples:

My friend was in Kennedy Hospital for treatment of a brain tumor. Two CAT scans showed this and need of surgery. Before a final dye-injection test, we prayed to St. John Neumann ... The test showed no sign of any tumor.

In January [1981] I was diagnosed as having cancer of the bladder. I immediately began a novena to St. John Neumann ... Just before scheduled surgery, the diagnosis was changed to simple inflammation of the bladder. Some people say "mistaken diagnosis." I say "miracle!"

A mother of six called the shrine for prayers as she had cancer of the thyroid. Tests were being made to see how extensive the malignancy was. The following day she called the Redemptorists back. Doctors now said there was no sign of cancer or tumor — just an enlargement of the gland, which was treatable medically without any surgery. The lump had been the size of a lemon before simply vanishing. She credits St. John Neumann's intercession.

In 2008 a young non-Catholic comes up to Fr. Raymond Collins at the shrine to report the results of her visit there a few weeks earlier when she was prayed with and blessed with a relic of the saint. The doctors can no longer find her two spleen tumors nor the four other lymphoma tumors.

Then there is this testimony of a Philadelphia woman:

I feel obliged to report what, in my mind, is an instantaneous miracle through the intercession of St. John Neumann ... Calling on my parish priest, while waiting for him, I noticed a statue of St. John on the table. I picked it up, held it to my left ear and prayed, "St. John Neumann, please restore the hearing in this ear." I am a senior citizen and have been deaf in that ear since childhood because of a punctured eardrum. Until that moment I had never prayed for restoration of hearing, the doctor having told me the situation was hopeless.

[From the instant of this prayer she could hear but, wondering if it was imagination, she asked her parish priest, in whom she confided, to say nothing about it until she could see a doctor.]

This I did ... [ten days later]. The doctor examined my deaf ear thoroughly and advised me that while I still have a punctured eardrum I am now hearing through my conductive nervous system. I no longer have deafness in my left ear. I will be forever grateful to God and St. John Neumann.

Her gratitude is shared by a huge number of people. In addition to these cures chosen from dozens of others in my files, there is an entire book of verified healings from one thirty-year period collected by Fr. Timothy E. Byerley: *Saint John Neumann: Wonder-Worker of Philadelphia: Recent Miracles, 1961-1991*.

Here is a condensed version of just one of the healings from that 1992 book:

In February 1988, twin boys Daniel and Matthew were born to Sharon O'Brien in Philadelphia, where the shrine is located. At ten months Daniel was walking, but Sharon and her husband Mike noticed that Matthew had a problem. He could stand but even one step and he'd fall, hugely frustrated. His legs and feet began to take a funny shape too, almost like a C. Specialists diagnosed two orthopedic abnormalities. The verdict was that toddler Matthew would need ten years of treatment including his legs being broken, reset, put in casts, and more, in hopes he might walk — but the problem would never be completely done away with. And treatment might not work at all because it should have been started much earlier than ten months old.

The parents felt as you can imagine you would if this was your baby. The options were pretty dire: never walk or lots of suffering and still maybe never walk. But while they tried to decide whether to put Matthew through all this pain and suffering with no guarantee it would help, they got the special orthopedic shoes the doctor recommended and worked with the toddler—fruitlessly. While Daniel was now running around, Matthew could only stand, fall, and, in frustration, crawl after his brother.

Then one day Mike's parents came by with a relic of St. John Neumann. Not a magic object—think of it as the equivalent of that treasured lock of hair of your dead loved one or those little baby shoes from your now-adult child you still keep in tissue in your dresser—it evoked thoughts of the saint and his wonderful goodness to children and love for them during his life. Touching the relic to Matthew's feet, legs, and knees as a sign of their call to St. John to pray for the tyke, the senior O'Briens and Sharon prayed over the little boy, begging God's healing.

The grandparents left. Then, on Mike and Sharon's typical tight schedule, Sharon left for work as Mike, exhausted and his mind on things he had to do, came in the door from his job. Like children immemorial, Daniel raced to his dad to be picked up. Racing right behind him was Matthew. Distractedly, Mike thought, "Those shoes are working."

The next day, Saturday, Sharon left again for work early in the morning after dressing the boys. Watching the twins, Mike decided to give Matthew's feet a break from those orthopedic shoes. It was only when he had taken them off and Matthew stood up and walked anyway that Mike snapped to attention. His toddler's legs and feet, he suddenly realized, were no longer misshapen. At that moment the phone rang, and he learned about his folks' visit and the prayers.

When the O'Briens gave their testimony in thanksgiving, the boys were three. Matthew's right and left leg were as straight as Daniel's, his right foot straight, and his left had just a slight slant—not enough to keep him from wearing regular shoes nor from being, sighed those who love him, "a terror!"

Like every one of the true stories in this chapter, it's a truly faith-building tale, but there is one thing that has to bother you. Considering the kid received a miracle, shouldn't his family call him a "*holy* terror"?

Chapter 7

Crazy about Jesus

"You have only two years to live," the doctor says solemnly to his thirty-nine-year-old patient.

The ethereal-looking little nun does not flinch. In her high clear voice she thanks him for his frankness. Fifteen minutes later, her small black bonnet once more covering the blond curls flattened by pulling them severely back from a middle part, Francesca Cabrini's diminutive figure in its long-sleeved, cape-shouldered black dress, a simple crucifix worn over her heart, heads down the streets of Rome to the convent of the Missionaries of the Sacred Heart.[81] If the sick woman looks as fragile as some delicate bird, her luminous blue eyes are nonetheless peaceful, her smile almost amused.

That afternoon in 1889, far from preparing for death, the young head of the order is deep in negotiations for leading her first missionary group to work among Italian emigrants in New York City, where the Americans will call her Mother—and one day Saint—Frances Xavier Cabrini.

"While I work I'm well; I get sick the minute I stop working," she will later laugh. If works of charity are the lamp she holds against the world's darkness—in the process somehow retarding her own physical

---

[81] The term *Sacred Heart* is an attempt to emphasize in visual terms not Jesus' human vascular organ, but his immense love—both human and divine—for humankind in His "laying down His life" for our human family and in the tender concern He has, with the Father and the Spirit, for each of us as individuals. Honor to the Sacred Heart is in no way distinct from the whole Jesus; it is worship of Him emphasizing the same aspects of His divinity and humanity exemplified by the older term *the Good Shepherd.*

disintegration—the oil for that lamp, as she says herself, is prayer. In the many hours of prayer a day she needs[82] to slake the spiritual hunger of her passion for Jesus lies some of the secret of how Francesca carries a workload that would daunt the healthiest individual. There also lies the key, no doubt, to her happy, even disposition when the doctor says she should be disposed to depression and mood swings with her ailments and sensitive temperament.

Mother Cabrini herself, with the sense of humor and simplicity that keynote her character, takes no medical prognosis as the last word. "I shall live as long as God wishes," she smiles and leaves it at that. Others believe she is so holy that, in her being, spirit dominates and lends strength to her emotions and body. Dr. Morini, who gives her two years to live, says he cannot fathom how a woman in her physical condition sustains her level of activity, besides having such psychological stamina. Astounded, this nineteenth-century man of medicine comes to a profoundly holistic conclusion: "God helps His saints," he ventures, "and [He] plays with them."

In fact one can almost hear the divine laughter as God chooses a rag like Cabrini's body and sends it out to cross malarial tracts in Central America, to climb muleback in the snow the immense mountains separating Chile from Argentina, and to trudge up endless stairs and down fearful alleys in the tenement sections of New York—all to bear His gifts to members of our human family.

And when some Goliath needs putting in place, the Lord sends the tiny, fragile nun as his David. With the temper she is born with purified of all malice in her recognition of her own need for God's forgiveness, she can stand toe-to-toe with the intimidating official who wants to stop an orphanage in New Orleans and say evenly, but with a salutary hint of fire, as she looks up at his imposing height: "Try to destroy this work if you dare, and you'll pay dearly for it." He withdraws his opposition.

Although she has not a dime and must beg for all her projects, God also uses the frail nun to confront backbiters like the society woman in Brazil who gets some straight talk from Cabrini right in front of her

---

[82] The exact number is impossible to estimate, as she did much of her personal praying at night when she was alone; in one crisis in Seattle near the end of her life, however, it is known she prayed fifteen hours straight.

fashionable and wealthy friends. The woman changes. And another school is established. If, in the process of her work for him, Cabrini gets malaria atop her other ailments, what does it matter? She is dying anyway. However, when it seems she *will* die on the ship taking her on one of her thirty-seven missionary crossings of an ocean, she has only to say to Jesus: "If You will only let me finish my journey!"

"He, so benign, listened to me; and now I feel well, and I've recovered my old energy," she writes her daughters. She is betraying no secret. The nuns who live with Cabrini know the ongoing miracle of her survival better than she. They say, "We couldn't help noticing that although Mother was so frail in health, she always appeared strong and happy" when working for the family of God—even if this means going all day without food to get auction bargains for a new school for the poor or getting thoroughly drenched looking for a site for one of her charitable institutions. To give herself this way to the Sacred Heart of Jesus, the focus of her congregation and her spirituality, she will pay with exhaustion and fever—but only after the work is done, they remark. For all of us in search of health or desirous to maintain our health, saints like Mother Cabrini are a good reminder of what doctors have long observed: people with very precarious health, even terminal conditions, can often live inexplicably long, productive, and satisfying lives when they have something important enough to live for.

In the case of genuine mystics, like Francesca, there is even a further dimension, a kind of supranatural sustenance given to saints apparently to reveal that their very energy often comes not from ordinary sources, but from their divine lover and Lord. As if to drive home this point, Francesca Cabrini is such a tiny eater that in no way can she be said to gain from her food adequate fuel for her undertakings. The spiritual source of her energy is also clear from her sleep patterns. She rises at four to begin praying, and who knows how far into each night she prays. In the early days, another nun shares her room but finds her bed moved elsewhere one day. Her error: when she awoke in the middle of the night and the room's darkness was flooded, *sans* lamp, with the Shechinah light of God's presence, she exclaimed to Mother Cabrini, "Do you see that?"

"It's nothing. Go back to sleep," Cabrini countered. But from then on she tries to be alone at night. However little she rests, she assures her daughters that her sleep is that of a child. Even awake, as the nun who serves as her traveling secretary observes, "No infant ever lay so safe in its mother's arms as Francesca Cabrini did in the Sacred Heart of Jesus." Today from books like Norman Cousins's *The Healing Heart* we have some understanding of what an antidote to illness a saint's level of belief in God's love and care is. "This trust in God," says the secretary, "was the secret of all her works." It is also, I suggest with her nuns and doctor, another part of the secret of her vitality and longevity.

When she is sixty, someone who works with her closely observes that Cabrini "enjoys perennial youth." In bouts, anyway. That winter to spring (1910-1911) the malaria she has caught on missionary journeys, on top of her earlier conditions, keeps her in bed several months. Yet when she hears the Holy Spirit's call she is up and off. Her "last two years" God will stretch to almost three decades. Occasionally that will require a minor miracle.

Once, confined to bed and in a high fever, after seven days. she has a dream or a vision of St. Joseph.

"I'm longing to receive Jesus in Holy Communion," she tells him. "If you could obtain for me to be free of this fever, for only an hour even, I could go."

The fever vanishes. She rushes downstairs and receives Communion. An hour later the fever returns, but milder. It is the turning point. A few days later she is back at work.

Two years later in mid-March she again collapses. Having made all the arrangements for her death, she lies calmly in what appear to be her final hours. Then, in the early hours of the next day, the feast of St. Joseph, there is an extraordinary change. She recovers.

A couple of years later, in 1915, on a train to Seattle, feverish with another malaria attack, she confides to her nun companion, "I didn't expect to make this trip again. But for some months the Lord has made me feel that He wants another project completed by me in Seattle. If He really wants it He will give me the strength ... It's true I'm not well, but I'd be worse if He didn't sustain me."

Sustain her He does — if at times barely — through a fury of persecution in Seattle, where even the bishop who invited her forbids her work. Eventually, after Cabrini has been wrung emotionally and physically to the last drop, Seattle gets a new hospital.

Not for nothing is Francesca Cabrini's lifelong motto: "I can do all things through Him who strengthens me." Her whole life is an encouragement that God really does choose the weak things of the world to do His mightiest works. Trained as a teacher but always longing to be a missionary, in her youth she is twice rejected by even a non-missionary order, who explain, "Face it, Francesca. You're just not strong enough for a nun's life."

In 1880 a spiritual director who has held her back for seven years on a project of his choosing finally says, "You want to be a missionary. I don't know of any missionary orders for women, so found one yourself."[83] Just then her always shaky health collapses; but she doesn't moan, "It's too late," just clings to her motto and says, "I'll look for a house."

Spiritually the thirty-year-old is ready. She has been formed during the preceding seven years, as all saints must be, by circumstances that either foster despair and cynicism or forge spiritual greatness. In her case she has carried the burden of straightening out a collapsing orphanage while working under the orders of the woman, probably certifiably insane, who is destroying it. From that debacle seven young women follow Cabrini as her first spiritual daughters.

By the time of her death in Chicago on December 22, 1917, sixty-seven institutions on three continents will be enlarging lives, rolling back the darkness of ignorance, poverty, illness, and prejudice. Among those her goodness touches are armies of street urchins and tenement dwellers in places like Newark, New Jersey, and New York City; disabled and working miners and their families in Scranton, Pennsylvania, and Denver, Colorado; Italian prisoners at Sing Sing and other penitentiaries; five thousand orphans in such cities as Los Angeles, New Orleans, New York, Denver, Seattle, Madrid, Paris, and London; upper-class boarding schools to influence those who can help Christianize their world in several Latin American countries; countless day schools in the Americas, Europe, and England; and one hundred thousand sick treated in the hospitals she founds in cities like Chicago, New York, and Seattle. Especially dear to her heart are the hostels for young women studying to be teachers that she establishes in her native Italy, knowing

---

[83] Hers is not actually the first.

a teacher brought to God is an instrument that may touch hundreds, even thousands, of lives.

Along the way, she has also almost singlehandedly changed the image of Italians in the United States from despised "dagos" and "wops"—eleven of these "white niggers" are lynched just before her arrival in New Orleans—to people like any others with their own right to share in the American dream.

For the most part, God spares her the terrible burdens of saints with the charism of healing, but occasionally He seems to use her in this way. A Mrs. de Luca knocks at the convent of a school founded by the saint in Rio de Janeiro. When the visitor learns Mother Cabrini is not in the country, she tells the nuns how she met the missionary on a ship crossing and confided her intense sorrow that after years of prayer she still has no children. Mother Cabrini ordered her to rejoice and have faith, "for you will have a son." Since Cabrini has that gift of many saints that often permits her to see the future, is this simply prophecy? Mrs. de Luca doesn't think so. She is accompanied by the son she insists "Mother Cabrini's prayers obtained for me from Heaven."

Another incident is told under oath by Sr. Maria Pastorelli for the Beatification process. This Italian nun, at work in Rio, got smallpox and was nursed back to health by Mother Cabrini. Sometime later, Sr. Maria, still teaching in Brazil, became ill with gastric troubles and headaches. Suddenly the sick nun seemed to see Mother Cabrini, who, in those days of slow, steamship travel, was definitely in Chicago. Sr. Maria felt Mother Cabrini remove the wet compress from her forehead as she scolded the young nun affectionately, "Why are you lying here, my daughter? Get up and go about your duties."

A moment later, Sr. Maria snapped out of the dream or vision. She found the cold compress inexplicably gone. More important, she was perfectly well.

While there is no need to make too much of the incident, it suggests that just as God sometimes sent His dead saints on healing errands to Francesca, He sent her while still alive—through a dream experience linked to ESP or the phenomenon known as bilocation—to carry His healing to Sr. Maria.

On her many missionary journeys—most of them demanding sea travel of one whose near drowning as a child had left her with a lifelong fear of water—Mother Cabrini nourished her far-flung daughters with chatty, affectionate, and humor-studded letters. In these are mystical outbursts betraying her ardent love of God, like her passionate statement that the "whole world is too small for all" she longs "to do for Him." But it is not such words which made the world acclaim her a living saint, but her deeds—above all the radiant goodness which showed in her every act. The miracles during her lifetime—putting out a fire enveloping a building full of sleeping children with a great Sign of the Cross, or multiplying foodstuffs, money,[84] even building supplies—were further signs.

After Mother Cabrini's death, from a burst blood vessel, God spoke in favor of holding her up before the world as a model follower of Jesus Christ by a number of inexplicable healings. One of the earliest that met all the Church's qualifications for an official miracle and was accepted for Mother Cabrini's beatification was the cure from blindness of Peter Smith, described in the prologue to this book. In those days, two to four miracles were needed for beatification. Here is a second official beatification miracle:

To the discomfiture of certain male biographers, Francesca Cabrini had a strong sentimental streak. Perhaps this was evidenced in the second beatification cure.

As a child, Francesca imagined the paper boats full of flowers she dropped into a river by her priest uncle's house were missionaries off to China.

Even as a child her longing to become a missionary was so intense that when someone teased, "Missionaries don't get any dessert, you know," Francesca promptly gave up all goodies, "to prepare myself." Yet if she had not been ordered to found her own group of missionaries by a priest who grasped something of her spiritual stature, Francesca Cabrini would probably never have reached her goal, since religious orders refused women with poor health like hers, who might prove merely a drain on their resources. With her mystic's view of reality, Francesca reacted strongly against this "sensible" outlook. She asked one order which had twice turned her down to refer their physical or personality rejects to her. If someone sincerely wanted to give herself to God, Mother Cabrini

---

[84] See some of these in my book *God Will Provide*.

would work with her so she could succeed. "And I will *never*," she promised her daughters, "send anyone away because of her health."

That open-door policy is probably the only way Italian Sr. Delfina Grazioli got to be a Missionary Sister of the Sacred Heart. Anyone but Mother Cabrini would have rejected someone who had had a rotten digestive system even as a kid. After every meal, Delfina didn't just belch; her stomach cramped. Sometimes she vomited. But she got along well enough even to be sent out as a missionary to Seattle, where Mother Cabrini and her daughters had established another Columbus Hospital[85] and a big orphanage with its own school on Beacon Hill, overlooking Lake Washington.

About 1913—this is still during Mother Cabrini's lifetime— the disturbances in Sr. Delfina's digestive organs became more acute; only twenty-four years old, during the next seven years, in addition to her overall digestive difficulties, she had all the pain of a serious gallbladder condition, which doctors eventually discovered was causing duodenal adhesions.

Let a physician who got to be on very familiar terms with Sr. Delfina's interior describe what should have been the last four years of the young nun's life. Surgeon Milton D. Sturgis reported:[86]

Sister Delfina was referred to me for an operation October 14, 1921, [after an x-ray showing] adhesions [that is, scarred tissue which can create problems such as obstructing food's passage, etc.] around the pylorus, duodenum, gallbladder and colon. It was clear she had these adhesions because she had suffered previously from severe infection in these areas [the reader will want to remember, this is pre-antibiotic medicine].

I removed the adhesions, as well as the gallbladder plus the appendix, which also was chronically inflamed.

[Sister Delfina] again came under my care when I operated on September 12, 1922, for obstruction in the area of the pylorus [that is, the outlet of the stomach to the small intestine]. I found

---

[85] Later renamed for the saint.

[86] I occasionally expand his abbreviated medical phrases to clarify a medical term or otherwise make what he is saying more intelligible to us nonmedical readers. Generally I bracket my explanatory additions, but not always.

extensive adhesions practically closing the pylorus radiating to the abdominal wall. This obstruction to the pylorus was so extensive it was thought advisable to do a gastro-enterostomy [a procedure in which a new opening from the stomach is created].

Following this operation she was for a time improved, but her symptoms then returned.

On the 22nd day of March, 1924, she was again operated on, at which time the opening from stomach to duodenum [small intestine] made in the second surgery was closed, while the upper four and a half inches of duodenum was removed.

… Her condition was not permanently improved, so again in February 1925 she was operated on by me for the fourth time for adhesions which produced an acute angulation of the duodenum with a physiological obstruction [that is, a blockage from a kinking of the intestine]. Again all the adhesions [that is, scarred tissue] were removed and I brought the upper part of the colon to where it belongs below the liver. As always her recovery from the surgery was without anything unusual but her general condition remained the same.

The general frailness of her physique, her lack of natural resistance and the unsatisfactory results attending the operation — [all made me] consider her case hopeless; and it seemed certain she would soon pass away. I remember that at that time I made such a statement to the authorities in the hospital.

The doctor who had referred Sr. Delfina to the surgeon concurred with Dr. Sturgis that the case was "hopeless." When Delfina refused a proposed fifth surgery, this physician, Dr. Leede, did not push the idea, since no operation had made any real difference in her condition. Instead he advised she be sent to a house of rest in the country. This was done, but perhaps this stress-relieving move had been made too late: at any rate, it had no positive effect on Sr. Delfina's digestive system.

Fevered, vomiting more and more frequently, and in severe pain, Delfina "declined rapidly." As her end neared, the Bishop of Alaska took an interest in the dying young nun.

"Ask God for a miracle through the intercession of Mother Cabrini, your foundress," he advised. Delfina did, her religious community joining in. No improvement occurred all of November, and at the opening of December 1925, she hung between life and death. December 4, she asked to go to Confession and receive the last sacraments to prepare herself for a good death. This was done on the fifth.

Invoking the intercession of their dearly loved foundress, the nuns—almost all of whom had personally known Mother Cabrini before her death this same month eight years earlier—and the orphans in their care began another round of prayers for Sr. Delfina's healing; but even to her fellow nuns it seemed the most pressing prayers should be for "a happy death," because, as one later testified, "this outcome seemed inevitable."

Then, the night of December 13 to December 14, Sr. Delfina had a dream. She was with her beloved Mother Cabrini, who was seated on a chair in the nuns' community room. A third nun, Sr. Carmela, was there as well. With a luminous smile and happy laugh, Mother Cabrini pointed her finger at this nun and said to Delfina, "I'll send you with Mother Carmela."

Immediately Sr. Delfina woke up. But behind it this numinous dream left no cure. Instead Delfina experienced more atrocious pain than ever, so much that she could no longer even talk, except for a word or two said so faintly that, to hear her, the listener had to put an ear to the dying woman's mouth.

In spite of all this suffering, Delfina had new hope, for Mother Carmela was in charge of the laundry, the garden, and the working men employed by the sisters. If Mother Cabrini said, "I'll send you with Mother Carmela," Sr. Delfina reasoned this meant she was going to be capable of work. "It's certain I'm not going to die," she said to herself. "Mother Cabrini must be going to obtain my cure."

With these wishful or heroically hopeful thoughts, depending on one's point of view, she endured the intensified suffering which continued December 14, 15, and 16.

On the sixteenth the dying nun still had enough faith in the dream message to whisper to the community superior, "Mother, our Mother Foundress is fulfilling the Bishop of Alaska's request for a miracle."

The mother superior, a nun named Mother Tranquila, later testified, "Yet even as she said this to me her condition was so atrocious that she was writhing in agony. And her voice was so feeble, the words gasped with such difficulty that I paid no attention. She saw that I hadn't understood, so she made an effort and said another time, 'Our Mother Foundress is going to obtain the miracle that the Bishop of Alaska has requested and cure me.' Hearing this from her and seeing that she was suffering immensely, I thought she was delirious and her death must be very near."

In her testimony, which I am translating from the Italian, the mother superior explains how she tried to be helpful to the young woman she believed delirious and in her death agony. First she prompted Sr. Delfina to simply accept whatever God desired for her. Be indifferent to whether you're cured or about to die, she urged.

"Perhaps Jesus, your Divine Spouse, is near," she hinted.

In answer she says, "Sister gave me a marvelous, unusual smile."

It was all Delfina could manage.

In spite of her longing to tell her dream, she had choked out all the words she could. Now she could only abandon herself to her agony.

Meanwhile Mother Tranquila went to phone Mother Cabrini's daughters at the other Seattle establishments so they could all unite in prayers for Sister's death hour.

But she hung on.

Early the next morning a priest came to give her the blessing for the hour of death. Afterward, as usual, someone brought her a little cup of coffee solely for her to moisten her dry mouth. She had a little and did not vomit, as she usually did if she actually swallowed anything. The dreadful pain was also easing, even beginning to disappear bit by bit. Saying nothing of any of this, at ten o'clock that morning Delfina asked the infirmarian to bring her a little orange juice.

Once more alone, Delfina drank the juice. When it, too, was not vomited, she knew: the mother foundress had obtained her cure. But still she said nothing. At noon, as usual, they brought her weak tea. As always, it was not to drink, but to moisten her dehydrated mouth. Not only did this not come back when she drank it, but Sr. Delfina was beginning to feel hungry. The pain was now entirely gone. In fact she no longer had any sense of illness.

Around three o'clock Mother Enrica, another nun, brought her a few sugared almonds, something she could suck to get a little saliva going in her dry mouth. To Mother Enrica's great surprise she found Sr.

Delfina sitting on the bed eating the grapes that were left by her bedside for the same purpose.

"What are you doing?" asked the startled nun.

"I'm eating grapes. I'm hungry." Then the hollow-eyed sister whose body had refused for so long to retain anything said, "Bring me something to eat. I'm cured."

Sugared almonds followed the grapes down the hatch. Whatever they brought, Delfina ate. That evening, she plowed her way through a full supper and felt strength begin to return to her emaciated body.

In her skeletal state, eating or not, she was ordered to stay in bed. But loudly proclaiming her miraculous cure, she begged the dead Francesca Cabrini to obtain for her the further grace to be out of bed on December 22, the date on which Cabrini had begun her heavenly life in 1917.

That grace, too, was granted.

December 22, Sr. Delfina was in the chapel receiving Communion. She continued to gain strength. And once well, she stayed well—better in fact than she had ever been.

Those most astonished by the recovery were the nun's physician and her surgeon.

Dr. Sturgis concludes his report quoted earlier by saying, "I can scarcely express my amazement at her final recovery and her restoration to normal health and activity." There is no doubt in his mind, he adds, that the cure was "miraculous in character and due to the spiritual means employed," not medical help.

Like Peter Smith, Sr. Delfina Grazioli was at the ceremonies for Mother Cabrini's beatification. Until her death, at age seventy-seven, on November 25, 1967, the woman whose digestive system had been a mess even as a child remained a living symbol that Mother Cabrini wasn't kidding when she held out welcoming arms to would-be nuns with rotten health.

Following those 1938 ceremonies, healings through Francesca's intercession continued. In 1945, the year before Mother Cabrini's canonization, Theodore Maynard, a biographer assisted by the sisters, refers to a number of remarkable cures. A few of these include a child dying of peritonitis healed in Chicago; a young woman cured in 1938 of meningitis in Lodi, Italy, the affluent Lombard town where Mother Cabrini's family were solid citizens; a nun recovered inexplicably from heart problems in New York City; and a doctor classed by himself and his fellow physicians at Seattle's Columbus Hospital as "terminal" from an unnamed disease, who turned to Mother Cabrini and was healed.

When the Church settled on the cures that would undergo the rigid inquiry to meet canonization requirements, two healings from Cabrini's hometown were the winners. Both happened in Lodi in 1939, the year following Francesca's beatification.

Let me detail one of these as a final sample of the caliber of healings with which God has at times since her death continued to use weak, little Francesca Cabrini, the Mother Teresa of Calcutta of her day, to bless His world.

Paolo Pezzini had been kicked in the stomach by a horse as a youth. From that time he suffered from gallbladder trouble. His symptoms at times included severe pain accompanied by hemorrhages. A strong, rangy-looking man, by the time he was thirty-two he actually spent a lot of time sick in bed.

Employed as chauffeur to physician Dr. Giampiero Pedronini, Paolo was treated by his boss with various medications the doctor thought might help. Relief was always temporary, however. In fact his problem was getting increasingly acute as years passed, and on December 26, 1938, while he was driving Dr. Pedronini's car, he was suddenly stabbed by such ferocious pains that he lost control of the car, which swerved into a canal.

Somehow, in spite of his pain, Pezzini got out of the car without injury, just soaked to the skin. This seems to have started a cold which within six weeks had become double pneumonia, as diagnosed by Dr. Pedronini on February 13, 1939. From the fourteenth to the sixteenth, in spite of his employer's treatments, the chauffeur's condition worsened. Besides the chills, fever, and abdominal pain, he now showed signs of a poisoning of his whole system. On the seventeenth he suffered cardiac arrest.

Dr. Pedronini felt there was no more hope. The patient was given the last sacraments. On the nineteenth the kidneys failed, so Paolo "became convulsive and delirious, then passed into . . . unconsciousness and coma."

All treatment beyond making Paolo comfortable was suspended as useless.

Meanwhile the friends of the patient, along with Dr. Pedronini, who knew better than anyone that only a miracle could save Paolo Pezzini, were making a novena to Bl. Francesca Cabrini, asking for either a healing or that his period of suffering be shortened.

On the evening of February 20, the comatose man was surrounded by friends praying the Rosary and invoking Mother Cabrini. Also present was Fr. Caesar Barzaghi, a Barnabite priest, who was reciting the Church's prayers for the dying.

Suddenly the man in the coma opened his eyes. He sat up in bed.

"What's going on?" He gaped at the priest in solemn stole holding the prayer book.

"Why are you all here?" he puzzled, looking at his friends. In the general awe and clamor of excited cries and explanations, someone ran to fetch Dr. Pedronini, who lived nearby.

He came in and immediately noticed Paolo had regained his natural color and his sight and was breathing freely with no sign of mucus-filled lungs. He was also moving with the ease of one who has no pain, indicating the uremia was gone. His mind was clear, if baffled to learn that he had just been on his deathbed moments before.

Asking the group to step outside for a minute, Dr. Pedronini gave his employee a thorough going-over. The lungs were clear. Kidneys were okay. Heart okay. To his astonishment, the doctor found there had been an instantaneous and perfect cure from the double pneumonia and every one of its deadly complications.

Still wanting to be prudent, the physician asked Paolo to remain in bed quietly for a few days. At the end of that period, he went over the chauffeur's body with a fine-tooth comb. The scrupulously careful examination only confirmed the complete healing. Paolo returned to work. He had no relapses.

More incredible still, as weeks and months passed, it became clear that in the second Paolo Pezzini was turned from a man in his last moments to a well one, he was also cured of his chronic gallbladder troubles. He never had another gallbladder attack.

This cure, instantaneous, perfect, and permanent, was seen by the Church's investigating medical commission as a very good sign that if Francesca Cabrini was crazy about God, if she literally couldn't do enough for Him—it's safe to say the feeling was mutual.

Chapter 8

"Who Said You're Going to Lose Your Sight?"

The apprentice machinist is handling a glowing red ball of molten lead. Suddenly it explodes in his face. From forehead to chin, from left ear to right, his flesh, kissed by the fiery metal, melts away. The horrified boss applies great gobs of Vaseline[87] and sends him home. The night is agony. The next morning, his face one great swollen blister, the condition of his eyes sends him rushing to an eye doctor. Grimacing in displeasure, the specialist orders dark glasses at all times and eight days in a dark room. Then he'll take another look.

Sitting in pain in the dark lasts one day. Young and impatient, unable to stand "being cooped up," as he later explains (I translate his French):

> I asked my fiancée to accompany me to the Oratory.[88] Minus seventeen degrees outside or not, I resisted all efforts to dissuade me. At the Oratory I asked Fr. Clément for Br. André.
>
> "He's having lunch at the monastery." Without being discouraged, I [went down the hill and] rang the monastery bell. Father Deguire, who answered, recoiled at the sight of me. I asked to see Br. André. He wasn't available. I pleaded, argued, and suddenly the good Brother himself came out into the hall inquiring what was going on.
>
> "Brother André," I said, "you can see I'm too young to lose my sight; you can do something!"

[87] A much recommended treatment for burns to the middle of the twentieth century; since felt to do more harm than good, by cutting off air.

[88] Literally: place of prayer; here referring to the Shrine of St. Joseph in Montreal.

He replied and I give you every word exactly as he said it: "Who said you're going to lose your sight? You have confidence in St. Joseph's intercession? Good! Go to the church, attend Mass, go to Communion in honor of St. Joseph, continue your [medical] remedies. Add to them a drop of oil of St. Joseph[89] and make the following invocation: St. Joseph, pray for us. All will go well. Good day now. Have confidence!"

I did exactly what he said. After Mass, I went to eat a little something in a restaurant. Seeing me, the lady who ran the place was touched to tears.

That evening, my fiancée carried out applying the oil and invoking St. Joseph. The next morning, oh, wonder, lifted as if they were leaves of cellophane, the scarred, blistered flesh came off my face; the area [even] of the eyelids was completely healed — my appearance, in fact, was as perfect as one could desire: there was no sign of wound, healing flesh, or scar; no pain. I went to work. And what a stupor [I caused] among my workmates!

The following Sunday, I returned to the Oratory to thank the good Brother André, who said, "Thank St. Joseph; continue to pray. Good day!" The most, well to me, comical thing was the lady at the restaurant, who kept asking me, "But are you really the gentleman who had his face so burnt last Sunday? I can't believe my eyes!" And she told the thing to everyone who would listen.

Lucien Galarneau's testimony from the dossier of the beatification Cause, dated April 23, 1944, cites a number of witnesses to the 1925 cure.

But did eighty-year-old Br. André Bessette — who, after all, gave only sixty seconds of instructions and didn't even use the words "I'll pray for you," let alone lay hands on the injured man — have anything to do with the cure? It would seem unlikely. Until one looks at the life of the featherweight (only five feet, three inches and fragile-boned, he weighed less than many children) French-Canadian known universally as "the Wonder Worker of Montreal."

---

[89] From the votive lamp burning before St. Joseph's statue in the shrine. Such things have no intrinsic healing power.

For some twenty-eight years (beginning when he was almost sixty), Bl. André Bessette's typical day saw him open by 8 a.m. his little eight-by-ten "office" in the shrine to St. Joseph erected by grateful recipients of favors. Standing all day for six and a half hours or more, he received several hundred people (two hundred to four hundred was usual, seven hundred one of his heaviest days), at a rate of about forty an hour, thus most for only a minute or two. Ignoring the chronic pain in his own stomach, the frequent headaches, and, in his late eighties and early nineties, heart problems that sometimes caused him to pass out and necessitated his being carried up the ninety-nine steps from monastery to shrine, he listened with bent head and lowered eyes to the world's troubles. Then with a voice so permanently damaged, he sometimes bled from the strain of hours of use, he whispered recommendations as banal as those received by the young burn victim.

"I came all this way and waited in line all these hours for *that!*" many thought; yet few left untouched, captured for God many times by what the old man was: a saint. Albert Cousineau, for one, has written[90] how as a ten-year-old boy with health problems he feared might prevent his becoming a priest, he came to Br. André expecting not only lengthy attention, but an instant miracle on his behalf. He got a few seconds' advice on prayer in a feeble, if affectionate, voice. Then "Next," and he found himself outside the door. Disappointed, the ten-year-old decided to hang around until the brother was completely free to attend properly to his important problem. But at day's end, along came a very sick man who obviously had an appointment. Since Br. André never closed his office door, the boy had no problem eavesdropping as the Holy Cross brother consoled and prayed with a man suffering from terminal cancer of the jaw. Soon young Albert slipped away.

"I was bathed in a profound peace," the later bishop of Cap Haitien remembers, "my mind ... at ease."

Occasionally Br. André laid hands on (children or men only) in a manner which often seems to have little relation to what we today know as the beneficial physical effects of loving touch.[91] While at times he rubbed vigorously an affected part such as an arm, leg, or neck either

---

[90] In the booklet "Brother André, as I Knew Him."
[91] See, for instance, *Therapeutic Touch*, by Dolores Krieger, R.N., a professor of nursing.

with the oil of St. Joseph or a medal of this saint to whom he recommended most of his cures, other times he simply passed his bare hand over the area without touching the individual. On one occasion even Fr. Clément, whose eyesight had been restored by André's prayers, questioned, "Surely you don't think you are going to make his feet work by rubbing these boards?" It was a case of a man so badly injured that his feet seemed only attached to his body by a bit of skin. The man's suffering was so great that he had two wooden boxes constructed to protect each foot from the jostlings necessary to be carried through the crowds to Br. André. Now the saint was rubbing these boxes! He kept a number of ill men in his own little room so they would not have to come and go. Perhaps this case was one of those, for the account says the brother spent some of his time for three or four days rubbing prayerfully on the wood. Then he said, "Now we're going to take off these boxes, and I believe your feet will be in fine shape." They were.

The oil, the medals—none of what he did in this line was necessary, he agreed when questioned. True, in some cases he might indicate the rubbing helped increase the circulation of the blood. And to one individual he said his hands produced the same effect as St. Joseph's oil—which is as close as he ever came to admitting he had the gift of healing. But, most commonly, he explained the value of the oil, the medals, or other tools of his trade as helping the sufferer to think about St. Joseph. From such thoughts and meditations, said André, "arises confidence in his intercession." That people found it healing just to receive André's attention or even be near him would never have entered that tired old head.

Unlike non-saint healers, who usually spend their time (up to an hour) with a client, eyes closed, concentrating on the treatment or prayer, most of Blessed André's interviews passed, on his part, in questioning[92] if the health seeker's relationship with God was what it should

---

[92] Work by the late London researcher C. Maxwell Cade and associates, using electroencephalographs to monitor brain waves, shows that individuals of very high spiritual attainments can be actively engaged in non-meditative activities, even intellectual debate on a subject like physics, while maintaining the brain waves associated with a contemplative state. This suggests that in cases in which individuals are cured by seemingly very mundane contact or conversation with a healer-saint, prayer *is* actually involved, because the saint's basic union

be. To his Holy Cross superior, the same Albert Cousineau who had once feared he could never become a priest, Br. André confided that if his visitors were on good terms with God, he began by advising such things as daily Communion ("God can refuse us hardly anything when He is in our hearts," he liked to say).

That he also advised prayer for the intercession of St. Joseph is well known. Less understood is how the saint saw St. Joseph. For André, God used St. Joseph as a bearer of healing. But in André's eyes, St. Joseph was still, as he put it to Cousineau, only an entrance hall to the mansion. The mansion was Christ, the King of Kings.

If Br. André sensed his petitioners were fallen-away Catholics, the good old man told them the story of the Prodigal Son. To incipient saint and great sinner alike, he often recounted in simple words, seasoned with the tenderhearted saint's own sobs, the story of Christ's Crucifixion for love of each of us.

He did this, he told his superior, because it is hard to love God if we don't often think about what He endured for us.

Although he was God's instrument for thousands of cures, Brother André encouraged many people not to seek "an end to your trials but only grace to bear them well," since "God will have an eternity to console you for any suffering here." To some (not all) priests, nuns, and his fellow brothers, he often flatly refused prayers for healing, declaring their vocation demanded reparatory suffering. Obviously he was not a man who had any ego need to say what people want to hear!

To a number of visitors he groused, "There's absolutely nothing wrong with you!" However taken aback or even insulted, these people found they were cured of the most diverse ailments even as he spoke to them in this way that adroitly forestalled any adulation of himself as their healer.

Men friends who had been cured or converted by one they considered a saint, by turn drove him during evenings around the area (except on Fridays, which he reserved for meditation on the Passion of Christ), so he could call on five or six more sick. "Often," one of these helpers remarks, "Br. André was in worse shape than the people I drove him to

---

with God is seldom, if ever, disturbed on the deepest level of his or her being, in spite of the activities on the upper levels of consciousness.

see." Still the feeble visitor took no precautions even with virulently infectious diseases. That, to him, would have lacked charity. He was also
fearless even on the iciest roads. He loved fast cars, it's recalled, because
that way he could call on more sick. Once, a friend remembers, their car
was almost turned over by the terrible winds of a winter storm; coming
back, ferocious lightning menaced them. The driver was terrified, but
Br. André, tranquilly saying his Rosary, didn't even seem to notice. He
lived what he used to say: "When one puts oneself in God's hands, one
gives oneself to whatever He wills."

His friends, like the sick he cheered by these visits, found him good
company. Quick with a witticism and gay of heart, according to his
insistence that merriment was of God, sadness of the Devil, a friend
has recalled that with little jokes and the laughter of a child the saint
covered his pitiful health and piercing fatigue.

Home anywhere from ten to midnight, the helpers still loved to follow the indefatigable brother to the chapel for his late-night, slow, and
prayerful Way of the Cross.

"A good evening: they were so glad to see you," André would say
after the hour or so of prayer in farewell, "and one cured someone ill,"
spoken, the friend testifies, as if *he*, not André, had been the carrier of
grace.

His friends gone, André prayed in his tiny cell, according to the
sick men he let stay overnight. The little room had an opening so he
could see the tabernacle in the chapel. Often he returned there to pray
penitentially, the tired old body erect, arms out in the shape of a cross.
Exhausted, he would fall asleep, then wake and pray again. Once, when
a fellow religious asked solicitously if the old brother couldn't just offer
God his well-deserved sleep as a prayer, André said solemnly, "If you
knew the state of those who ask my prayers, you wouldn't suggest that."

Sleeping often only a couple of hours, some nights not at all,[93] he
was up again before 5 a.m. to pray some more. By preference he liked
to serve six or eight Masses a morning, but in later years, with his office
hours, he could attend only two before he had to grab a quick breakfast
and open the door to the first sick.

---

[93] Unreasonable as this seems, experiments with electroencephalographs
show that certain states of the brain in prayer can apparently give the
benefits of sleep.

If his prayers took up most of his spare moments starting long before he joined a religious order (an early employer already remarked this habit), it was not a case of intercessory prayer being part of his healing ministry. His healing apostolate was the overflow of his prayer, the love in deeds of his union with Christ. And those prayers were so efficacious, his friends saw, because of his great, simple, and rocklike faith. That faith left him calm while hurtling through the night on icy roads. It let him remark, "Dying today or tomorrow, what's the difference?" to shaken friends in New England, when his heart almost gave way in his late eighties.

Throughout his life, he did things which in one with less faith would have been superstitious or (recall rubbing the boxes) the act of a mad-man, but in his holiness were symbolic gestures of childlike confidence in God's goodness and the intercessory claim on God's heart of His saints. Thus to a group of religious just entering the area who asked his prayers for needed vocations, he asked, "How many do you want?" They looked at each other.

"Twenty," one ventured.

"Well, cut out a paper chain with twenty figures and put it around the neck of St. Joseph's statue in your chapel."

They got their postulants. Exactly twenty.

A priest was sweating blood to pay off the mortgage on an orphan-age. Br. André asked, "Whose name does the place bear?"

"St. Joseph's."

"Write a paper: 'St. Joseph, pay your bills,' and put it up in front of his statue." With trepidation, the moneyless priest put a much politer note to St. Joseph before the statue. From the most unlikely source he could imagine, money came to pay the mortgage.

To buy the mountain next door to the Holy Cross School so the healing shrine to St. Joseph could be built there, Br. André and friends "seeded" St. Joseph medals all over the area. Stubborn owners eventu-ally capitulated.

The gestures, of course, did not cause the events; they merely ex-pressed the real mountain mover, André's faith and unceasing prayer. In that faith the tiny religious could say, "If one knew what recompense awaited one in Heaven for the least suffering borne well, one would demand on one's knees to suffer." But he was aware that most people are not spiritually mature enough for reparatory suffering, even for their own ills and sins, to say nothing of suffering—as André did—for others'. Filled with the compassion of Christ, "who healed all who came," the old brother gave himself to prayer and to penance for the ill and the sorrowing. He lived in the hope that healing would either open them to God's reality and love or establish them in grace.

Perhaps the definitive source of information, including numerous statistics, on Bl. André and his cures, is the out-of-print, eleven-hundred-page French work *Le Frère André, 1845-1937*, by scholar Canon Étienne Catta. For a typical year of André's ministry, 1926, two of Catta's figures hint at the magnitude of the humble old man's work: 7,334 people go to the effort of writing or coming in person to speak of favors received at the shrine; 1,611 of these are physical cures. Many who are healed never write or return.

Some do not even stop to say a word of thanks, like the man who arrives with legs so lifeless they swing like boughs in a breeze as he maneuvers his crutches. Cured completely, he rushes down the hill and jumps onto a tram. A friend of André's watches from a window at the shrine. No one has even gotten the cured man's name. Around this time, André's mail ran to eighty thousand letters a year. Cures reported included every possible human ill, from alcoholism to gross physical deformity or the last stages of heart disease or cancer. By no means were all healed. Some failures he put down to sin, like the blind man weeping for a cure who refused to give up another man's wife; many he ascribed simply to destiny, since we all have a time to move into the next life.

It became necessary at times to send the elderly wonder worker away for a rest. Often this was to the United States, where André had two married sisters, a brother, and cousins. Unfortunately on these trips his presence was usually discovered, like the time a cousin invited him to a dinner at a New England hotel and found that a thousand people had joined them. At the impromptu prayer meeting, a miracle occurred. Such events led more pilgrims to Montreal and made André's life ever more a holocaust to others' healing. Ordered to Pasadena, California, in 1921 for a week's rest, he was asked by the pastor of St. Andrew's Church there to pray for some people. Five hundred showed up, and seven known miracles took place, including cures of the blind, the deaf, and someone whose crutches the saint carried back to Montreal to add to the two roomfuls already left as mute witnesses by those cured.

"Brother Andrew cures only by prayer," the Los Angeles papers reported.

"St. Joseph is the intercessor," he corrected. When a man in Montreal blurted out, "St. Joseph's worthless; you're the one who gets graces for us," the saint became so upset he shook with chills and had to be put to bed.

Sheltered under the glory of St. Joseph, the tiny, seemingly ageless old man never seemed to have any idea he personally had a thing to do with the thousands of pilgrims, the cures, or the erection of the largest church in the world dedicated to St. Joseph.

"Those people are so stupid to think Br. André works miracles," he complained often. "The good Lord works miracles. St. Joseph's prayers obtain them." To avoid such misplaced attention, he made himself scarce on big feasts or processions outside office hours. He liked particularly to hide behind the high altar, where he could pray for hours unseen. When a homilist on one big occasion eulogized "the venerable old man who presides over this sanctuary," André completely misunderstood. "How well he preached about St. Joseph!" he remarked happily.

If he "considered the impossible not at all unfeasible," as someone said, his expectant faith, like his compassion, was rooted in his French-Canadian backwoods heritage and tested in the crucible of personal suffering. In truth Br. André Bessette is one of the most unlikely of healers, as must be evident to anyone familiar with studies of such people. He had neither health nor energy to give. Charming with friends, he was shy and had little personal charisma with strangers. To avoid adulation, he further affected an irascibility that often offended even while someone was cured. Finally, his whole life from birth was one of such physical weakness, radical poverty, and neediness, that he seems more a candidate for healing than one able to dispense it.

The eighth child of a poor rural family, Alfred, as he was christened, was such a pitiful specimen at birth that he was baptized on the spot. Possibly he was born with some defect in his stomach. He failed to thrive physically in spite of an exceptionally nurturing mother, who, rather than aggravated by his weakness, loved best her puniest offspring. Fatherless at nine, by his twelfth year his mother was also dead, a victim of TB brought on by poverty and grief. The relative who took him in was a robust, hearty man who frowned when Alfred couldn't work as he did. In fact, try as he would, Alfred proved too weak for every job, whether baker's or shoemaker's apprentice in Quebec, factory work in several New England towns, or even such easy jobs as horse groomer. People liked him but had to let him go when tasks proved beyond his strength. His big-hearted mother, known for her lovely smile and quick song, had seen her ten living children split among relatives after her husband's tragic death under a falling tree; yet she never became embittered or despaired of God's love. An utter failure at life, Alfred's poverty, too, only drew him deeper into the heart of God, with its mysteries of suffering and healing, poverty and riches of grace.

Almost totally illiterate, he came to the Congregation of the Holy Cross, an order dedicated to education, recommended by his parish priest as no less than a saint. But, again, he could only agree with their evaluation that he had nothing to give. He neither could teach nor was he robust enough for manual chores. He could not even make a claim to sacrifice if they took him. For having succeeded at nothing in the world, he had nothing to give up. Holy Cross turned him down, then relented. After his novitiate, they declared that his health made him too great a liability to be kept. Finally, they accepted him as a sort of charity case when his spiritual director harrumphed that if Alfred, now become André in honor of his old pastor, became too weak to work at all, he certainly could still pray for the rest of them. That he knew how to do.

Assigned to answer the door, the new porter remained the same miserable physical specimen. He was unable to digest much more than flour stirred into boiling water. Yet he found the energy to race all over the boarding school to summon this pupil or that priest. He also delivered the laundry, ran everyone's errands, and washed and waxed miles of floor. He was the last to bed, because he had to lock up at night. Somehow, amid all this, he maintained a prodigious prayer schedule and quietly carried on a vast, discreet apostolate to the sick.

For his humility, one suspects, God would always leave him in the utmost poverty, whether of physical health, of learning, of status and ability as the world judges, even of reputation (many would call him "the old nut" and "charlatan"). His very personality showed the deprivations and poverty of his life. The backwoods semi-illiterate remained marked by shyness and timidity. If his union with God let him remark with assurance to comfort someone, "It isn't necessary to study for fifteen years to love God," the fact remains that he lived with students and teachers and always remained aware of his inadequacies. He was uncomfortable, to a degree, with the learned and the important. He was overly sensitive to slights even though he bore them charitably. He hid unease under brusqueness.[94]

And to further humble the humblest of men during the last few years of his lifetime (he lived to ninety-one), the nervous and physical strain of standing on his feet listening to his endless stream of petitioners—some of whom would have made anyone impatient, so inane were their requests or remarks[95]—was sometimes so great that a quick retort escaped him.

"I've made someone cry again," he would sorrow in his "feeble, hoarse, almost extinct voice," often weeping himself in distress and begging his confessor to tell him whether it was "all right" for him to dare receive Communion.

"Will you pray for my conversion?" he felt the need to petition on his deathbed. Out of that spiritual poverty, that naked, hungry dependence on God for sustenance and healing, have come so many thousands of miraculous cures, even with a second chapter, I can give only a brief sampling of the healings during his lifetime and since his death in 1937.

---

[94] How much of this was the result of shyness and how much deliberately to stave off those who wanted to idolize him is impossible to separate, but his Holy Cross confreres believe shyness played a role.

[95] For instance, the girls who ask him to prevent their brother's marriage because he supports them and they do not want to go to work; the man who inquires whether it is magic or hypnotism that works the cures; or the woman who claims God owes her a healing at once because she goes to daily Mass.

Chapter 9

Wonders in Montreal

I was very sick. According to my doctor I was going to die this same night [this is 1923 or 1924] of peritonitis. Azarias Claude, my boss, brought Brother André to me. At this time, I had been unconscious for three days.

The first knowledge I had of the brother's presence was his shaking my hand three times. He asked, "How are you doing?" I replied with a groan. Shaking my hand again, he repeated, "Things not so good?"

Then I replied, "They're really bad."

The third time, still holding my hand and squeezing it, he said to me, "It's going to get better."

At this moment, I experienced a sensation of relief, as if a weight broke loose from my brain to slide down my shoulders, along my body and depart through my feet.

... I asked Brother André, "Am I going to sleep?"

"Yes, you're going to sleep and tomorrow morning you're coming to the Oratory."

I asked, "Will I be *capable* of coming to the Oratory?"

"If you're not sick, there's nothing to prevent you."

Then Brother André, accompanied by Mr. Claude, left my bedroom. The nurse returned. She took my temperature, which had become normal. She telephoned the doctor, who told her, "I'll be right over. Prepare his wife, because when the temperature falls that means death will follow quickly."

[The doctor arrived and found the "dying man" sleeping peacefully.]

… I slept the entire night until nine-thirty in the morning, when Mr. Claude woke me up, saying, "Get dressed; we're going to the Oratory."

I felt very well. I dressed. The nurse made no objection to this visit. Mr. Claude drove me in his car to the foot of the mountain. We went up from there to the shrine on foot [note that this is ninety-nine steps], and I was able to climb without any fatigue. In Brother André's office I said simply, "Good morning, Brother."

"Good morning, sir," he replied.

The rest of the account tells nothing more dramatic than Br. André's counsel to get a medal of St. Joseph. The man who should be dead goes to the gift shop and buys one. He returns to ask the saint if it's okay to eat, since he's hungry. The saint says, "Sure. Eat whatever you want. You'll come and see me again."

At home, the nurse has orders he should have nothing to eat. He sneaks something anyway while she is taking a nap, but is caught with a bowl of tomato soup. Telephoned by the nurse, the doctor says emphatically, "If he wants to die, let him go ahead and eat." He eats and, by evening, the doctor throws in the towel: "As a physician," he says, "I cure with medicines. But Br. André can work miracles."

Only then, says Moses Roberts in his testimony before the beatification tribunal, does it hit him that the simple, undramatic events of the past twenty-four hours actually add up to a miracle.

"You'll come see me again," Br. André had said. Moses does. An honest man, he confides: "I know you cured me, but I still have no confidence in you and I don't want to be a hypocrite."

Normally any reference to the saint himself doing anything puts the little brother in a fury, but this time he only says, "What would I have to do to give you confidence?" and Roberts says he'd like to see someone's cure with his own eyes.

"If you come more often to the Oratory, you'll have the chance to see something," André smiles. Then, "Next." Moses drops by daily from then on. And the fourth or fifth day after his conference with Br. André, the brother calls him into the little office.

A man about thirty years old arrives, an English-speaking veteran of World War I. For the past ten years or so he has borne his war wound, a forearm completely bent back and rigid against the upper arm. Br. André assumes an irascible air. "Do you understand French?" he questions.

"Yes."

"Take off your coat." This requires help, and it is Moses who gives it.

"Arms at your side!" Brother André barks in the manner of a sergeant at drill. Grabbing the stiff arm with one hand, with the other he strikes a blow full strength to the elbow joint. Immediately the dead forearm falls to the man's side. Without missing a beat, the tiny brother continues his commands: "Arms in the air, arms behind your back, arms straight out ..." With complete suppleness the arm, dead these many years, functions perfectly. Then the saint grumps, as much to Roberts as to the war veteran, "You're not sick: why do you come here making me lose my time?"

Hastily, without any help, the newly healed individual grabs his clothes and clears out. Roberts scurries away too, but as Br. André has undoubtedly foreseen, he will be back, three to five nights a week, to put himself at the disposal of the ministry that saved his life: he has seen with his own eyes, and he believes.

Photographs of the dead André in his coffin will clearly show the walls of the shrine literally "papered" with crutches hung there by those cured through his intercession. A typical case is that of Joseph Jette, twenty-two years old when the scaffolding he is climbing collapses, leaving him with a fractured spinal column: he will be a cripple for life, say physicians. At first his mother keeps the pair going by selling off some property. Soon they are destitute and faith brings them to Br. André. The young workingman must be carried up the steep steps to the shrine. "After praying for several minutes," Joseph recalls, "I went to see Br. André; he ordered me to put down my crutches and walk. I obeyed. I was cured!"

The mother, the son, onlookers all wept. Br. André disappeared without a word.

One of André's many friends was due for an operation: a cancerous ulcer was eating away his thumb. Even a touch caused profuse bleeding. Br. André rubbed the diseased part a moment, and lo, once more a perfect thumb! He joked, "The remedy you've been using relieved the pain for a minute; the doctor relieved you of your money; now St. Joseph has relieved you of everything!"

While his cures of wage earners favored the poor, Br. André also cured a number of medical men. His own physician, Dr. Lionel Lamy, one of those, was treating a case of fatal diphtheria and caught the deadly disease. Br. André arrived at the doctor's home that evening worn out, holding the banisters with both hands so he could pull himself up the stairs.

"It appears you're sick," he said to his doctor. "I'll give you a rubbing." For about a quarter of an hour he rubbed the sick man's throat.

"His hand," later recalled Dr. Lamy, "was cold and rough."

"Courage! Have confidence in St. Joseph."

The night passes very well for the sick man. In the morning he coughs up a great deal and is saved. Several days later, he discovers Br. André has left a little note that twits him good-humoredly: "What do you think of a doctor who gets himself cured by a charlatan?"

Besides helping men who needed their health for livelihood or good works, Br. André also seems to have favored children in his cures. For instance, there is his friend Camille Gravelle's nineteen-month-old child who swallows lye, burning the interior of mouth, throat, and esophagus. Even after six months of medical care, the child's esophagus is so contracted that only a few drops of milk can be taken at one time — and that with the aid of a tube. Br. André declares she will be cured. Soon another doctor is shaking his head and mumbling, "I don't know what the little guy did!"

Alphonse Metivier, one of the boys who will grow up to join the Holy Cross Order and become a missionary in Bengal, witnesses in 1963 that as a young student his vocation was in peril due to his deafness. Sitting under the professor's very nose, he still couldn't hear. "My parents," he testified, "brought me to see Br. André at the College of Notre-Dame. We prayed together for St. Joseph's intercession for about ten minutes while the brother rubbed my ear with a medal. My father heard a little cracking sound in my ear. I heard!"

Then there is the two-and-a-half-year-old whose parents have been told he must have eye surgery. "Will you guarantee this will save his eyes?" the father has asked the doctor.

"No, those eyes are finished," is the heartless reply. The mother, Mrs. Albert Cardinal, later recalls: "I took my poor little one . . . ; I put him in the arms of Brother André and he took him . . . and said that there was nothing wrong. He [the son] has wonderful eyes ... He has never had any [more] eye trouble."

A child paralyzed from polio is carried in. Br. André orders Mrs. Comtois, the mother, to have little Rita walk. The toddler is afraid to try. "But I've put your boo-boo in my pocket," the saint encourages. Nothing doing! The poor mother leaves discouraged, carrying her two-year-old. But when they reach the sidewalk below the shrine, Rita demands to be put down and immediately begins to walk.

A young Holy Cross scholastic is brought in by a priest.

"What's that on your face?"

"Eczema, and the doctor says he can't do anything more." He is told to rub himself with a medal and drink a bit of the oil from St. Joseph's lamp "to purify the blood." Quackery? Whatever, the young man follows the instructions, and the next morning his skin is perfect and remains so.

From California a mother brings a child of six. The boy is in a plaster corset from which a shaft of iron juts out to grasp his head. He suffers from degeneration of the spinal column. The mother says to the tiny old man, "I have confidence in St. Joseph and in you to help my child."

"He's cured," Br. André replies simply.

The woman of faith immediately begins trying to wrench the child out of his plaster dungeon. Fr. Clément has himself had his eyesight given back through André's hands, but he protests, "Watch out, Br. André, or you'll be dealing with the police."

"You ought to have more confidence in St. Joseph," retorts André.

But Clément worries: What if the boy takes off his support and collapses? Even if the mother forgives André, what about the father? Especially if the child sustains further injury from being without his brace — it can't just be slipped back on — it would be understandable that the out-of-towners ask the police to close the shrine as one of those bogus places where charlatans encourage people, to their injury, to ignore medical help.

Trying to deflect the mother from her purpose, the priest urges her to go pray about the matter. She goes into the chapel, followed a moment later by both Fr. Clément and Br. André. Has she vanished? No, from the sacristy comes plenty of noise. She has put the child on the counter and with whatever comes to hand, she is pounding relentlessly on the plaster, breaking it open. Out of deference to the priest, André is silent. But the child freed, he gives him a hand down, and orders, "Walk!" The child does. Whereupon a new witness intervenes and demands, to prove the cure, that the little boy climb on a chair and *jump* to the ground. Three times the child does; then he runs off to joyfully race up and down the walk by the chapel.

Fr. Clément finds his legs trembling uncontrollably. As for the audacious witness, he says: "Father, I want to go to confession. It's been a long time ..."

André prays for some little ones at a distance. For instance the eight-month-old whose pneumonia has gone into meningitis; the right arm and foot are paralyzed; the poor head oscillates continuously on the pillow. The doctor says the baby will not last this night. The nurse counsels relatives to consult André. He sends word to rub the child wherever he has symptoms with a medal of St. Joseph. From the first contacts of the medal, the head stops its movement; the next morning, the limbs work again. Only a fool, of course, will be deflected by the rubbing from considering Br. André's prayers the real cause of the change. The physician is the first to call it "a miracle," according to the mother, Mrs. Armand Grothe.

Mothers were another group who could always count on André's compassion. Rather than a number of capsulized examples, I give one case in some detail because it shows the impossibility of suggestion, and the power of saints to heal at a distance. A very early cure of his ministry, it was done when very few — certainly neither the recipient nor her husband — knew Br. André had the gift of healing. He was known then merely as the good-natured little porter of the Holy Cross boys' school in Montreal.

In that guise he opens the door one day around 1880 (André is then about thirty-five) to a dour man who answers to his "How are you? How are things going at home?" with "What does that matter to you?" There to see two sons, the visitor stalks off. When he passes the brother on his way out after the visit, André confronts him: "You seem in a bad mood?"

"I've good reason for it."

"What's the trouble?"

"I've got two boys in school here that cost me a bundle; my wife has been sick for years, so I have to have a nurse for her; the doctors cost me ..." As he spills out these troubles, with the gait of a man in a hurry, he keeps walking toward his carriage. André follows him all the way. He says, "At this very hour, things are better at your home. You'll give me news [about it] the next time you come to see your boys. So long."

The pressured husband drives away, he reports years later, paying no attention to what the Holy Cross porter had said. On his two- or three-hour drive to his home, he has many other things to mull over.

At that home, at the moment the little porter is speaking to her husband, the sick woman, bedridden for several years, suddenly says to her nurse, "Bring me a chair. I want to sit up."

"But you can't get up," the nurse objects. "You aren't capable."

The patient answers, "Yes, I am capable. I feel better." The chair is brought. The wife next says she thinks she would like to take the air on the porch. Would someone bring her chair out there? And the bedridden woman walks out to the porch, seats herself, and waits for her husband to bring her news of their sons.

As he nears home, the husband has no expectation of anything but finding his wife in bed. He has not thought of Brother André's remark at all. But as he pulls into his property, where the house, with a big porch, sits well back from the road, he notices someone on the porch. "Who could that be?" he wonders. The nearer he gets, the more it seems to resemble his wife.

When he sees it *is* his wife, he drops the reins, leaves horse and carriage, and runs to the porch. Only then will he give thought to André.

Years later, as an old man, and his wife still in good health, he will confide the whole story to Azarias Claude, one of André's coworkers. Claude will relate it to Br. André, who admits: yes, it is true.

Another group who seem to have a special place in Br. André's heart are those who have no faith. In fact he will tell a friend that he believes whereas individuals like the man healed on his twenty-second visit to the shrine are often people of great faith who are tested in the fire, so to speak, to increase their virtue even more, many instant healings are given to those with no faith. This is to heal them of their spiritual weakness. Again, I give just one example in some detail to stand for a whole group of healings. I give the testimony of Sr. Saint-Jacques of the Order of Sisters of the Holy Family as she gave it in 1958 (my translation from the French):

I was sick at the mother house [at Sherbrooke, Quebec, Canada] since 1925. All the doctors had said my case was incurable. In 1934, driving to the States, Br. André said to the driver, "Let's stop at the Sisters of the Holy Family."

The infirmarian proposed to me to see him. I refused, saying, "I'm going to the infirmary chapel. I don't want to see him because I have no confidence." My spine was interiorly twisted and I didn't want to hear, as I knew Brother André often said, "You've nothing wrong with you," or something of that sort. [Note: In the text there is no final quotation mark; I have arbitrarily placed it at what seems to be the end of her remarks and the beginning of her interior thought.]

But it happened that the infirmarian told him, and I couldn't get away. He was there, probably praying, at the statue of the Virgin Mary. "Try to walk," he said to me. I wasn't capable. "Go on, then; sit down," he said, and he began to pray some more. Then he came back toward me. He said to me with a tone of authority, "Get up and walk!" This [tone] produced an enormous change. My knees began to swell, as did my hands and my face. But I started to walk.

"Go thank St. Joseph."

I was so astonished to be walking without crutches! "Would I be able to go to the big chapel?" I asked. It was so long [since] I had been there.

"Go to whatever chapel you want!" he answered. I came back [later] to Br. André. My knees, my hands, my face were not losing their swelling. "Am I going to become paralyzed?"

"No, that's just blood that hasn't started to circulate." And indeed I got over everything. I don't even believe I thought to thank him.

Later, she not only thanked him; she worked at the Holy Cross institution where he lived, along with others from her congregation. And in fact, when she broke her arm three years later, in 1937, and he was on his deathbed, she would be the last person Br. André saw in this life for healing.

Her account continues:

I asked myself, "Why did it happen that I was cured when I had no faith?" Another sister replied, "He came to give you faith."

I am the only sister that he cured in that visit to the infirmary, and there were many sick there. The infirmarian told me, "He came expressly for you."

If one figures a very modest ten thousand cures—an estimate by his Holy Cross Congregation—for the roughly sixty years when his healing ministry was in full swing (and cures were very possibly more than that), Bl. André can confidently be termed one of the greatest healers the Catholic Church has produced among her saints. Yet when his friends wondered aloud what they would do after his death, he assured them, "I'll be able to help you a lot more after my death, because I'll be much closer to God than I am now." In 1937, when Pope Pius XI was in danger of death, ninety-one-year-old André offered God his life for the pope's.

"But the Oratory still needs you," someone complained.

"When someone does good on earth," the venerable old healer remarked with typical impersonality, "it's nothing in comparison with what he'll be able to do when he gets to Heaven."

Those words began to come true as soon as the pope had unexpectedly recovered and Br. André had quietly died. In his lifetime it had been said that perhaps his most extraordinary gift was that of inspiring others with something of his own boundless confidence in God. In the seven days of his funeral services, the more than a million people who filed by his bier showed something very like his fervor. Even a dying man was brought in on a stretcher. Conversion had always been the cure he sought most avidly; and while conversions are healings outside the scope of this book, let it be noted here that the confessionals were full day and night.

But there were physical cures too. An asthmatic on the point of death after six years of sufferings is healed instantly; likewise, a four-year-old child is held up by his father, touches the dead saint, and is instantly able to take his first steps. A young girl in a wheelchair is another who hears the saint's silent command with the ears of faith—and is healed. Eight-year-old Arthur Ducharme, in an accident five months earlier, has had the nerves and muscles of his right arm cut to the bone by shards of glass. The hospital surgeon's recommendation: amputation.

That step vetoed by the mother, the arm heals as far as the wound's closing is concerned but remains inert; a sling is necessary to support it. Various treatments have been useless; there is no way to rejoin the severed muscles and nerves in 1937. Young Arthur touches the saint's body and is instantly able to use his arm. He demonstrates by carrying chairs around the sacristy. There remains a certain flabbiness, but the limb will serve him for all his needs in the years to come, even playing hockey.

The first of several days' triumphal rites for the humble brother is broadcast January 6, the day André dies. Among the listeners is retired policeman François Lecuyer, of Montreal. Lecuyer, in nineteen years as a traffic policeman working near the shrine, has become so crippled by rheumatism in his joints that he has had to retire early as an invalid. No treatments have helped. Periodically his feet swell, causing terrible sufferings. At such times he can walk only with crutches or cane. As the Lecuyer family respond aloud to the radio prayers, the father, who has been praying to Br. André as to a saint, from the moment he heard of his death, feels himself sicken. His coloring becomes like that of impending death and tears run down his face. Painfully the family haul him out of the living room; they fear he is having a heart attack. But as the prayers end, Lecuyer sits up. He reaches for his cane, his crutch, realizes they remain by the radio in the living room, gets up without either, and begins to walk. He says later it is only after seven or eight minutes that it hits him that he is cured and that Br. André has obtained this grace from God.

Excitedly he calls to his wife to bring his shoes, and the still-shaken woman exclaims, "You know very well you can't put on your shoes! Your foot is too swollen." But Lecuyer's foot slides easily into the shoe. Together he and his wife go to the Oratory, where he squeezes the saint's foot in thanks as they pass, part of the endless line of people who ignore the January cold to pay their respects to the body of a saint. Later Lecuyer remarks that while he was praying along with the radio, "I had never prayed like that. At that moment I had confidence as I had never had it before." Similarly, listening to the same service, a deaf boy who joins in the prayers is instantly healed.

On January 8 a mother rushes to the corpse. Her daughter is in extreme danger in a hospital from peritonitis. She prays and touches to the body several objects of piety which she will give to her daughter to evoke faith in André's intercession. Arriving once more at the hospital, the word is still, "The child won't live through the night." But by evening she is already on the mend.

The end of the funeral ceremonies by no means halts the cures. From January to October that year, letters testify to 6,700 favors, 933 cures. And that is only the beginning. A few years later, 1941 to 1943 for instance, the Oratory receives 10,408 letters giving thanks just for *cures*. Of these, 6,610 specifically cite Br. André as intercessor. A medical bureau along the lines of the stringent one at Lourdes is set up to examine the most extraordinary cures. Eight physicians under direction of Br. André's old doctor, Lionel Lamy, select to investigate 791 impressive cases of claimed healing in the next fourteen years, that is, 1944 to 1958. Of these, forty prove so beyond any possible medical or human explanation that they are set aside to be submitted to Rome, already moving to beatify the man who laughingly called himself "St. Joseph's little dog." Here is one:

Beginning in 1933, a young girl of fourteen, Thérèse Cousineau, suffers more and more from a deviation of her spinal column. From this period her stomach also refuses to keep down food. It is necessary to give up the plaster corset that aims to squeeze her into normal shape. Then the deformity of the shoulder increases and a hump bends her into a hunchback. Beginning in 1937 she suffers convulsions. On January 11, four days after the saint's death, Thérèse is brought to his coffin; but she only gets worse from the effort. Still as March begins, she and her parents begin a novena following precisely the use of St. Joseph's oil as Br. André often used to recommend it, but asking Br. André's intercession specifically. Again she gets worse and is unconscious nearly three hours. The physician believes it is the end, and she receives the last rites. But, beginning the next morning, her stomach starts functioning.

She is hungry, eats, and digests easily. The spinal column, however, is still as before. On March 22 the family begins a second novena, begging daily, "Br. André, obtain her cure!" Her sufferings she offers God as a prayer for His servant's beatification. Four days later, the pain is less. Thérèse sleeps. Waking, she is much better. "Doctor," she challenges, "I bet I'll be cured at the end of this novena."

The month dedicated to St. Joseph ends. So does the novena. The morning of April 1, as her mother rubs her back with the oil beloved of Br. André, suddenly, with loud pops and cracks, the bones of the spinal column simply realign themselves. The hump is gone. Besides the delirious joy of Thérèse and her parents over the complete (and permanent) cure, her cousin Albert, last superior of Br. André, is unspeakably grateful to his old friend for one more favor.

The cures are not all local. One child's inexplicable healing takes place in Africa. And the estimated three million annual visitors to the Oratory come from all over the world. In the early days of his ministry they asked simply for "the porter" or "Br. André." After 1978 their prayer requests addressed *Venerable* Br. André, his heroic virtue verified after long, thorough study of his life.

Beatification came only four years later. The cure chosen from among so many was a miracle given by God twenty-four years earlier to someone who for much of his life had never heard of Br. André. Joseph Audino was an immigrant, with his family, from Italy to the United States. Living in Rochester, New York, in 1950 he made a pilgrimage to the eastern Canadian shrine of Sainte-Anne-de-Beaupré. Extending his trip to Montreal, he followed the suggestion of a hotel porter that he shouldn't miss an important site for visitors to the city called the Oratory of St. Joseph on Mount Royal. Only there did Audino learn about another porter, Mount Royal's Br. André.

Flash forward to 1954: Joe Audino began having health problems. By 1957 they had intensified. By the next year, 1958, the advanced form of reticulum cell sarcoma was throughout his body. Radiation could no longer keep pace with the cancer. Joe was face-to-face with death, his diagnosis "terminal" and his death expected within thirty days. He was in too much pain to make a confession or receive Communion, he says. He simply lay hopelessly in bed, too weak to walk, with a football-size liver. In his troubles he thought of Br. André. And no matter how bad he felt, he never stopped praying for Br. André's help. "I knew he'd be able to help me," he says.

He consented to an experimental treatment that never helped anyone else. But shortly after, he was cancer free. His doctor Philip Rubin, chairman of radiation therapy at the University of Rochester Cancer Center, says, "There is no clear scientific explanation for his cure."

Rubin also wrote in the *Journal of Nuclear Medicine* with a second doctor who was involved, that the treatment given Audino "is essentially of no use in the treatment of reticulum cell sarcoma and can lead to death. Remission at this stage of the disease (other than that seen in the case of Mr. Audino) is unknown." Dr. Rubin was so struck by this patient's inexplicable return to health he was willing to testify to a miracle. In 1965, two years after the five-year cancer-free landmark, new, non-involved doctors began going over the case. Finally a dossier of 585 pages of testimony, medical reports, and 150 x-rays was packaged and sent to Rome for study by medical men there. The whole medical end of the process was not concluded until June 1980. That's when the Italian consultants agreed with Dr. Rubin that what had happened to one of their countrymen through invoking the prayers of a little French-Canadian porter of established heroic virtue was explainable only as a miracle.

Next a theological commission verified intercession in Joseph Audino's case was clearly André's, the only one invoked for prayer, not André's *and* St. Joseph's. Beatification following in 1982, prayer pleas now went to *Blessed* André until October 2010. Following the same kind of intensive study and ultimate acceptance of another medical miracle, the featherweight porter was canonized. Pope Benedict XVI presided at the ceremonies for *Saint* André Bessette. (Details of this authenticated miracle were kept under wraps due to an altered media climate, in which miracle recipients were sadly often hounded, losing any hope for privacy.)

To those who know Him, it seems God definitely has a sense of humor: in this case, the first canonized saint for the Holy Cross Congregation of educators was their sole largely illiterate member. In other ways, too, St. André Bessette's story definitely proves truth is far more astounding than fiction. Here was an uneducated French-Canadian, too frail to succeed in any work he tried until, at twenty-five, he gave himself full-time to God's service. He then spent decade after decade—living to ninety-one—like the stoutest packhorse carrying souls to God and God's healing to souls. Long years after asking on his deathbed, "Will you pray for my conversion," he continues an avenue for God's healings. Credit for those owed purely to St. André's prayer intercession is still often hard to disentangle from credit due to a mix of his prayers and those of St. Joseph. Considering their friendship, it seems a sure thing André likes it that way.

Chapter 10

America's First Homegrown Saint

All saints are healers. But their cures may take vastly different forms. In the case of St. Elizabeth Ann Bayley Seton, America's first native-born saint, had she lived today her passionate compassion and activism might well have led her into a ministry of physical healing. But in God's designs, Elizabeth lived her life as a Catholic in the early nineteenth century, an era when ideas of God's giving physical cures were little mentioned.

It would be almost a century after Elizabeth's death in 1821 before Bible students began pondering that Jesus healed all who came to him (cf. Matt. 12:15) and never spoke of illness as one of the crosses His followers are meant to bear. In Elizabeth's time the Church acknowledged miracles *could* happen without *expecting* they would; the big thing in illness was to pray, not for healing, but for resignation to God's will (which was seen as the cause of the illness even in cases most today would trace to very human factors, such as lung cancer in a heavy smoker).

The American spiritual landscape was also sombered with Puritanism as well as the residue of a dour European Catholic heresy, Jansenism. God was stern, much of life's good things were to be feared as traps of Satan, salvation was hard to come by, and the smart thing to do was opt for pie in the sky and live in this "vale of tears" as self-denyingly as possible, accepting all suffering as always willed[96] by God.

In such an atmosphere, Elizabeth Seton's sanctity understandably flowed into spiritual healings. And a particular sphere became spiritual

[96] Recall that Catholic theologians distinguish that from what is merely *permitted* to honor free will.

care of the dying. In fact if anything is characteristic of "Eliza" or "Betty" Seton, it is the strength and tenderness with which she helped those she loved so passionately die: from her personally immature, professionally heroic physician father; her charming, slightly spoiled, and irresolute husband; a number of the friends of her heart, including three young, unmarried sisters-in-law, the youngest of whom she had raised from the age of ten; and both the oldest and the youngest of her five children.

Still, neither inborn courage nor precocious spirituality spared Elizabeth from the normal human progression of growth. When, in her twenties, she helped her first loved one, her adored, irreligious father, die, for all her piety she was still spiritually confused and immature. In her anguish and her fear of Richard Bayley's possible damnation, she lifted her baby toward the heavens and offered its life to God in exchange for her father's salvation. Did God laugh at her earnestness? Or weep that the young Episcopalian believed him so implacable? At any rate, her father did turn to Christ before dying, the baby, Catherine, became Elizabeth's healthiest daughter (she lived to be over ninety), and Elizabeth went one step deeper into realization that God is *really* love.

Death, for all of us, is potentially the great final healing of our earthly lives. But, sadly, the dying *process* can be far from smooth or peaceful, due to a number of factors, including the average person's lack of spiritual preparation and people who can be helpful facilitators for birth into the next life. The more Elizabeth advanced, in spite of her confusions and imperfections, in the knowledge and love of God, the more her heroic self-giving, sacrifices, and prayers joined the example of her own faith to bring this literally vital kind of healing to the dying.

Even individuals who had not been "religious" died healed, that is, convinced of God's love and able to turn with hope and trust to Him. In instances in which her influence had been long, as with her daughters or through drawn-out illnesses, those tended by Elizabeth Ann Seton died exceptionally holy deaths. Both her daughters, I believe, died saints.

Did the holiness she gradually achieved mean Elizabeth Ann Seton became an otherworldly creature spared any suffering in losing loved ones? Far from it. Even after she had been through many deaths and was considered a saintly woman by many, Elizabeth broke down emotionally when her oldest daughter, Anna Maria, lay dying at age sixteen of tuberculosis spread to the bones. Ten-year-old Rebecca and twelve-year-old Catherine sent their mother to the chapel during their sister's last moments because of Elizabeth's anguish. Although she had been cared for night and day by her mother, Anina, as the family called her, died in her younger sisters' arms. For at least three months following, in spite of her intellect's sincere "Thy will be done," the mother felt she might go mad with grief.

Four years later, her youngest child, Rebecca, died at age fourteen after developing a tumor in the thigh following an ice-skating accident.

"How will you live without me, Mother?" warm-hearted Rebecca asked ingenuously just before her death. Only in this last great sorrow did Elizabeth achieve an inner strength so heroic she did not break down but simply soothed the child in her arms. "Don't worry, darling; Mother will soon wear away and follow you."

Five years later, only forty-seven, Elizabeth died peacefully of TB.

Far from being immune to her losses, they had molded her. The theme of St. Elizabeth's life, beginning with the loss of her mother in childbirth when she was a toddler of two, became the search for God, in whom alone is permanence and freedom from partings, sorrow, and loss. Already at the death of her two-year-old baby sister when she was four, the lonely little girl explained she wasn't crying because "Kitty is in Heaven. I wish I could go too [to be] with Mama."

Her life one long deathwatch, Elizabeth Bayley Seton became a saint because even her most agonizing losses spurred this passionate woman to throw herself into God's arms, rather than turn away in bitterness or despair. And instead of contracting in self-centeredness, her heart expanded in grief so that others in need could find a shelter there from life's storms.

⌒

Born into the upper crust of old Dutch-English New York City when such a world represented high moral standards as much as social prominence, Elizabeth Bayley was the most admired beauty and charmer of her generation. A brilliant-eyed, petite debutante with masses of dark curly hair and lovely, finely cut features, she smiled and laughed through balls and society luncheons. Yet even in the gayest moments of her youth there was absolutely nothing shallow about Betty Seton.

Spurred by the early bereavements, rejection from her stepmother, and long periods of total neglect by the career-absorbed physician father she adored, from early childhood, hers was a rich inner life with a strong spiritual bent. The little nominally Protestant girl (actually her only living parent was a humanitarian with no real religion) wore a most un-Protestant crucifix around her neck, bowed her head at the name of Jesus, and wondered why her playmates thought it funny. How could she explain to them she was born with a soul that cried out for God in the same ardent way her oversized heart cried out to give and receive human love?

Her marriage when she was nineteen to handsome William Seton, son of a prominent and much-loved wealthy businessman, was a social "event," as was the ball at which the young newlyweds were among the official hosts greeting General Washington. Gratitude one of her strong traits, a happy marriage, and the first true home she had known since her mother's death only turned Elizabeth more toward God. She followed her physician father, who would give his life for epidemic-stricken Irish immigrants, in her deep affinity with the poor.

Those who saw her and "the friend I can tell anything," her sister-in-law Rebecca Seton, going out many mornings with food and medicine for New York's poverty-stricken, dubbed her prophetically "a Protestant Sister of Charity." At the same period, her wonderfully vivid, witty, and charming letters to friends or her father (separated from his second wife) reveal the doting mother who is sure her babies (there were five in seven years) are among the wonders of the world.

Any wife and mother reading these letters and the notes as banal as our own ("My love: I send your toothbrush and comb which I forgot this morning ...") can relate absolutely to this woman, so maternal, so earthily in love, so willing to share her troubles with her intimate friends without that false pride which maintains a front of unreal competence and confidence, so grateful for her friends' support, and so willing to give it lavishly in return. From long-ago-penned pages, Elizabeth smiles so warm and witty a friend, so perceptive and intelligent an adviser, so stouthearted and steady in a crisis like her husband's bankruptcy, even as she openly admits her fears and inadequacies, so gifted with good humor, optimism, and sheer charm that it is impossible not to cry across time and space, "Elizabeth, be my friend!"

At the same time, how one longs to ease her sufferings as one sees her across time. As in a photo album, certain pictures stand out. The lonely motherless child, rejected by her stepmother, lavishing her love on little half brothers and half sisters. The young wife quarantined under guard in Italy with no way to keep warm or decently fed her dying tubercular husband (who has insisted this trip will restore his health) or the child with them, their eight-year-old oldest, Anna. Elizabeth laughs to raise the others' spirits and prays like an angel to turn William from thoughts of his bankruptcy to spiritual preparation for his death. When she weeps in the night, she is careful not to make a sound.

In New York a year or so later, she lies on her bed in an agony ("My God, show me Your truth!") over whether the Protestants or Catholics are right in claiming, as both do in that bigoted era, that only they have the key to salvation. It is a day when a WASP turning Catholic dies to family and social status. Although she can be sure a few Protestant women friends will remain loyal, however saddened, the penniless young widow, trying to teach school to support and educate five children, knows she will cut herself off from financial and community support, as well as chance of remarriage; and there will be no place in the New York of her Bayley, Barclay, Charlton, Seton, and Roosevelt kin for her Catholic children, either. But once convinced that Catholicism is the mother Church of Christianity, Elizabeth joins the Irish maids and grooms in worship at their dirt-floored church, even though she soon loses her teaching job and finally is driven from the city to refuge in Catholic Maryland.

As her children grow, one sees her enduring heartbreak and humiliation time and again over her sons, both unsteady, irresolute characters. She is always trying to get them settled in life. To her embarrassment, they use her devoted friends and their connections not to achieve but as ne'er-do-wells and drifters who dip freely into the fruits of others' labors. In her lifetime she will never get them turned around.

Along the way of her arduous life it seems almost incidental that Elizabeth Ann Bayley Seton begins the Catholic parochial school system, opens the first Catholic orphanage in the United States, and starts the first American religious community, an American branch of the

Sisters of Charity, who will serve the young nation in schools, hospitals, and child care across the land. Perhaps Elizabeth's accomplishments fade next to her relationships, because whether with the poor children she educated, the postulants of her order she guided toward spiritual wholeness, her many lifelong friends, or her own five offspring so dearly loved, Elizabeth Ann Seton is foremostly a maternal woman: one who will always be more attuned to relationships than to projects for their own sake. Out of her greatest love relationship, that with God, she gladly becomes a nun, but only on the unheard-of condition that she can keep her children with her and retain full control of their rearing. In her daughter Rebecca's battle with cancer, Elizabeth will run her religious order and all its undertakings for months from the young girl's bedside so as not to abandon her child for an instant.

In spite of her ardent love, she could save neither Rebecca nor Anna Maria from agonizing deaths that tore her own heart to shreds. And among her dear spiritual daughters (including Harriet and Cecilia, two young Seton sisters-in-law who followed her into the Church in spite of the ostracism of the Seton family, and [Cecilia] into religious life), the death toll was very high due to the poverty of the infant order. But after her own death the greathearted mother could answer the cries for help of her nuns—Seton's spiritual daughters—and of mothers with dying children with even more powerful prayers. And she did.

Her own darling Rebecca had died of a tumor. And cancer is the disease the majority of Americans fear most. It seems doubly fitting, then, that St. Elizabeth Bayley Seton, America's first homegrown saint, should have been beatified after cures of two cancer victims were attributed to her intercession.

Early in 1934 Sr. Gertrude (Korzendorfer), the Sister of Charity who ran De Paul Sanatorium, New Orleans' 250-bed psychiatric facility, was nauseated and in terrible pain. Dr. James T. Nix, a doctor in whom she had complete confidence, was consulted and removed her gallbladder on April 14. In the sister's words:

> After,... I felt some relief from pain and nausea, but I never felt entirely well nor physically able to fulfill my duty. I was continually losing weight. In October of the same year my condition grew worse. I had sudden spells of intense pain in the right side

of my abdomen, followed by chills and attacks of fever; and my temperature rising to 103. These attacks occurred at intervals of approximately one week. I became dark yellow.

On December 25, after a more serious spell, [Dr. Nix] ... ordered that I should be transferred immediately to the hospital.

Sr. Gertrude's fellow Sisters of Charity were very concerned. The nun, who was about sixty years old, was "a treasure to the community" because "of very fine qualities of mind and heart." Now the other nuns saw:

the hospital treatment was unable to bring about any improvement in her condition. She continued to fail rapidly. Unable to receive nourishment her weight melted away daily. Her normal weight up to this illness was about one hundred and sixty-five pounds. Now she was reduced to one hundred and eighteen pounds. A consultation of physicians was called ... Three other physicians together with Doctor Nix agreed on the pre-operative diagnosis that Sister had a cancerous condition of the pancreas [because of her symptoms] ... An exploratory surgery was recommended ...

Dr. Nix later recalled the operation, which took place on January 5, 1935, with gastroenterologist A. L. Levin and surgeon Marion Souchon observing:

The entire abdomen was examined through a median upper abdominal incision. All structures were normal excepting the head of the pancreas which was enlarged to three times its normal size, presenting itself as a firm tumor mass and having all the appearances of carcinoma of the pancreas. There was no other pathology ...

It was impossible to do surgery of any kind because of the extent of the lesion. Even a cholecystduodenostomy or a cholecystgastrostomy[97] was impossible. It was my opinion at the time that if any further surgery were attempted, the patient would have died promptly as a result of it. She was extremely emaciated, ane-

[97] Operations to bypass the tumor-created blockage of the bile duct.

mic, and deeply jaundiced. No corrective surgery was done. The abdomen was closed.

... From gross appearance Sister Gertrude had an inoperable carcinoma [cancer] of the pancreas, the mortality of which is 100%.[98]

Tiny tissue samples had been cut from the tumor mass and were now sent, for purposes of absolutely accurate diagnosis, to three separate pathologists: Dr. Maurice Couret, director of the Hotel Dieu pathology lab, Dr. John A. Lanford of Tulane University of Louisiana, and Dr. W. H. Harris of the University of Tulane School of Medicine. All three reports agreed the tissue was a carcinoma, that is, a cancerous tumor.

Both the operation results and the pathologists' reports merely confirmed what the Sisters of Charity, women who ran the Hotel Dieu and other medical facilities in the country, could see from their years of medical experience by just looking at Sr. Gertrude: She "was wasting away almost hourly" and medical science could do nothing about it.

These medical workers were also women of prayer, their feet as firmly planted in things unseen as seen. The moment exploratory surgery confirmed fears of Sr. Gertrude's terminal condition, they began a novena. For the next nine days they placed their petition for Sr. Gertrude's restoration to health in the hands of their dead foundress, Mother Elizabeth Seton. They believed she was a saint. Her prayers must be powerful. Let her ask God for this grace.

Exploratory surgery itself is a trauma to the body, and Sr. Gertrude was extremely weak, jaundiced, and anemic. Yet from the very beginning of the novena, that is, just the second day following surgery, the dying nun later recalled:

> I felt neither pain nor nausea. I was able to eat with relish and retain any nourishment presented to me. My strength returned. I gained weight and I was discharged from the hospital February 1, 1935. However, my Superiors thought it would be better for me to remain there a month longer, which I did. I returned to

---

[98] Overall five-year survival rates from this killer is still less than 4 percent. Where the tumor is truly localized to the pancreas (less than 20 percent of cases), the five-year survival rate rises to 6 to 12 percent, depending on the tumor's stage.

my duty the 1st of March. Since then I was able to follow the common life and to attend to all the duties of my office as Sister Servant [i.e., superior] of a 250-bed hospital for the insane.

I have never had any relapse of my former sickness, and I attribute my cure solely to a novena made to Mother Seton in order to obtain it.

Could the pious nun be mistaken? Could the exploratory surgery, cutting into the tumor, have triggered a spontaneous remission? On this point Dr. Nix says, "I do not believe the cure could be in the least attributed to any surgical intervention," and he reminds questioners that in 1935 cancer of the pancreas had a 100 percent mortality. Furthermore, as information on Sister's case notes:

The common experience in surgery is that whenever a cancer is cut and the growth has not been completely removed there follows what surgeons call a metastasis, that is, there is generally a spreading of the cancerous infection throughout the system. In Sister Gertrude's case, the cancer was cut, the growth in its entirety practically speaking, remained in the pancreas but instead of the infection spreading throughout the system, the disease was arrested and a complete cure effected. This contrary to all the expectations of the medical men in attendance.

For seven and a half years, the well-loved nun continued her stressful work as sister superior of the large psychiatric facility. Then, in 1942, while eating a meal at the Villa Saint Louise in Normandy, Missouri, "life left [her] as suddenly as a light goes out when you press the switch," according to a Sister of Charity with her.

Because of the suddenness of her death and the earlier extraordinary cancer cure, an autopsy was performed at De Paul Hospital in St. Louis, Missouri. Dr. Walter J. Siebert, hospital pathologist, found the immediate cause of death was a massive pulmonary embolism, a condition totally unrelated to either the pancreas or cancer in any form. The biopsy of 1935 had been sent Dr. Siebert from New Orleans. He agreed "there is no question but that the biopsy section removed from the head of the pancreas ... shows an adeno-carcinoma ..." However, seven years later, careful autopsy shows "no evidence, whatever, of this cancer and furthermore does not even show evidence of a scar in the pancreas where this tumor had been."

Understandably the cure of Sister Gertrude was accepted as an authentic miracle in favor of Elizabeth Seton's beatification.

Chapter 11

A Dying Little Girl—Who Didn't

Born in Baltimore, Maryland, on October 7, 1947, Anne Theresa
O'Neill was a healthy child until early 1952, when she was four years
old. Then her parents, William Richard O'Neill and Felixena Phelps
O'Neill, discovered with alarm "blood blotches" covering the little girl's
neck. They rushed their firstborn to the family doctor, E. W. Johnson,
M.D., who did a blood test, looked somberly at the results, and sent the
child at once to St. Agnes Hospital.

Admitted to St. Agnes on February 17, 1952, Anne "was very sick,
extremely pale, lethargic and had enlarged glands in her neck." The
following day a bone-marrow test provided the deadly diagnosis "acute
lymphatic leukemia." Two weeks of blood transfusions and other treatments proved futile. The parents were given the heartbreaking news
that it was only a matter of time before the end.

Unwilling to accept that, Anne's parents looked for new medical
advice. They turned to Dr. Milton S. Sacks, of University Hospital
(the University of Maryland), a brilliant physician and authority on
leukemia.

Dr. Sacks was using a new drug, aminopterin, on leukemia victims.
Anne was admitted to University Hospital on February 28. But aminopterin proved no miracle drug.[99] Her condition only got worse. After
three weeks in the hospital her suffering was intense, her little face
swollen way beyond normal proportions. Her case judged "hopeless,"
she was sent home on March 27. But Dr. Sacks kept her under his per-

---

[99] The National Cancer Institute has not listed it among leukemia chemo-
therapies for many decades.

sonal care and in a desperate bid to keep the dying child alive, after only three days at home he rushed her back to the hospital for another blood transfusion. After the transfusion he wished to keep Anne at the hospital, but the O'Neills insisted on taking their daughter home. If they could not cure her, at least they could give her the comfort in her last days of care at home.

But even that began to seem impossible. Within a couple of weeks Anne had sores all over her body. She smelled like something decaying. Her fever was high. Nutrition was no help: She was able to take only sips of Coke. In that pitiful condition, the little girl came down with chicken pox. Not even just chicken pox, but, according to Dr. Sacks, one of the worst cases he had ever seen. During Holy Week of 1952, Anne gasped for breath, and the end seemed very near.

April 9, she simply could not breathe. This time the parents phoned Dr. Johnson, who rushed her to St. Agnes for oxygen. Once there, however, her breathing eased somewhat. Still Sr. Angelica (Inez) Howell, who saw Anne, could later testify that she "thought the child was about to die, so critical was her condition."

Sr. Mary Alice Fowler, supervisor of the children's ward, reports: "Anne Theresa was in a pitiful condition. She was very pale, her face was swollen, she was irritable and was so weak that she could neither sit nor stand. The diagnosis this time was "'advanced leukemia ... [with] chicken pox ...'"

Although the hospital was run by Sisters of Charity, the O'Neills had never heard of Mother Elizabeth Ann Seton. But Felixena understood about saints and their prayer power. She was a great friend of St. Thérèse of Lisieux. She had been enlisting Thérèse's prayer support and felt St. Thérèse had given her a sign in some roses that Anne would not die. As she clung to this belief—extremely unrealistically as things appeared—those around her thought "the poor distraught mother has just lost it." Thus things stood on Easter Sunday.

Sr. Mary Alice took a completely different view of Felixena O'Neill. She later wrote:

> Little Anne's mother was a woman of great faith. When I saw Anne's condition ... the thought came to me that this case would be a good one for Mother Seton to show her power with

God and, if it be God's holy will, … [to obtain] the cure of this incurable disease …

I talked to the mother and told her what I wanted to do. I also told her what Mother Seton had done for another patient I had for whom all hope of recovery had been given up and that this patient is living today in wonderful health.

The faith-filled, if anxious, mother and compassionate nun concocted a plan. Sr. Mary Alice would get the Sisters of Charity and the children in the homes and schools run by the order started in a crusade of prayer for Mother Seton's intercession with God. Felixena would get as many people as she could to join in. A novena as well as informal petitions to the saint began from that moment.

Sr. Mary Alice testifies: "During the novena Anne seemed to show some improvement. She began to eat and to take notice of things about her. Later she began to sit up and within a few days she was allowed to be up and walking."

By April 27, eighteen days after she had been admitted in critical condition from what was at that time an incurable disease, Anne O'Neill was discharged from the hospital with healthy blood. The doctors diagnosed "a remission."

The family did not drive straight home. Instead they went first to Emmitsburg, where Mother Seton had watched her own daughter die of cancer. At the saint's tomb they prayed with fervor, aware that in 1952 no child with Anne's disease had ever escaped death.[100]

Dr. Sacks had the heavy knowledge that the reprieve was certainly temporary. Remissions in acute leukemia did occasionally occur, particularly following a viral infection such as the very severe case of chicken pox Anne had. But the remissions were always brief. In 1952, even when aminopterin worked — and it had not worked on Anne at all — the longest remission had been two and a half years. Typically, spontaneous remissions, which occurred in 1 percent or less of his cases, Dr. Sacks knew, lasted less than one year.

Weeks and then months passed. Anne remained well. Again and again the O'Neill family returned to pray by Elizabeth Seton's tomb or

---

[100] In 2013: 95 percent will go into remission, up to 80 percent of those will have long-term (five years or more) disease-free survival.

invoked her prayers at home. Sr. Mary Alice and others continued to pray. The year 1952 ended. Then 1953. Blood tests continued normal. In 1956 and 1957 the child went through the painful ordeal of bone-marrow punctures. Results: normal. In 1957 she passed the five-year cancer-free mark. At that time the longest remission in Dr. Sacks's records was about two and a half years.

Ten-year-old Anne, "an intelligent child loved by all because of her genial and pleasant disposition," had made medical history.

Still, for a cure to be an official miracle, there must be no doubt it is permanent. Only after ten years was this designation deemed safe and the word *miracle* used by the Church. And that only after a final bone-marrow puncture when she was fifteen so the Church medical investigators could be positive. Anne's parents left undergoing this up to their daughter because of the pain; decades later Anne would brush off her heroism saying, "I couldn't disappoint my mother." The next year, at sixteen, she and Felixena attended the beatification of Elizabeth Ann Seton, based on Anne's cure and Sr. Gertrude's.

Sixty-six years old in October 2013, Anne is alive and well. The mother of several adult children, she has eight grandchildren. Jewish spirituality has a tradition that the one who saves a single life saves a world. It is a goose-bumps moment to reflect that the little world of Anne's children and grandchildren and descendants ever on owe their lives to this miracle through Mother Seton. The family are certainly devoted to this saint. William O'Neill, for one, always carried her relic in his pocket as a point of prayer contact and drove the family the hour or so to Emmitsburg so many times that Anne's next-youngest sister, Jeanne (two and cared for by relatives when Anne was ill), says she grew up feeling that place an extension of home and the Sisters of Charity there part of the family.

Long years after the miracle Felixena was still praising God for His goodness and Mother Seton's prayers in her oldest daughter's cure. When you love someone, you like to have his or her pictures around. Pride of place in the O'Neill living room went to a portrait of Elizabeth Ann Seton painted by the O'Neills' artist daughter Celine,[101] along

---

[101] Celine made a duplicate for Sr. Mary Alice Fowler which hung in one of the Daughters of Charity homes for young women and their babies for years.

with the original small statue of Mother Seton given the anxious parents by Sr. Mary Alice during Anne's illness.

The saint continued a friend. William O'Neill was ill with cancer many years before his death at age fifty-nine on December 21, 1977, two years after Mother Seton's canonization. Felixena credited many blessings from God during this hard time to Mother Seton, whose husband had also died leaving a family of five and a homemaker wife. Daughter Mary Margaret, the child Felixena was pregnant with during Anne's illness, points out as one of those blessings that William was able to continue to work with cancer for over fifteen years, supporting the family in an era when married women had many skills lost today but few for the marketplace. No wonder Felixena says emphatically "Mother Seton is very important to this family."

The daughter Felixena still lived with in her nineties, second child Jeanne, echoes her: "Mother Seton has been very big in our lives [and] continues to be working very much in the family." Jeanne mentions her own daughter's devotion to the saint, then speaks of other saints family members love, giving her opinion that all the saints work together.

Anne named her daughter after another person who was a bridge to God's saint and thus to God: Sr. Mary Alice Fowler. In studying these cures through saints, oftentimes there is someone like Sr. Mary Alice, a friend of a particular saint and a person of prayer, who—acting like a bridge—brings together God's friend, the saint, and someone needing a miracle.

This Daughter of Charity nurse who first introduced the O'Neill family to Mother Seton—linked by their love of God and His saints and their powerful experience of His grace—became Felixena's best friend. Jeanne speaks of how beloved Sr. Mary Alice remained throughout her life to the entire extended family, right down to Jeanne's own daughter. "When we go to Emmitsburg, we always take flowers and visit her grave," she says.

Centered in God, the O'Neill–Sr. Mary Alice–Mother Seton friendship begun in His name when a little girl was dying has turned into a multigenerational one. Why go into this? Because it is valuable knowledge that when any of us ask for a miracle, we are not being selfish: as I've said before, a miracle is never just for the one who receives it. Like a stone in water, it ripples out, many times beyond anyone's wildest imaginings.

Dr. Sacks's experience with remissions triggered by viral infections was that these were short-lived. Research by other physicians makes it legitimate to raise the question as to whether the particularly virulent case of chicken pox and accompanying high fever could be factors in Anne's cure. I refer to the work of doctors such as William B. Coley, regarded by many as the father or grandfather of immunotherapy, who practiced at New York's Memorial Hospital until his death in 1936. Dr. Coley found a positive relationship between spontaneous cure of cancer and infection. By deliberately infecting individuals who had inoperable cancer with strong toxins, he achieved some extraordinary cures. In the 1980s the use of Coley's toxins at Beijing Children's Hospital, the largest pediatric hospital in the world, achieved complete disappearance of extensive inoperable cancers in some children. Research along these lines was also done at some United States institutions, including a program under physicians Herbert Oettgen and Sanford Kempin at Memorial Sloan-Kettering Cancer Center in New York. Walter J. Urba, M.D., Ph.D., a researcher and Director of the Robert W. Franz Cancer Center at Portland, Oregon's Providence Hospital says that in the twenty-first century "many scientists continue to work on what we think are likely to be the active components" of Coley's toxins.

Other researchers, noting that a fever of over 105 seems to be a factor in infection-linked remissions, have pursued the role of fever. Among their findings: fever stimulates the immune system, restricts the circulation of iron, which cancer cells require, and is deadly to cancer cells, which cannot take heat like normal cells.

To note the possible role of virus and fever factors in Anne's case is not to say either prayer or a saint's intercession were credited inappropriately with her healing. Chicken pox could have played a role in God's honoring Mother Seton's prayers, in response to the many faith-filled prayers of the living. It is certainly strong evidence for Mother Seton's intercession that dying Anne's totally unexpected improvement began on the first day prayer was specifically directed for Mother Seton's intercession. Bursting with faith, Anne hates things like viral infections or fever even being mentioned, lest they lessen someone's faith, but this very nonjudgmental woman tells me, "Do what you have to do." I mention virus with fever because some (not all, by any means) of you, I know, are familiar with those factors in relation to cures and may think they were the means by which God healed Anne. Recall, however (see the introduction), those Church guidelines for an approved miracle, including the one that demands "the cure must not be preceded by any crisis of a sort that would make it possible the cure was wholly or partially natural." So this was one of the things looked at by Rome before proclaiming Anne's case an official miracle. Those Vatican medical investigators, following a thorough study of the case, could only conclude with her own doctors—and remember the primary one, Dr. Sacks, was an authority on the then always fatal disease—that there was *no natural* or medical explanation which could account for the survival of this one child alone where all the others in her situation, *including those with viral infections and high fever*, died.

Chapter 12

"Hey, You, You're a Mother!"

For some reason known only to God, the shrine of Mother Seton does not seem as oriented to healing as some other North American shrines. Still St. Elizabeth Seton has continued to help mothers and their children after her canonization no longer necessitated asking, "Is this cure a miracle?"

Here is the detailed testimony of one of those healings, written by the grateful mother, Mary Porter, in June 1977, when the family still lived in Lakewood, Ohio. It was first printed in a now defunct periodical of the Daughters of Charity.

> On Sunday, July 6, 1975, at 11:30 p.m. my twenty-one-year-old son, James, was riding home on his newly purchased motorcycle when a car that had been parked at the curb ... pulled out in front of him. Jim's bike smashed into the car, sending Jim soaring thirty feet into the air. He landed headfirst onto the street.
>
> The impact forced brain tissue through his skull and out through his right ear, inside the helmet he was wearing.
>
> The neurosurgeon, Dr. David Lehtinen, told us Jim had sustained a massive brain injury, both sides of the brain had hemorrhaged massively, and parts of his skull on both sides of his head had to be removed to allow for the tremendous brain swelling that ensued.
>
> "I was working on a dead man," the surgeon said, "working only for survival."
>
> Thanks to the prayers of over seventy young people and relatives who gathered at Lakewood Hospital emergency room that night, Jim did survive the operation. Minimally. His brain

remained swollen, heartbeat and temperature were out of control, breathing needed mechanical aid, and seizures shook his body. He sank into a deep coma and his healthy, uninjured body started wasting away.

The atmosphere at the hospital was *pray for his death*. The staff worked hard to keep Jim alive, but I think it was only because of our deep belief that a miracle could, would happen. As sincerely, as kindly as they could—including the neurosurgeon and other consultants—they insisted that even if Jim could come out of the coma, nothing but existence in a vegetable state was possible for him.

Nothing more medically could be done for our son. He was merely being kept alive. After only three weeks in the Intensive Care Unit he was moved to a regular hospital room and removed from the extraordinary life-sustaining devices of the Intensive Care Unit. There was no discussion about "let him die" at this time, but I knew this was the feeling. Jim continued to hang on to life.

On September 3, 1975, Jim had to be moved to another facility for long-term care, Highland View Hospital, in Warrensville Heights, Ohio, about thirty miles from our home. At this time we were told again by Dr. Lehtinen that in his opinion *our son would never wake up*.

As a family we were devastated. We had already buried a six-year-old daughter, Patsy, twelve years before; and when Jim's tragedy happened we were just recovering from the death of another son, Hal, aged twenty, who was killed in another automobile accident two and a half years before Jim was struck down.

Physically, mentally, emotionally, and yes, spiritually, we were exhausted. We went through the motions of living, but my husband and I, and Jim's two older sisters especially, were just empty shells traveling those sixty miles every day to pray over that comatose skeleton ...

We ranted and raved, and screamed and cried and stormed at an unjust God—and relented and repented and begged His Son, His angels and His saints to have pity on us and our half-dead, half-alive son. But the pain continued.

On September 8, 1975, I read in our diocesan paper, *The Catholic Universe Bulletin*, about some woman, an American, who'd had five children and was going to be canonized on September 14. Another saint. I, we, had prayed already so much ... [asking] so many [saints] to intercede for us, and we were still hurting. Oh God, the hurt!

But this Elizabeth Seton was the mother of five. Surely she could feel my feelings if anybody could. She knew the trials and suffering involved in raising a family She would know my agony ... wouldn't she? Hey, you! Mother Seton! You know I'm dying inside. You know how desperate I am. Don't you? Please, can't you help me? Please, Elizabeth Ann Seton! Please help me! Please, please, please, God, work another miracle through this new saint of Yours. Let her glory be even more, God. Please give her a miracle for her canonization day. Come on, God! Come on, Mother Seton! You can do it! ... Won't you?

My tears soaked that September 8 newspaper. Elizabeth Ann Seton, first American saint, mother of five children, help my child. Mother Seton, help my child. M.S., help my child. Every page of the diary I was keeping about Jim's ordeal, from September 8 on, has this brief prayer scribbled at the bottom of the page — Mother Seton, help my child.

On September 12, when I arrived once again at Highland View, I found our neurologist Dr. Patawaran and an eye specialist buzzing around Jim's bed. Through the brain trauma his right eye had been irreparably damaged. *If* he woke up, ever, from the coma, that eye as the organ of sight would be useless, since the cornea, iris and pupil were plastered together in one layer. Our doctor, another ward doctor and the eye specialist were amazed and mystified. Dr. Alan Moss, the eye doctor, declared that some kind of "spontaneous remission" had taken place: the eye was healed. At the bottom of my diary's September 12 page it reads: "M.S., keep working."

September 14, 1975 [diary]: He was aware. Seemed to hear us. Attentive, concentrating. Was he?

September 16: Got relic of Mother Seton from Sister Patricia Newhouse, principal at St. Mel's. This is too much! M.S. is the founder of her community and they're teaching at our school!! Diary reads: Left relic over his bed after I rubbed it all over Jim's poor head. New strength in neck and spine! Lifted his head and body completely over on his side by himself. A spastic kind of movement, without intent, but his head did not flip-flop like a rag doll as it had done all these months if not supported!

September 22: Staph infection worse. Mother Seton, clear his infection—please.

September 23: High fever, ear draining all night, pus and fluid.

September 27: Brain swelling gone!! Was this the reason for fever and draining? Thank you, St. Elizabeth Seton!

September 30: Mother Seton, bring him sight and hearing.

October 2: Holy God, we praise Thy Name! Staph infection gone, disappeared … completely! He is awake!! He is aware of us in the room, seems to be able to see something straight ahead. Mother Seton, intercede. Mother Seton, thank you!… Give him comprehension. Please, God. Please.

October 12: Thank You, God. Thank you, Mother Seton. Jimmy very awake … a look of knowledge or understanding in his eyes. Or is it recognition? The dull, vacant, robot stare is gone. Holy God, we praise Thy Name!

October 14: Very, very awake! Tongue moving in and out like an infant. Ready to eat food, to talk, God? Thanks, God, Mother Seton and everybody!

[Thirty-five years later, in 2010, his older sister Sharon recalled that, although he was being fed through a nose tube, she put a tiny bit of a Reese's peanut butter cup to his lip. Her comatose brother grabbed her arm and pulled it to his mouth, wanting more! She told the doctors and the next day he was in a wheelchair when she arrived.]

October 16: He's trying to communicate! When I talk to him he forces air out the trach.[102] He is truly awake, knows I'm there and is answering me. Mother Seton, you are something else. You are a miracle-worker!

---

[102] Mary refers to a tracheotomy, the opening into the windpipe made through his neck enabling Jim to breathe without use of nose or mouth.

Highly skilled doctors believed Jim would never wake up, his staph infection would never yield as long as he lived, and *if* he ever regained consciousness, he would be blind in the destroyed eye. But when this writer spoke to Mary Porter, mother of eight and a freelance writer herself, twelve years after Jim's accident, he was alive and well, had held various jobs, and was able to share the physical work of the farm where he lived with his family near Erie, Pennsylvania. If his vision was not twenty-twenty, he still had the use of both eyes.

Once he began regaining physical health, Jim was able to start functioning mentally, says Sr. Patricia Newhouse. This Sister of Charity of Cincinnati not only organized prayer for him but is the one, Mary Porter said, who "brought our devastated family back to life." Sr. Pat, retired in 2008 but busy working with seniors in Okemos, Michigan, keeps in touch with the Porters. She still talks of Jim's highly successful volunteer work with children in the school where she was principal when he was retraining himself following the massive brain injury.

"How the kids loved him," she recalled to the writer. "A case in a thousand," says his original neurosurgeon. Sharon recalls that every one of her brother's doctors, not just his neurosurgeon, agreed. Jim's waking up and being capable of being brain retrained (although he could remember how to fix your carburetor, Sharon says, he had to learn his ABCs from scratch) the doctors found beyond any human explanation. "They called it," says Sharon, "a miracle."

Mary Porter's grateful assessment of her son after recovery, "He is *slightly* slow normal. *We* know he sustained a massive, killing brain injury; strangers cannot tell."

All the medically unexpected improvements which began with the strange "putting back together" of his mashed eye, his mother emphasizes, "took place within the first month of Mother Seton's canonization! And usually as I specifically requested them."

"Why did our prayers go unanswered until I became aware of her existence?" the mother muses in her written account. Did God pick us to spread her fame? Or was it, as I believe, she heard the awful anguish in my cry: 'Hey, you, you're a mother!'"

They might agree his case was a miracle; still doctors predicted a life span of no more than fifteen years for James Porter. Yet almost forty years after his brain-shattering accident, the miracle recipient, pushing sixty, was alive and well, although lonely, having outlived both his parents. With aging, he has developed short-term memory problems and lost his driver's license, a blow to anyone living in the country. But his sister Sharon points out that Jim's memory loss is by no means completely disabling. For one thing, he still plays weekly competitive team pool, and he is still the best player on his team. Out in the Amish-dominated, relatively isolated northwestern section of Pennsylvania, twenty-five miles south of Erie, with not a whole lot to do within walking distance and no buses, Jim does his best to keep busy. He helps the farmer across the street who has a hundred cows or joins his retired brother-in-law, Sharon's husband, in puttering in his garage. When he can get a ride he likes to attend weekday Mass. This is no easy task. This is not Catholic country. For instance, there are only two Catholic schools in the large county, a hundred miles apart, and no accessible Catholic high school. Sharon's older children were educated in Catholic schools in Cleveland, Ohio. Her youngest child, Billy, now married with three children, went to Catholic school in Pennsylvania too—but only by riding four buses.

The Porter siblings do not forget Mother Seton. And she does not forget them either, it appears to those of us who do not believe in coincidence. The Catholic school Billy took all those buses to was named for St. Elizabeth Ann Seton. In front of it is a huge statue commemorating the American heroine.

Some things are too deep for a lot of words: to this day, when Jim accompanies Sharon somewhere that necessitates passing the school, as soon as the statue of Mother Seton comes in view, he blesses himself, grins, and chuckles, "There she is! There she is!"

Chapter 13

"Maybe He Wasn't Really Dead"

On a sunny spring day, Fr. John Bosco was in Lanzo, Italy, paying a visit to one of the schools he had founded. When he arrived, seven boys were in the infirmary, quarantined with smallpox. Sick or not, their faith in one they believed a saint was so great they were sure that if Don Bosco, as they called him—*Don* being Italy's title for priests—would only come up and bless them, they would be healed and not have to miss the fun and entertainments scheduled for his visit. From their sickroom, they sent out an urgent request that the visiting priest come see them.

With his usual total unconcern for his own well-being—he once snapped at a hovering woman, "Madame, I did not become a priest to look after my health"—the saint entered their off-limits quarters.

With cheers and roars, all the boys began to clamor, "Don Bosco, Don Bosco! Bless us and make us well!"

Boys were never too raucous for this saint. He only chuckled at their exuberance. Then he asked if they had faith in Mary's intercession, for like all saints, Bosco never attributed his cures to his own prayer power.

"Yes, yes," they chorused. If Don Bosco was praying, they were full of faith.

"Let's say a Hail Mary together then," he proposed. Perhaps he reminded them that, as at Cana when Jesus worked His first public miracle at her request, when Mary asks her Son for a favor, she gets it. At any rate, only *after* the prayer which asked for the cure through Mary's prayers, not Bosco's, did he bless the sick students in the name of the Father, Son, and Holy Spirit, from whom all healing comes.

As their hands completed the answering Sign of the Cross, the boys began reaching for their clothes.

"We can get up now, right?"

"You really trust our Lady?"

"Absolutely!"

"Then get up!" He turned and left, and six boys, ignoring the deadly pustules that still covered them head to foot, hopped into their clothes and raced out to the festivities.

The seventh boy, John Baravalle, was a worrier. Might he not get worse if he got up? he stewed. After all, the school doctor had been insistent on bed rest and complete quarantine. Anxiously John decided to see if the school's priest director would second Don Bosco's permission. Although Baravalle was no sicker than the other boys, the director, seeing the pupil's lack of faith, advised he should probably stay in bed. It took him the twenty quarantined days to recover. As for the six imprudent, roof-raising rascals who dashed out to the fun and games with complete confidence, their pustules began to disappear as they played. The only near-casualty of that day in May 1869 was the poor conscientious school physician, who almost had a heart attack when he saw the smallpox patients "infecting" the entire school with an often fatal illness. While he was understandably furious, in fact no one caught the disease.

$\backsim$

"He likes me best!"

"Liar!" Dark eyes spit fire from one neglected slum child toward the other.

"I can prove it. Look, he gave me this slick new comb and a pile of doughnuts this high and—"

"Hah!" the other interrupts. "That's nothin'! Don Bosco's gonna get *me* a job as a 'prentice."

"So!" The too-thin face thrusts forward belligerently. "That's only 'cause you're too dumb to get your own—"

A roar and a lunge connect the two undersize bodies in a twisting tangle, each heartily pounding the one who dares question his special status with the young, curly-haired priest who comes running to separate them, his laughter and warmth easing the hunger for love beneath each grimy, brawling exterior.

Many years later, as clean, decently clad, well-mannered adults, long deflected from incipient delinquency into honest workingmen and stalwart Christians, the same pair and hundreds like them, plus many slightly better off boys like those seven at Lanzo, would recall Don Bosco with the same fierce, if less combative, love.

"How he loved us!"

"Remember his fatherly smile."

"And his gentleness. Wasn't he more tender than a mother?"

"He had so little to give us actually: a handful of doughnuts or chestnuts, maybe a cheap comb—but those days with him seem to me like Paradise."

There is even a testimony to this Holy-Spirit-filled magnetism from America's shores. The late Italian-born pastor Alfonso Volonte of Corpus Christi Church in Port Chester, New York, has told how, even when Bosco was old and unwell, the sight of him at one of the schools for poor boys he founded would cause "a free-for-all to get near him." One of Fr. Alfonso's most precious memories even in great old age was the day, as one of those youngsters, he actually managed to grasp the hand of the saint, who smiled "as only Don Bosco could smile" and let his free hand rest on the young Alfonso's head while saying a few treasured words to the boy.

The man whose love healed lives and sometimes bodies as well was canonized as St. John Bosco in 1934. It was only forty-six years after his death in 1888, in spite of all the miracles required at that time. His had been a life on the fast track too: Bosco was years ahead of his time—and ours. A master psychologist, nurturer, and educator, his boys' clubs and schools—whether academic, technical, or seminary—lovingly educated the whole child, intellect, emotions, soul, and body, with remarkable results.

Bosco founded technical schools to augment or replace the system of apprentice training of the young, midday retreats for workers and students, and vacation camps for Christians. Beginner of Italy's Catholic press apostolate, he knew how to turn every available medium of communication or entertainment—from almanacs and magazines to theater and music—to Christian use. One of the most winning personalities among the Church's saints, he was gifted by God with perhaps more charisms than any nineteenth-century saint, from prophecy and reading of hearts to the working of all sorts of miracles, including healing minds, souls, and bodies.

Fatherless himself at two, already in his ninth year John had been given his life's work in a numinous dream in which Christ and Mary showed the Piedmont farm boy he must turn wayward boys from wolves into lambs. Founder of the Salesians, today the second-largest and one of the Church's most vital orders, Bosco and his spiritual sons and daughters have saved hundreds of thousands of young people living in poor neighborhoods and slums all over the globe from meaningless and/or destructive lives. But before this vast enterprise took off, the peasant boy himself underwent an arduous spiritual conditioning that taught him to hope when all hope seems futile. Not only could his widowed mother not afford to send her youngest child to school and seminary, but the oldest of the three Bosco boys, John's half brother, Anthony, the son of the dead father by his short-lived first wife, flew into rages at the very sight of young John with a book.

"We're peasants. We don't need this kind of foolishness. Get out in the fields, where you belong," and Anthony would throw his youngest half brother's reader as far as he could.

By the time John was fourteen and still out of school, Margaret Bosco had to send him out on his own to escape the abuse. Working as a hired field hand, John saw his dream apparently recede farther and farther. But instead of giving up, he went deeper and deeper into prayer, mining toward that golden lode of trust in God and abandonment to Divine Providence which later formed the treasury for all his extraordinary works.

When the boy's remarkable intelligence—for one thing, he was gifted with a photographic memory—and immense charm brought him to the attention of a saintly priest who promised help, the man soon died. No human can help you—trust only in me, John later revealed God seemed to say to him at this time. It would take him many years, sometimes fighting discouragement and certainly not always aware of the character and virtues he was developing as he surmounted obstacles, to make it through school. During those years it is said he mastered thirty-seven trades. Certainly he held every kind of job, from tutoring to janitor at a pool hall, where he slept in a cubbyhole under some stairs.

When he finally completed his training as a diocesan priest and began his apostolate, critics sprang up at once. What was the young, handsome priest doing hanging out in areas known as hotbeds of vice?

Why was he seen entering a tavern late at night with a vicious gang and standing these young hoodlums a round of drinks? Had John Bosco no thought for the dignity of the priesthood? Why, most priests, some reminded him, forebore even to *speak* to slum people or any young person in order to maintain the proper awe toward their sacred calling.

When Bosco told his fellow mid-nineteenth-century clergymen that he was going to form a cadre of laymen and priests "in shirtsleeves" to live in the slums and work with the young spawned there, kids who would otherwise end up dead of drug or alcohol abuse, jailed for violent crime, or victims of the gang system, some fellow clergymen were horrified. They actually made arrangements to have "poor unbalanced Don Bosco" confined to a mental institution, but the quick-witted Bosco outfoxed them.

Another hardship was the political situation. It was a period of political instability. The small kingdoms of Italy were breaking up interiorly or being invaded by foreign powers. The entire Italian Peninsula was moving toward unity as a new nation.

Church and states, particularly Piedmont's government, were locked in battle over everything, from the pope's earthly kingdom, the Papal States, to the role of religious orders in the new era. Many anti-clericals in government looked with a jaundiced eye at the muscular, athletic young priest, a spellbinding speaker who could lead boys—and men—anywhere he proposed. When he marched through Piedmont's capital city, Turin, with several hundred young slum toughs on their way to the country to hike or picnic, sinister political maneuvers and the building of a personal power base were suspected.

On all sides, criticism or misunderstanding. No substantial help anywhere. His mission seemed doomed before it got off the ground. Finally came the crisis on Palm Sunday 1846, when he was going to have to tell his hundreds of followers they were being evicted from even the bare field he had rented as their meeting place when they had been thrown out of every building in Turin. Only in this last great temptation to despair, when he was asked to trust a God who seemed both deaf and cruel, did Bosco interiorize a faith so heroic that nothing could defeat it and a humility bottomless enough to defeat every impulse to pride in his enormous human and spiritual gifts. That same afternoon he was offered the lease on a dirt-filled shed leaning against a brothel across from a tavern. From this beginning, his mission never looked back. Neither faith nor humility failed him in the years ahead as he built playgrounds, schools, workshops, and training institutes, seminaries, churches, and living quarters all over Italy and in mission lands with no means of support but trust in Divine Providence.

His splendid body—he could pound a nail into the wall with his bare hands and into old age easily outran all comers in the footraces so dear to his boys' hearts—he literally wore out in service to the young, so that a doctor described him at sixty as like a coat become so ragged it is good only to hang in the closet.

"You must give up all work and do nothing but rest," the physician ordered

"That, Doctor, is the one thing I cannot do," the saint answered with his wide grin. And he went on with his killing schedule for another dozen years although nearly blind, suffering emphysema, and weak in almost every organ and system.

To reduce himself to such a state from the superb health that was his from birth, he had been guilty of self-abuse. Very early in his apostolate he wore himself into such a run-down condition that he caught pneumonia, the disease which had killed his strong young father when John was only two. Don Bosco's young toughs prayed, fasted, and wept to no avail until, on the night the doctors said the priest would die, a friend browbeat him into a single prayer that, if it were God's will, he might recover. The next morning he was pronounced out of danger. Medical advice was for many quiet months in the country to recoup his wasted strength. Bosco went to his home village, but aware that without his guidance boys could resume their former deadly habits, he returned to the slum before his body was fully recovered. For this loving folly he paid with bouts of emphysema the rest of his life. His eyes he ruined by overuse, never sleeping more than four or five hours a night, and staying up for years one entire night a week to answer letters and work on his books and articles (as today, youth needed Catholic literature to counter the paganism of the times), and making no allowance until almost blind for the weakness caused by a direct hit from a bolt of lightning.

Yet God assisted him. For instance, if Bosco could not see with his eyes, God gave him other means. Take the testimony of a boy making his confession to the saint. Don Bosco, who had been in the church hearing confessions for hours, informed him in which building on the large property he would find a boy hidden away and smoking an illegal cigarette.

"Don Bosco asked me to go to this fellow and tell him he should think about coming to confession."

When the messenger stepped gingerly into the dark hallway, he saw no one but smelled cigarette smoke. He called out the message hurriedly, because he wanted no dealings with the older, bigger youth. Then he dashed outside, hid in the bushes, and a moment later saw the boy named come out the door and head for the church.

Letters that the saint sent to various Salesian institutions throughout Italy and in other countries sometimes gave detailed advice about people and events there while he was far away, noting casually, "I dropped in on you in the spirit." Besides bilocation, Bosco's ailing eyes also got another assist. Consider this testimony:

[Don Bosco] was writing and I sat down near to him, watching him keenly, studying a certain movement he made while he was writing: he turned his head slowly from left to right, to accompany and follow the movement of the pen across the page. I did not understand why ... As soon as he stopped writing ... I [asked] ... "Why did you turn your head to the right to accompany the movement of the pen when you were writing?"

Don Bosco smiled as he answered, "This is the reason why ... [I] can no longer see with this eye, whereas the other eye, too, sees only a very little."

"... Then, how was it that, when I was quite some distance from you the other day in the courtyard, you looked at me very directly and keenly, as clear as a ray of sunlight?"

"Come, come now! All of you imagine things ... whereas there is really nothing at all ..." ... We began to talk about [another] matter. ...

But now to return to this topic of his look. I was at recreation in the playground one day. As usual, I was completely absorbed by the game. As I stood still a moment, I heard some boys talking with great animation. I turned around and espied Don Bosco surrounded by a crowd of boys at some distance from me. There were a great many of them, as there always were whenever Don Bosco came down into the playground, and they were all talking loudly and merrily with him. Absorbed as I was in the game I was playing, I did not feel like joining them. So I stood there hesitantly, and looked toward them again, where Don Bosco stood. Then all of a sudden I was struck by the brilliance of his eyes, as he looked toward me. I really could not describe it. I stood at least some thirty paces from him, and was not even directly opposite him, but found myself at a lateral angle of his vision. Don Bosco was literally besieged by the boys, and held the hands of several. I recall these things very clearly ... I say that his eyes were like a ray of light, like a shining ruby, a diamond, something quite unconceivable, and which could be compared to a flash of lightning. I was quite entranced by what I saw, and quite automatically, without knowing what I did, I approached the group. As I reached him, I felt Don Bosco take my hand, although I had not tried to push my way through to him.

The account, by Peter Fracchia, speaking many years after the fact, in 1937, makes it clear that Don Bosco could use his nearly blind eyes like the most keen-sighted of individuals at times. Spirit dominated flesh, one might say.[103] Or looking at it another way, like one who is at the same time both infirm and healed, he possessed, as Scripture says, in God's grace a strength made somehow more perfect in his weakness.

Lovable, human Don Bosco exemplifies in still another way that people madly in love with God can still behave as foolishly as the rest of us. Don Bosco not only acted as a priest, a catechist, and a teacher of subjects from music to metrics to his first slum kids, he also took many homeless or abused boys to live with him. He cooked for them, cut out and sewed their suits, barbered their hair, made their beds, and in all ways acted as both a mother and a father. Surely this was enough self-giving, but not for the saint. When a boy came to him moaning piteously with a toothache, an earache, or another infection in those pre-antibiotic days, Don Bosco would ask God to heal the kid by giving the

---

[103] For similar cases, see the description of cellist Pablo Casals in Norman Cousins' *Anatomy of an Illness* or of Pope John Paul II from the *Los Angeles Times* in my book *The Sanctified Body*.

pain or the illness to him. God, of course, may answer our idiotic prayers as well as our sage ones. Finally, when Don Bosco couldn't function for his hundreds of boys because he was incapacitated by the terrible toothache he had taken on for one boy, he came to his senses. He realized that this love that cries out to bear physically the loved one's pains and troubles, spiritually speaking, was a youthful excess. From then on, when led by the Holy Spirit to pray for healing—certainly not always the case, for he assisted many people in their deaths—Bosco prayed people well with the assumption God could spare the cure: it did not have to come, physically anyway, out of Don Bosco's hide.

Of course he reserved the right to make occasional exceptions, like the time he arrived at a Salesian school to find that the youngster who was to take the lead in the evening's entertainment had lost his voice.

"I'll lend you mine for the evening," the saint said. For the rest of that night the boy projected his voice beautifully, while Don Bosco was hoarse as a foghorn.

Because his sanctity was so widely known, in spite of his efforts to keep himself out of the limelight, Bosco's door often opened to people in search of healing. How many miracles occurred in the little room where, in his later years, he received his visitors for three hours a day, or on his many trips, only God could say. It is suggestive, however, that at his death, one hundred thousand turned out for the seventy-two-year-old priest's funeral, while it took thirty-four thousand pages to record all the testimonies of those who came forward two years later and asked to enter into the official record under oath their stories of Don Bosco's sanctity shown in heroic virtue *and* in what he had done for them and theirs. Many of these testimonies included healing.

One well-authenticated cure took place the same year the six boys were healed of smallpox at Lanzo. It occurred about 5 p.m. on May 16, the evening of Pentecost, in the Church of Mary Help of Christians, which Don Bosco built[104] next to his complex of homes and schools

---

[104] In this church put up by the penniless priest at a cost of a million lire in only three years, 110 favors—including cures of the caliber of the one I give here—had been recorded in 1875, only seven years after the mother church of Bosco's Salesian order opened its doors.

for boys in Turin. Maria Stardero, a blind girl of ten or twelve, was led by her aunt into the church, where dozens of boys were standing about or kneeling in prayer as they waited for Don Bosco to arrive for confessions. Fr. Francis Dalmazzo, one of the first Salesians, spoke to the woman. In his testimony he later recalled, "I was grieved to see that the young girl's eyes had no corneas and resembled white marbles."

When Don Bosco arrived, he questioned the girl about her condition. She had not been born blind, but as a result of eye disease her sight had been completely lost two years earlier. When he asked about medical treatment, the aunt began to sob that they had tried everything, but doctors could only say the eyes were "beyond hope."

"Can you tell whether things are big or small?" the saint asked.

"I can't see a thing."

He led her to a window. Could she perceive light?

"Not at all."

"Would you like to see?"

"Oh, yes! It's the only thing I want," and she began to sob about how miserable she was.

"Will you use your eyes for the good of your soul and not to offend God?"

"I promise I will, with all my heart!"

"Good. You will regain your sight," the man whose own vision was in need of help assured her. With a few sentences he encouraged the visitors to have faith in the intercession of Mary. With them he recited a Hail Mary and another prayer to Mary, the Hail, Holy Queen. Then, urging them to have absolute trust in the prayers of the Mother of Christ, he blessed the girl. After that he held a medal of Mary Help of Christians, in front of her and asked, "For the glory of God and the Blessed Virgin, tell me what I'm holding in my hand."

"She can't ..." the elderly aunt began, but Don Bosco paid no heed, while the girl after a few seconds shouted, "I see!" Immediately she described the detailing on the medal. When she stretched out her hand to receive it, however, it rolled into a dim corner.

The aunt moved to retrieve it, but Don Bosco motioned her back.

"Let her pick it up to see if the Blessed Virgin has thoroughly restored her sight," he insisted. Unerringly the girl bent into the shadows and picked up the tiny object. As the many witnesses looked on, awed and profoundly moved, Maria, beside herself with joy, bolted for home, while her aunt thanked Don Bosco profusely with sobs now of joy.

If Maria Stardero was so wild with joy she forgot to even thank the one whose prayer obtained her cure, she returned soon afterward to make her small donation to his work and offer thanks. Forty-six years later, in 1916, when some Salesians checked on her, she still had perfect vision.

The cures he worked for his individual boys were even simpler. For instance, a teenager who lived at the boarding school in Turin suffered a sudden mental breakdown. Far adrift in some interior world, the boy was brought for the saint's blessing before being sent home.

Blessed, the comatose-appearing teen suddenly started as if coming out of a trance.

"Where am I?" he asked, looking around bewildered.

"You're here in my office," Don Bosco smiled. "You weren't feeling well. How are you now?"

"Fine, but I'll bet I'm late for Latin," and the boy dashed off to class. That was the end of his breakdown.

Many of the saint's cures were worked while he traveled to beg funds for his works, to oversee their development, or while on missions for the Church. In Paris in 1884 he healed the son of the Marquise de Bouillé after the child had already received the sacraments given when death is imminent. Ignoring the doctor's sentence of death and the youngster's condition, Don Bosco gathered the family around the bed, invoked Mary's intercession, prayed with them, and left, assuring the parents the child would soon be convalescent; the next day the boy began to recover.

A few days later it was a dying girl of twelve, whom the saint prayed over, who was cured.

Such healings electrified the usually blasé Parisians. The coachman driving Bosco in the city muttered, "I'd rather drive the Devil than drive a saint" on one of the occasions he was unable to budge his vehicle because of the mob attempting to get close enough to touch the priest or scissor off some handy portion of his shabby cassock. As for Bosco, keeping a wary eye out for people wielding scissors, he murmured disgustedly, "These people are nuts."

Born poor himself, Don Bosco dedicated his order to work for the poor; but some of his miracles God gave to the wealthy, who often responded generously to support his undertakings. One such cure took place in Florence. A rich noblewoman there had a very young godson she loved as if he were her own child. While Don Bosco was visiting Florence, it happened that the little boy fell ill. When the doctors said he was dying, this woman went into a frenzy. She sent messengers everywhere searching for "the saint," and she rushed out herself to join the search. By luck, it was she who found Don Bosco. Being given a tour of their boarding school by some priests known as the Somaschi Fathers, he was suddenly confronted in this sedate group of clergymen by a madwoman, her hair undone, her clothes improper for outside the home, shrieking out her grief and pleas.

Understandably, the priests conducting the saint around their institution were not thrilled. But Don Bosco was not repulsed.

He excused himself and went at once with the wailing woman.

At the child's house, they found the little boy had just died. On his tiny bed, the small corpse lay glassy-eyed and still. Almost in a whisper, Don Bosco invited those in the room to beg the intercession of Mary Help of Christians. Then he blessed the little body. At the last word, the chest began to move. After a few more breaths, the child yawned, then opened his eyes. He smiled at the stupefied faces hovering over him.

In a short time he was perfectly well.

His godmother became such a benefactress to Don Bosco and his Salesians that they referred to her as "our good Mama in Florence."

Years later, Don Bosco was present at her dinner table when she began relating the story to other guests. Head bowed, his eyes never left his plate during her tale. Only when she finished did he speak, murmuring softly, "Perhaps he wasn't really dead."[105]

Among the other cures that seemed to be given by God to gain benefactors for the humble priest's work were a number in Rome. For example, when Don Bosco had great trouble there getting approval for his radical new congregation, God used the saint to give healings to

---

[105] To Bosco is also attributed a similar miracle in Turin.

several important church officials who opposed approval or to members of their families. For all today's theology about not bargaining with God, God seemed himself to barter the cures for approval of his saint's congregation. Among these cures a key opponent, Monsignor Svegliati, was healed overnight of virulent influenza following the saint's visit; Cardinal Antonelli, in great pain and immobilized by gout, when Don Bosco called on him was well the next day; and the eleven-year-old nephew of Cardinal Berardi, dying of typhoid, was inexplicably healed after the saint came to pray over him. To each of these churchmen, before working the cure, Don Bosco made it clear that their vote was expected in return. These changed votes gave the Salesians approval.

Like all the saint's projects, the Church of Mary Help of Christians, in Turin was paid for by donations, from pennies to large sums, by people who wanted to help Don Bosco save poor and troubled youths; but many gifts to his building fund came from individuals the saint cured or promised protection from illness. For instance, during terrible cholera epidemics, Don Bosco liberally promised freedom from infection, in Mary's name, to his donors. He said he was acting on instructions from the Virgin and, in fact, although hundreds died in some neighborhoods, none of the donors was among them. Even odder, he promised immunity to those of his boys who would join him caring for victims of the disease which was so infectious and so deadly that its sufferers were often abandoned by their own families—as with AIDS in its early days. Although they should have been infected by their close contact, not a boy sickened.

Unbelievers were also among those healed by the saint. I think of the prominent doctor who came to visit Don Bosco. After a few social remarks, he said, "People say you can cure all diseases. Is that so?"

"Certainly not," the saint answered.

"But I've been told—" The well-educated man was suddenly stammering. Fumbling in his pockets, he pulled out a tiny notebook. "See. I've even got the names and what each one was cured of."

Don Bosco shrugged. "Many people come here to ask favors through Mary's intercession. If they obtain what they seek, that's due to the Blessed Virgin, not me."

"Well, let her cure me," the doctor said agitatedly, tapping the notebook on his well-clad knee, "and I'll believe in these miracles too."

"What's your ailment?"

"I'm an epileptic." His seizures, he told Don Bosco, had become so frequent during the past year that he couldn't go out any more. In desperation, he was hoping for help beyond medicine.

"Well, do what the others do who come here," Don Bosco said matter-of-factly. "You want the Blessed Virgin to heal you. So kneel, pray with me, and prepare to purify and strengthen your soul through confession and Holy Communion."

The physician grimaced. "Suggest something else. I can't do any of that."

"Why not?"

"It would be dishonest. I'm a materialist I don't believe in God or the Virgin Mary. I don't believe in miracles. I don't even believe in prayer."

For a space the two men sat in silence. Then Don Bosco smiled, as only he could, at his visitor. "You are not entirely without faith—after all, you came here hoping for a cure."

As the saint smiled at him, something welled up in the doctor. Don Bosco knelt, and he knelt too without another word and made the Sign of the Cross.

Moments later, he began his confession.

Afterward, he declared, he felt a joy he would never have believed possible. Time and again he returned to give thanks for his spiritual healing.

As for the epilepsy, that simply vanished.

After Don Bosco's death, there were many miracles to testify to the sanctity of this great friend of God. Ignoring those involving after-death appearances by the saint[106] because I treat this subject at length in another book,[107] and ignoring those in which the saint's relics played the predominant role, I offer as examples the cures of two women.

Sr. Mary Joseph Massimi, of the convent of Santa Lucia in Selci, Italy, was about to die in 1928 of a duodenal ulcer. Her confessor gave this Augustinian nun a relic of Don Bosco, who was not yet beatified,

---

[106] See p. xxi for reference to one case.

[107] *Messengers: After-Death Appearances of Saints and Mystics*, retitled *Apparitions of Modern Saints* for the condensed paperback.

and advised that she make a novena for his intercession. During the novena, instead of improving, her condition got worse. It was obvious that her recuperative powers were simply gone. But the nun's faith was unshaken. She simply began a second novena.

This time, too, she deteriorated further. It appeared her death would occur any moment. Still, on the fifth day of the second novena, May 15, she dreamed Don Bosco said to her, "I've come to tell you you will recover. Just be patient. Suffer just a little longer. On Sunday you'll be granted the grace [of healing]." Sunday was then four days away.

Friday, May 18, she dreamed again. This time Don Bosco carried the black habit that her order's nuns wear on holy days. He repeated the promise of a Sunday cure. But her condition as Saturday faded into Sunday left room for only one conclusion: Sr. Mary Joseph had been the dupe of wish dreams with no real numinous content. Sadly on the very day her dreams had promised healing, her confessor was forced to give her the last rites.

But as the sister received the sacrament, her whole body suddenly "shuddered from head to foot, and in that instant she felt as though she was recalled from death to new life."

Occurring as the Church's experts, in the final act before beatification, were weighing two other cures attributed to Don Bosco for supernatural content, Sr. Mary Joseph's healing caused a chuckle among those who recalled how God had so many times furthered Don Bosco's projects with healing miracles.

Within twelve months of his 1929 beatification, there were already two new post-beatification miracles considered able to meet the Church's criteria. As study proceeded, however, a cure from Innsbruck, Austria, was set aside as not completely verifiable. In its place was offered at once the 1931 cure of Mrs. Catherine Lanfranchi Pilenga.

Catherine Pilenga suffered from serious chronic arthritic diathesis, particularly in her knees and feet. The organic lesions caused by the disease did not threaten her life, but they practically paralyzed her lower limbs. For twenty-eight years, she had battled the condition; not a single treatment since 1903 had given her any relief.

In May 1931, she made her second pilgrimage to Lourdes. It was no more successful than her first. As she prepared to leave the shrine, Catherine prayed, "Well, Blessed Mother, since I haven't been cured here, obtain the grace for me that, because of my devotion to Blessed Don Bosco, he will intercede for my recovery when I'm in Turin."

She arrived in Turin from France in her usual serious condition. It took her sister and a male helper to get her out of their vehicle and into the Church of Mary Help of Christians, where she sat down to pray in front of the urn that contained the mortal remains of Don Bosco.

Deep in prayer, at some point without noticing what she was doing, she knelt down. After remaining on her knees about twenty minutes, she stood up, walked to the altar of the Blessed Virgin, and knelt again to continue her prayers. It was only at that point she suddenly realized, in kneeling, she was doing something impossible for her—and knew she was cured.

People who had seen this woman laboriously assisted into the church because she was unable to move about by herself now watched in amazement as she moved freely not only on level ground, but climbing and descending stairs. Her disease had simply vanished. It was a permanent, instantaneous, total recovery, verified by three doctors as well as a medical commission appointed by the Church, from a condition that nearly thirty years of medical help had failed to cure. Heaping joy upon joy, Mrs. Pilenga's cure was eventually picked from the many healings God has given through Don Bosco to be held before the world at his canonization as an authentic miracle.

In 2010 Don Bosco's relics went on world tour, including a number of places in the United States. This was in anticipation of—and the opening of events in celebration of—the saint's two hundredth birthday in 2015.[108] A new round of God-given healings and other graces, such as those that poured out for his beatification and canonization, appears likely as more people are reminded to ask the warm-hearted saint's prayers.

---

[108] This author's biography of Bosco and his Preventive System of educating whole children will appear before this date as her contribution, in gratitude for his helping me raise my own children.

Chapter 14

"I'm Not Leaving Until You Cure Me"

In New Orleans' historical Irish Channel district, every early October and again in January, people fill the old pews of St. Mary's Assumption Church for a special Mass. In January they are celebrating the birthday of beatified saint, joy-filled priest-healer Francis Xavier Seelos with a healing Mass. In October they commemorate his death. In both they celebrate the happy life of service of Fr. Seelos, a Redemptorist born in Bavaria in 1819. Seelos died in New Orleans on October 4, 1867, and was buried near St. Mary's altar. Since beatification his body has its shrine in the church. A 2012 article in the New Orleans *Times-Picayune* credits him with "a rock star's following in the Irish Channel."

This did not start with beatification. Crowds keep getting larger but were coming year after year before Fr. Seelos attained that status. Back in 1986, just before this book's first edition came out, the *Times-Picayune* featured an article and photo of the Mass. The newspaper noted "a rare sight in inner-city churches these days: a full house, more than 1,000 strong," and quoted one of the sixteen priests who joined a bishop in the Mass: "The man's still getting a church full of people 119 years after his death in a town where he worked barely a year. I don't know what it is but it's something beyond the normal."

Among those in the crowd, the newspaper concludes, is a woman who credits the long dead priest's intercession with saving her life. What they don't know is that people crediting Seelos with saving their life is commonplace, whether during his life or today. As far back as a 1900-1903 collection of testimonies by those who knew the Redemptorist, almost 40 percent of the witnesses offered accounts of graces and cures received by invoking Fr. Seelos's prayer intercession, according to today's shrine director, Redemptorist Fr. Byron Miller. From these and other testimonies witnesses have left, it was common knowledge during his life that Fr. Seelos's prayers worked healing miracles and that something beyond the normal—in people's widespread opinion, his sanctity— filled churches wherever he went, whether that was New York, Chicago, Detroit, Pittsburgh, Baltimore, Cincinnati, or any of a myriad of small American towns and villages from Wisconsin to New Jersey.

To understand Xavier, as his large, devoted family called him, one has to accept that, while in general saints are made, not born, it is also true that in the spiritual life, as in music, there are natural geniuses. They also have to grow to their full powers, but it seems easier for them—or at least they grow faster and go farther than the rest of us. By the age of five, under his father's instruction, Mozart was a prodigy. Similarly, under the direction of his mother, frail little Xavier Seelos very early showed the kind of spiritual precocity one would see seventy years later in small Francesco Forgione (Padre Pio).

The sixth child, fourth living, and second son of ten children who would grow to adulthood, Francis Xavier Seelos entered life in the picture-postcard little town of Füssen, sixty miles southwest of Munich in the Bavarian Alps. The family was a happy one. It was also one with a tradition of healing given in answer to prayer.

A pregnant paternal grandmother had lost both her previous babies to miscarriage. In May 1782, when Pope Pius VI passed through the town of fifteen hundred people, the young wife rushed for a papal blessing that this child might live. It did, her only survivor, for she died, with her next baby, in childbirth two years later. The one living child, Mang (after St. Magnus, patron of the town's Benedictine monastery), became Francis Xavier's father.

After Mang married, he became so ill with some virulent disease that his life trembled in the balance. His wife, Frances, fell on her knees and vowed a pilgrimage to the great Einsiedeln shrine in Switzerland, if his life was saved. In Mang's *Hausbuch*, one can read his grateful "Praise God! The prayer of my dear wife was heard."

Their little Xavier, born January 11, 1819, was in bed much of his early childhood with various ailments, convincing his mother, who had already buried twin girls, that he would not live to grow up. Perhaps for this reason, she talked to him a good deal of Heaven's glories and took special pains to share with him her love of prayer. But early training is not the whole story. Mozart's sister got music lessons too. Mrs. Seelos would later remark that she tried to spiritualize all her children, but Xavier took to such things beyond the others, including two girls who became nuns.

Some see a spiritual prodigy as a somber child. This is the exact opposite of reality: Xavier was a merry, giving child— among his family's simple memories is one of the day the tiny boy "borrowed" the coat his father had been married in and paraded down the streets, sleeves flapping, tail dragging, entertaining his friends. He liked to make people happy. When he went away to school, always necessarily on scholarships, he was called by his friends "the banker," for what little he came by, they could always draw on. One of them says that Xavier had the rocklike faith of his mother melded to the quick-to-laugh, urbane geniality of his father. Those who knew him as a university student in Munich picture someone far along the road to spiritual greatness.

It was no great surprise to his fourteen-year-old brother, Adam, to arrive at his brother's quarters for tutoring and be told by an excited Xavier, "We won't be studying today. Our Lady appeared to me last night." In his youthful elation, Xavier shared with Adam that he, Xavier, was not to remain in his homeland, but to go far away. A year later, in 1843, he left Bavaria forever.

In an age when many people thought loving God meant you didn't love anyone else, Xavier wrote his next-in-age sibling, Antonia, who had been his natural confidante and playmate: "Love has bound us two together for time and eternity. Here on earth we will remain united in our hearts and in our prayers for each other—and there in heaven we will be eternally united without the least fear of separation." In that same long farewell letter with its separate warm notes to the family members, he admits writing in tears. Heavy-hearted, he tells Adam in another letter, "If it concerned my own wishes, I'd stay with you always but I can't resist the inner call—I freely follow it."

Like St. John Neumann, whom he worked under as a young priest in Pittsburgh and loved "like a father," Seelos joined the Redemptorists, missionaries who ministered to German-speaking immigrants. Actually, Seelos would serve people of every ethnic background, just as Neumann did.

Redemptorists who knew him declared that Seelos was already considered a saint in the order's American novitiate. The American people agreed. Hearing him give one of his first sermons in not-yet-mastered English, an Irish immigrant remarked that, while she couldn't understand him, it did her good just to see that "holy priest" struggling to preach. In Pittsburgh and New Orleans, parents predicted to their children that Fr. Seelos would be canonized one day. Bishops concurred. Bishop Michael O'Connor of Seelos's first major post, Pittsburgh, wrote to Rome, "This priest is a man of truly remarkable sanctity" and asked that Seelos be named his successor. In Detroit, Bishop Lefevere said of Seelos, who served there for ten months, "One only has to look at him to know he is a saint."

Early in his priestly career the whispers began concerning physical cures. Michael Curley, a Redemptorist biographer, with access to many first-person, under-oath testimonies, notes: "In asking God to cure people of bodily disease ... Seelos seemed to have no doubt his prayer would be answered. This was quite apparent on several occasions in Pittsburgh when the people brought their sick children to him. He said a prayer over them before the altar ... with such calm assurance that the bystanders were struck by it. They were more surprised when those for whom he prayed were cured."[109]

One of those cured children was a little Protestant boy whose mother sent Fr. Seelos a gift in thanks. Another was Philomena Roehlinger, whose epileptic seizures, beginning in infancy, had gradually become so severe her mother privately asked Fr. Seelos to pray her child would die. Instead the saint worked a total cure as described in detail in the pamphlet *Meet Blessed Seelos* by John Vaughn. Years later the family's second child was instantaneously cured of an eye affliction five years of doctoring had failed to help. God, testified Mrs. Roehlinger, had given Fr. Seelos "great power."

Another woman testified that when Fr. Seelos was stationed in Pittsburgh, her condition was such that death seemed near. She told the priest she was not afraid to die, but she was worried about her young children. Fr. Seelos, she said later, told her to begin a novena to Jesus in His eucharistic form and to receive Communion with the same confidence in

[109] In *Cheerful Ascetic: The Life of Francis Xavier Seelos*.

healing displayed by the woman who touched the hem of Christ's garment. Inspired, the sick woman prayed with faith and was healed.

Because of events like these, a crippled man came to see Fr. Seelos. "Cure me," he pleaded.

"Now, now, I'm no doctor," Fr. Seelos began. But the visitor was not about to be denied. Picking up his crutches, he heaved them out the rectory window.

"I'm not leaving until you cure me," he said determinedly.

Seelos shook his head but fetched his Bible. He had the man sit and then settled himself. He began to read in the Gospel of St. John. Finally, he stopped, closed the book, and began to pray ardently.

Next he prayerfully recited the Church's blessing for the sick. Only then, when he had done all he could to sidetrack any healing from connection with himself, did he bless the man.

Immediately the petitioner felt a strange feeling pass through his crippled legs. Sobbing with joy, he began to walk as he cried out his thanks to God and to Fr. Seelos for his cure.

That same rocklike faith in unseen realities that was at the service of the sick gave Fr. Seelos words for a couple who told him their child had died.

"Your child is not lost to you," he assured them. "Your child is saved for you for all eternity."

Those coming to Fr. Seelos for healing or consolation often thought him robust, because he accomplished the work of a strong man. Actually he seems to have experienced a kind of ongoing healing, somehow continually recharged by his union with God so that he could serve others in spite of his bodily weakness. In Lent of 1857, however, as if God were signaling the need for a rest, the preacher broke a blood vessel in his throat and hemorrhaged for three days. His death expected, he wrote a "last letter" home. Later his sister said with great emotion to a visitor, "He, who in his whole life hurt no one, asked our pardon." Soon he was back at work but forbidden to preach for some time.

Christlike goodness like Seelos's heals, but it also triggers attack by those it threatens. Some of these are simple "bad" people like the man who lured the priest out at night on a sick call in order to beat him to near unconsciousness. Others are "good" people who are *forced* by the purest motives, they would tell you, to act against someone. Thus the newspaper that reported with high-minded horror Seelos's having gone in the dead of night to a bawdy house. The priest, who had answered the call to a dying prostitute, said simply, "Well, I saved a soul."

Much loved in his religious order, he had been made novice master, then prefect of students. His fatherly treatment of his students—things like letting American seminarians with inadequate Latin take their theology exams in English—incensed one Redemptorist, who wanted Americans rigidly held to every European custom. By a secret letter campaign to Rome, this fellow priest discredited Seelos as "too good" to be effectual. Suddenly stripped of his offices sans explanation, Seelos took the demotion with the happy assurance of a saint who knows God is doing him a good turn whatever happens.

Without any rancor, he went on being "too good." When another priest gloated, as they preached a mission together, "Boy, I'm going to castigate them today," Seelos objected. "That's entirely out of place." In a day of "hellfire and damnation" sermons, Seelos's talks emphasized God's pity and love as reasons for childlike confidence in our heavenly Father. If any soul was lost, he assured his hearers, it was never from a sin too big, but only from too little trust in God's mercy and forgiveness. And if anyone was afraid his or her sins were too many or too awful to confess, he promised to hear that person with special gentleness. No wonder two-hour waits before his confessional were common, while in some towns mobs of eager penitents almost tore his confessional door off its hinges.

In such an atmosphere, not only conversions but physical cures flourish. For instance, in March 1860 two doctors declared that a woman of Cumberland, Maryland, was going to die from diphtheria. This Mrs. Brinker no longer could feel anything in her hands or feet. Given the last sacraments, she lingered some weeks without improvement. By May 2, when someone asked Fr. Seelos to visit her, she was unconscious. She later told how she came to, to find the priest praying on his knees next to her bed. To her surprise she could feel again. With his kind smile, Fr. Seelos told her he was going to make a novena for her. He felt sure, he said, that God would restore her health. From then on she improved. By July 4, she was well.

Several years later the same woman's life was endangered again by some illness whose main symptom was a terrible cough. Passing through

Cumberland on one of his preaching tours, Father Seelos seemed to be amused. "What you need," he grinned, "is another powerful blessing." He blessed her and instantaneously the cough disappeared, never to return.

We have no date on the second visit, but it may well have been in 1865, for he stopped in Cumberland that year according to testimony by the Simon Sell family. Sell, a workingman, fell from a scaffold that June 6. Worse than his broken hip and ribs and the deep wound in his side were the internal injuries. With his crushed kidneys and other internal damage, three doctors told the family, he was beyond medical skill.

On June 10, Fr. Seelos, visiting the Cumberland Redemptorist house, was called out to give Sell the last rites. The workingman sorrowed to the compassionate priest that he would leave his family destitute, since he had nothing for their support beyond his labor. Fr. Seelos was moved. In the next few days, he returned several times to see the Sells. Then one day he said to the children, "Let's kneel down and ask God to heal your father."

On his knees he led them in prayer. The family experienced him as approaching God like a child begging a kind father for a special favor. They were all weeping when Fr. Seelos stood up and said, "Mr. Sell, you're not going to die. To support this home for your children, you're going to get well."

Sell did not die. In three months he was out on crutches. A little later he was back at work.

⌒

In September 1866, Fr. Seelos was on a train to a new post in a trilingual parish in New Orleans. Sr. Maria Largusa of the School Sisters of Notre Dame was on the same train. She noticed that the priest did not use the sleeping car but sat up all night. He seemed, she said, immersed in prayer.

"Will you be in New Orleans long, Father?" she asked the next morning.

He smiled. "I'll be there a year. Then I'll die of yellow fever." Speechless, Sr. Maria filed that conversation away as one to remember.[110]

---

[110] The July 24, 1866, diary entry of a Redemptorist friend notes that Seelos said the same thing to him.

In New Orleans, too, people were soon talking of this man who so affected people's lives and telling each other about inexplicable cures. Among these was the case of the three-year-old daughter of the George Segel family. She was very sick, refusing all nourishment, when the family doctor confessed he could do no more and advised calling in a specialist. Instead the parents wrapped the sick child and carried her to Fr. Seelos. Rather than an instant cure, when the priest prayed over the child, she seemed to be violently affected. He advised the parents to go home and assemble their workers to pray for the little girl. They followed this odd advice and the child fell into a deep sleep that lasted so long and was so sound, it was feared she was dead. She woke better. Again her parents bundled her up and took her to Fr. Seelos. He prayed over her a second time, and she was further improved. After a third prayer session she was completely well and remained healthy thereafter.

Another testimony collected for the pre-beatification investigation and reported in Curley's official biography tells of the Redemptorists' widowed washerwoman, Maria Jost. She was bringing the fathers' laundry back to the rectory, balancing a large basket on her head, when she was hit by a horse-drawn trolley. After two months in bed unable even to move without help, the doctor gave her the good news that in another month she might be able to sit up for brief periods.

"I'd rather die than lie here helpless another month," she exploded when Fr. Seelos visited and said something about patience. Without further unwanted advice, he prayed and blessed her. The next morning, she was up and well.

⌒

In the fall of 1867 the city and the Redemptorists living there were decimated by yellow fever. Two Redemptorists had already died in the house when Seelos was given the news that the doctors judged him past recovery.

"Oh, what pleasant news!" he exclaimed. While the *Daily Picayune* reported each morning on his condition, Xavier weakened slowly. His humor remained. Asked if he needed to make any arrangements with his brothers and sisters about a family inheritance, he answered, "Before I came to America we arranged this in really brotherly fashion. I get nothing and they get nothing."

To a brother who, sure this was a saint dying, kept badgering him, he admitted yes, the Virgin Mary was appearing to him on his deathbed. Of course the Redemptorists are quick to add, Seelos may have imagined this in delirium.

One thing they do know for a certainty: Fr. John Duffy, the pastor under whom Seelos was working at the time, did not have yellow fever, but he was just about out of commission anyway. As a child of eight or so, he had cut his knee so badly with an ax that several doctors agreed amputation was necessary. Aghast, his mother begged the intercession of a saint, and the boy was healed. The leg served him well for years, but under the strain of the epidemic, making constant sick calls — the city death toll was then about eighty a day — and caring for the ill Redemptorists, the knee went out. Suddenly he could not walk and had to beg a passing wagon to drive him home.

Fr. Seelos, who had been his novice master, was delirious when Duffy came silently into his room. He never knew that the younger priest knelt by his bed on his one good knee and begged God to cure the bad one through the merits of the dying Seelos. Duffy left that room, he later testified, healed completely of the lameness and the pain. And, in spite of backbreaking work during the rest of the epidemic, he had no further trouble.

Fr. Seelos did know that Br. Louis, the interrogator on his inner life, wanted a cure. The brother said bluntly, "Now you cure my knee. This running up and down stairs all day is killing me. My left leg's giving out."

"You sure have peculiar ideas!" Seelos grinned. But he said nothing more when Br. Louis grabbed the sick man's hand and put it on the ailing leg. He even smiled and pressed gently on the sore spot. Br. Louis said the pain vanished immediately and did not return until some days after Seelos's death.

After several days of passing nothing but blood, his face bright with joy in the hymn being sung by his friends, Francis Xavier Seelos died at age forty-eight. He had been in New Orleans just a year.

Chapter 15

In New Orleans: "Our Most Amazing Case"

In life Fr. Francis Xavier Seelos smiled engagingly for his official priestly photograph while his fellow Redemptorists, in nineteenth-century style, assumed expressions ranging from sober to downright grim. In death, too, Seelos's expression people found benign and inviting.[111]

In spite of the ongoing yellow-fever epidemic and a hurricane that blew through New Orleans that day, immediately following his death on the afternoon of October 4, 1867, hundreds rushed to St. Mary's Assumption Church, where his body lay on view.

Redemptorist Br. Louis feared the coffin would be overturned by the eagerness of the crowd pressing to reach the body. He noted that people, including the Redemptorists, were drawn to *touch* Xavier Seelos's corpse, for there was a general conviction that this was no ordinary body, but the physical portion of a saint whose extraordinary relationship to God carried God's healing love to others.

Among those saying openly that a saint had just graced New Orleans with his death was Christine Holle. Christine had been in bed for a month when she heard the bells tolling Fr. Seelos's death. As she listened something welled up in her, and she felt a great desire to get to St. Mary's. Ignoring the excruciating pain racking her abdomen and hip, she dragged herself out of bed and into some clothes. What disease she had is unknown to us today, but we have her testimony that it caused ongoing agonizing pain. Somehow she made it to church and through

---

[111] A coroner has assured me that corpses have no expression except as set by an undertaker, but testimonies in dozens of cases convince me that the death of saints habitually breaks this rule.

the pressing crowd to fall on her knees by the coffin. Reaching up, she touched the dead priest's hand. At that moment the terrible pain in her abdomen and hip left, never to return.

The next morning, as the body was being moved for burial in front of the altar area, a grandmother with a baby in her arms called out to Fr. Seelos in prayer. Would he intercede for this child already marked by impending death? From that moment occurred what one who saw it called "a great cure."

While individual Redemptorists like Fr. Duffy and Br. Louis were certain Fr. Seelos was a saint, they knew that only after both a stringent examination of a person's life and verified miracles as signs by God will the Church make such a pronouncement. Hoping an official scrutiny would be initiated by the Church, they dared do little to promote it. Any suspicion on Rome's part that a religious order is drumming up the looked-for popular enthusiasm on behalf of a dead member stops a Cause cold. So while Br. Louis, in New Orleans, and other individual Redemptorists such as Seelos's former seminarian Fr. Bernard Beck, in Detroit, made careful notes on what people said to them of Fr. Seelos and the healings recipients attributed to him, publicly the order remained quiet on the dead priest.

It was ordinary people who had known Fr. Seelos who spontaneously turned to the dead priest as a powerful prayer partner in Heaven. They shared the view of the writer for New Orleans' secular newspaper, the *Daily Picayune*, that Fr. Seelos's "only human weakness was his overflowing sympathy and charity for poor, erring humanity." In prayer, they put Fr. Seelos's sympathy and charity to the test and were not disappointed.

In New Orleans the parents of Cecilia Villars asked the dead priest's prayers when their sixteen-year-old daughter became sick on November 17 during a smallpox epidemic that battered the city late in 1869. Cecilia's "impossible" overnight cure from physician-verified smallpox was followed within a month by her equally inexplicable cure from other life-threatening problems, including a lung tumor.

With what we know about the links between mind and body, it would today be possible to theorize that Cecilia's trust in Fr. Seelos's intercession triggered remarkable and rapid changes in her body without anything supernatural involved at all. If so, this would also be a wondrous thing that many a victim of infectious disease or tumor would like to experience.

But a cure in Pittsburgh in 1872 shows that healings through the intercession of saints often take place in situations in which the mind-body link cannot be cited—and in which, in fact, spiritual explanations seem the most plausible.

On that April 11, a twenty-month-old baby, Julius Stephi, was literally pulling his hair out in the agony of meningitis. The child also had pneumonia. Both were complications from a severe attack of measles. Three physicians, Drs. Hoffman, Foligney, and Clark, had fought for the child's life—and lost. The little one was in prolonged death throes when his grandmother, Mary Magdalena Vogel of another Pennsylvania town, came into Pittsburgh and stopped by on her way to Mass at St. Augustine's Church.

In this pre-telephone era, Mrs. Vogel did not know her grandson's condition. She was shocked to see her daughter and son-in-law waiting in torture for the writhing baby's death agony to be over. During the Mass, Mary Vogel testified later, the pain-racked little body in the crib was continuously before her eyes. Just as the priest reached the solemn moment of the Mass when, Catholics believe, the bread and wine offered are changed into the Body and Blood of Christ (John 6:51-56), Mrs. Vogel suddenly saw another face in her mind: that of Fr. Seelos, who had been her confessor years earlier. The late lay writer and former Redemptorist John Vaughn relates:

> In this particular church they would ring the bell in the church tower at the moment of the consecration during the Sunday High Mass. As the bell rang she said: "Father Seelos, while you were on earth you had the power to change bread and wine into the body and blood of Christ. Now that you are in heaven, you are not less powerful. Please ask God to heal my grandchild." Then she promised to make a novena in honor of Father Seelos and have a Mass said if the child would either end his agony by a quick death or recover.

Mass ended and Mrs. Vogel rushed back to her grandson. Her daughter met her at the door. "Mother, Mother, the most wonderful thing's just happened. Just after the consecration bell rang in the tower of St.

Augustine's, little Julius stopped writhing. He's asleep as quiet as a lamb. I think he's going to be all right!"

An hour later the toddler, who had refused all food for two days, woke up ravenous—and well.

⁂

Cures like this led to opening official investigation into Seelos's sanctity, which observers during his lifetime predicted. From 1900 to 1903, testimonies were taken under oath in the places where Father Seelos spent much time: Augsburg in Germany; and Pittsburgh, Baltimore, and New Orleans in the States. His Cause for official sainthood was then sent to Rome.

A cure from around this time was that of a handicapped individual, a pious, if perhaps eccentric, old woman known as "Holy Oil Mary." Mary Bauer got her nickname because this staunch believer in prayer for healing used to anoint the sick with oil according to the command of the apostle (James 5:14). Using her black-enameled crutches, she made her way each morning into St. Mary's Assumption Church, where Fr. Seelos is buried. There, after Mass, she spent most of her day praying. Apparently one day God spoke to her about her own crippled condition. While every day she paid a visit to the tomb of Fr. Seelos in the church, this day she asked his intercession for her *own* cure, stood up, set her crutches aside, and walked off without them. For roughly the next seventeen years—witnesses place the cure about 1905—until her death on March 11, 1923, the prayerful woman in the old-fashioned black dress walked unaided.

John Ducote, Grand Knight of the Redemptorist Knights of Columbus Council in New Orleans testified that in June 1938, when he was six and a half years old, he caught infantile paralysis. Known familiarly as polio, this dread children's disease of that pre-vaccine era rampaged through the little boy's body, leaving both his legs and both his arms completely paralyzed.

The reader will recall the Notre Dame nun who had ridden on the train with Fr. Seelos when he moved to New Orleans. Her order still held the dead priest in great veneration, and when John's mother reported her son's condition to a Notre Dame nun named Sr. Gertrude, Mrs. Ducote was counseled to ask the intercession of Fr. Seelos. The mother took this advice. She not only frequently asked Fr. Seelos to pray for John, but she made repeated visits to his tomb with her request.

In John Ducote's own words: "I remained totally paralyzed until approximately the end of August. Then one Sunday morning I called for my dad to come to me. He did not hear me because he had the radio on. I then got up and walked through two rooms to the side of my dad. These were the first steps I had taken in three months! I have always felt that I am walking today because of my mother's prayers to Father Seelos [for his intercession]."

In the second decade of the twenty-first century, mail and phone calls pour into the Seelos National Shrine requesting prayers for every kind of condition. Pouring *out* are monthly newsletters, which, shrine director, Redemptorist Fr. Byron Miller tells me, are "requested by thirty thousand households in all fifty states and beyond." They feature letters of thanksgiving—at least half a dozen, each month year after year—for answered prayers. Many of these are striking accounts of physical healings, considered by their recipients miracles received from God through the intercessory prayers of Fr. Seelos.

For instance, a Galveston, Texas, individual's life had come to "an abrupt halt" after a stroke in 1999 and then became unbearable from untreatable and inoperable pain from a syrinx[112] in the spinal cord. The person writes in 2012 healed of both after being prayed over by someone invoking Seelos's intercession. The doctors in Houston are "thrilled."

A woman is diagnosed with incurable stage 4 lung cancer, adenocarcinoma.[113] Metastasizing to her spine in 2011, it is being treated with chemo just to keep the misery from spreading or growing in size, when the cancer goes into inexplicable remission. "My tumors are shrinking with no activity" to make them shrink, she writes. She has been prayed for at the Seelos Center and says, "I feel Fr. Seelos has guided my husband and me in ways to promote this surprising healing."

There are scores of other cancer healings, improvements, and changed diagnoses. A nurse writes her gratitude that the mass in her two-year-old's foot proved noncancerous after prayer invoking Seelos. The mother

---

[112] A syrinx is a pseudo-cyst creating a blockage to the normal flow of body fluid transporting nutrients and waste products through the spinal cord.

[113] The most common of the many types of lung cancer in women and non-smokers. It is increasing, perhaps due to air pollution.

had been so frightened she could neither eat nor sleep, knowing what cancer of this type could mean. She shares Fr. Seelos with a friend whose child's mass then also proves benign.

Childhood Kidney IGA neuropathy is incurable in June 2013; "it might get a little better or a lot worse," but it is there for life. Then the little boy with this shattering diagnosis is blessed for healing at the Seelos Center. Now his kidney doctor finds there is not even protein in the child's urine, something he has never seen happen. The doctor says, "I don't know what angels you have watching over you, but this is a miracle!"

Little ones get other breaks too: a father writes from Brooklyn about the healthy new son named Francisco Xavier in honor of Seelos, to whose prayer intercession they credit the change from the diagnosis of the serious syndrome Trisomy 13 and heart problems for over six months of the pregnancy to a completely normal sonogram at eight months. (Most babies with T-13,[114] also called Patau Syndrome, are never permitted to live but aborted after parents are told about 80 percent will die shortly after birth from severe neurological and heart defects.)

Another family has only a 1-percent chance of a child without severe genetic/physical disabilities from the twelve-week ultrasound confirmed by a neonatal specialist. Attending Masses at St. Mary's Church, where Seelos is buried, and with the mom prayed over at the Center, Christian (middle name Seelos) is born perfect and, when the testimony is given in June 2013, at two and a half remains so.

Then there is the Florida child born with four congenital heart defects, including a hole in the heart. Surgery must be done ASAP but before that Grandma and Grandpapa and the baby's mom circle the infant and invoke Fr. Seelos's prayers: after pre-op, the surgeon does a last EKG and says the baby is fine and can play football someday if he wants to. Another pediatric cardiologist proclaims this "nothing short of a miracle."

A person writes to "praise God and thank Fr. Seelos" that the total paralysis to the left side of her face, stage 5 Bell's palsy, diagnosed as perhaps permanent, is now 95 percent gone. She had asked Fr. Seelos to intercede with Jesus for her.

---

[114] Trisomy 13, the number referring to an extra copy of chromosome 13.

Given 1,000 grams instead of 0.1 milligram of a medication, the victim of a pharmacist's admitted mistake is comatose and on life support without a good outlook until, after six days, Seelos's prayers are invoked. Docs and nurses agree the return to health is "medically impossible."

There are inexplicable heart cures too: a man suffering "serious heart problems" gets access from his cardiologist to some medication from France and gets "over three years some improvements but nothing resembling a cure." But after some Seelos novenas, studying the saint's life, and being blessed with a relic, he reports in 2012, "After an EKG, my cardiologist entered the room smiling broadly and shaking his head. He said, 'I'm trying to believe it: your heart is perfectly normal!'" The healing recipient ends his testimony: "Since I didn't anticipate the healing, I was as surprised as anyone." Another gentleman who has been hospitalized in 2011 eight times due to atrial fibrillation never responding to any medication, suffering a small stroke, enduring treatments ranging from a stent and balloons to being shocked (CardioVert) to having a defibrillator/pacemaker implanted is already in an operating room for still another procedure, an ablation operation, when—this time Seelos is being invoked—the doctor declared "no operation was necessary" because the heart rhythm had returned on its own to completely normal, where it remained when his wife wrote her thanks.

A woman seeks Seelos's help in 2005 for a son with multiple sclerosis (MS) and a workaholic son-in-law needing a heart transplant. The son's MS, when she writes in May 2013, has now been eight years in remission, and the heart is still going with just medication, no transplant, in spite of no change in the son-in-law's workaholism.

From Erin, Tennessee, another mother writes: "My son was in a very bad car accident. The doctor said at the time he didn't see how he was alive. He had a crushed pelvis and left leg … At that time he was told he'd never use his left leg and live a normal life because of his crushed pelvis. Well I asked for your prayers and I began to pray to Fr. Seelos [for his]. Today my son lives a normal life and walks fine even without a cane. Fr. Seelos again has helped. God be praised."

There have been cases like these for years, including large numbers of inexplicable remissions or cures from terminal or advanced cancer. From time to time in the pre-beatification period one of these healings would be forwarded to Rome in hopes it would meet the Church's stringent criteria for formal miracles (p. xxvi). These included a young college student's healing, which looked like the first recorded cure of sickle-cell anemia, a disease that even in the twenty-first century has yet to be conquered by medical means. But even this case would not hold up to be named the official miracle.

That would be the extraordinary cure of Angela Boudreaux from terminal liver cancer after exploratory surgery gave her two weeks to live. Reproduced here is the author's summary of Angela's experience written initially for this book's first edition from long interviews with Mrs. Boudreaux by phone and then a number of times in person as I was a guest at the Seelos Center, invited by its priest director, and staying, as their guest, at the Boudreaux home. At that time — that is, well *before* her healing was chosen as the official miracle for Fr. Seelos's 2000 beatification — Angela reported an entire saga of healings within her nuclear family in response to requests for Fr. Seelos's intercession.

These begin with a "cure" which seems rather minor — unless you've ever cared day after day, night after night, for a baby screaming, scratching, and crying with the pain and itching of severe eczema. That was the case with the Boudreaux's fourth child, John, who about a year after his birth in 1964 developed an allergy his mother says "was so bad that any creases in the body, such as those of elbows, knees, armpits, the back of the neck, etc., would crack and bleed with an odor like a drainage ditch." Because he scratched and bled all night, crying all the while, his mother had to rig up cardboard restraints when she pajama'd him so he would be unable to bend his arm to further gouge his flesh. This nightmare had gone on about a year, starting not long after he was weaned from breastfeeding to canned formula; yet the pediatrician and another specialist assured the mother it had nothing to do with any food allergy.

Angela says she had reached the end of her rope when she found a pamphlet from the Seelos Center in nearby New Orleans. The pamphlet offered a Redemptorist priest from the center to visit anyone hospitalized and pray over them for a cure through Fr. Seelos's intercession.

Little John wasn't hospitalized but his distraught mother, she could later kid, felt *she* might soon be. Two days after his second birthday, on

Friday, March 4, she carried the miserable child to the Seelos Center. To her dismay, she found the lone priest (not the gracious man there now) little inclined to pray for the baby; if he extended his offer to the non-hospitalized, he explained, he feared he would be overwhelmed. Angela begged and pleaded that he just bless the child with Fr. Seelos's crucifix in God's name.

"You're looking for a miracle," the priest accused as if this were a grave offense.

"I'm asking God," corrected the determined mother, "for a doctor who will find out what's wrong with my child so they'll cure what he has or keep it under control."

Only after half an hour's wrangling and Angela's firm promise not to run out and tell other people her non-hospitalized child had been prayed for at the center did the priest reluctantly bless the scabby-skinned two-year-old.

The next Tuesday, March 8, a nurse working for the specialist who had been ineffectually treating John suddenly took advantage of her boss's absence to recommend that Angela consult another doctor, who, in turn, immediately sent the little patient to dermatologist James Burke.

Dr. Burke sandwiched the toddler into his day's schedule. To Angela's joy and relief, as soon as he looked at him, he said offhandedly, "Oh, we can get that under control." He ordered John off all soap and a number of foods such as the milk formula, orange juice, egg, and chocolate. For temporary relief he gave a shot. Although allergists would not expect food-triggered eczema to clear up until some days after the last offending item was eaten, that night when Angela bathed John with the recommended over-the-counter soap substitute, the eczemic scales floated away with the bathwater.

Put to bed without any restraints in his pajama sleeves, the toddler slept peaceably—as did his grateful parents and siblings.

From then on, he neither scratched nor bled. For John Boudreaux, himself a parent today, his childhood eczema is only a story.

☞

Five months later, in the first days of August 1966, unpleasant symptoms of her own sent Angela to nearby New Orleans Sellers and

Sanders Clinic. There Dr. Alfred J. Rufty took her history, palpated her abdomen, swollen to proportions of a six-month pregnancy, and found a liver nine times normal size.

Angela had excellent rapport with her doctor and told me, "I trusted him to the fullest," but when he tentatively diagnosed, "My guess is you have cirrhosis of the liver —"

"I sat up and said indignantly, 'Doctor, I don't even drink.'"

The amused doctor countered that there are all kinds of cirrhosis, some quite unrelated to alcohol.

But the truth was to prove worse. A precautionary biopsy under local anesthesia retrieved no liver tissue at all—only malignant cells. A follow-up extracted liver tissue but saturated with cancer.

Exploratory surgery was scheduled immediately for August 8 at Southern Baptist Hospital.

"How long will the operation be?" Angela asked.

Because Rufty respected her wish "to know everything," he told her frankly, "It'll be one hour if there's no hope; if it's five hours long (because removal of the cancer appears possible), you'll be flat on your back for at least a year."

"Well, when I come out I'm going to ask what time it is. Then I'll know exactly how I stand," Angela said with characteristic resoluteness.

Both Dr. Rufty and Dr. Freeman, the surgeon, were non-Catholics but the latter, a genial six-foot-six-inch Methodist, was willing to wear a memento of Fr. Seelos, as a symbol of prayer for his intercession, on his surgeon's cap while operating (Angela was allowed nothing on herself). Asking that intercession, the young mother of four put herself in God's hands.

The operation took one hour.

Dr. Freeman found the liver simply "replaced" by a malignant tumor (90 percent tumor, 10 percent liver, Angela would be told). The huge liver "contained multiple nodules of tumor," reported Freeman, "in both lobes." To have cut all the diseased organ away would have been to leave the patient liverless. Freeman could only sew her up. His report ends, "Prognosis: poor."

To verify his findings, the Southern Baptist Hospital pathologist, Dr. Frankie M. Slay, sent tissue samples taken for biopsy during the operation to other pathologists, including Dr. Will Steinberg at Tulane and doctors at the Armed Forces Institute of Pathology, in Washington, DC. All agreed the liver's invader was malignant. Furthermore, because only children usually have liver cancer by itself, the pathologists agreed it would be very surprising if there was not another, primary (that is, parent) tumor in Angela's body of which the liver cancer was merely a deadly offspring.

Experiments have shown that a doctor shaking his head worriedly over a patient can lower that individual's resistance significantly as measured by white cells. Now Dr. Rufty, whom Angela trusted so, told her that she would most likely be dead of total liver failure within two weeks. In fact she would probably never leave the hospital.

"I'm a very positive thinker," Angela has said. Instead of turning to planning her funeral, Angela's mind went to Fr. Seelos's prayers and how they had obtained just what she sought for John.

She looked the doctor in the eye.

"What will you do for treatment?" she asked.

"Fifteen pathologists from throughout the United States will study the malignancy and recommend what type of chemotherapy we might try as a treatment if"—his voice underlined the word—"you're still alive in two weeks."

Not only alive, but with her liver improving rather than failing, Angela was home by her August 26 birthday. On her way, she had stopped at Fr. Seelos's grave, in St. Mary's. There, although she had been told she could not kneel, kneel she did—to give thanks.

Meanwhile the consulting pathologists, probably figuring that the object of their deliberations wouldn't be alive long enough to profit by them, took their time. It was well over a month after exploratory surgery revealed her terminal condition, before the hospital called to say the recommendation had been received.

Proposed was a purely experimental treatment for the liver tumor (to the physicians' chagrin, in spite of every possible exploration—was this the first part of a miracle?—no other cancer site could be found).

Beginning that fall, a derivative of the deadly World War I chemical-warfare poison mustard gas, called thiotepa, was given Angela once a week through intravenous glucose solution. She was counseled soberly that she must prepare herself for severe side effects, including terrible nausea, the loss of her hair, possible loss of teeth from loosening, bleeding gums, and so forth. She would, Dr. Rufty told her again, be flat on her back for a whole year, suffering greatly and unable to do anything. And there was, with all of this, little hope that the experimental treatment would do anything but add to her miseries.

To say Angela surprised her physicians is putting it mildly. She had absolutely no side effects to the derivative of the gas that decimated both German and Allied troops. Further, once recovered from the surgery, she was up and doing. That Thanksgiving—four months after being given two weeks to live—with help she was cooking Thanksgiving dinner for her family of six and guests. Christmas, she had out-of-town guests who stayed on into January so she could show them all the sights of nearby New Orleans.

Literally she never looked back, except to tell her story to interested people for the glory of God and to honor the prayer power of Francis Xavier Seelos.

Five years later, in October 1971, Angela elected to have surgery for gallstones, predicting that something extraordinary would be found when her liver was once more exposed to a surgeon's view. It was: Dr. David Weilbaecher's report says he found only tiny scars on the liver surface. There was no sign of any tumors. Both a needle biopsy and a wedge biopsy were done. Like a liver scan done at the same time, they showed only a normal liver.

A follow-up report sent to the Armed Forces Institute of Pathology received the noncommittal comment, "The apparent cure following treatment with thiotepa is remarkable."

Was the chemotherapy the cause of cure? The men who can best judge that, Angela Boudreaux's physicians, don't think so. For one thing, she had already lived on in an inexplicable way before chemotherapy ever commenced. Then, according to Dr. Rufty, her liver shrank and returned to normal too rapidly for the chemotherapy to have been the agent of change. The Protestant presented her case to a group of medical colleagues and said, "This case is definitely a miracle." He and other non-Catholic doctors cooperated fully, as did Catholic David Weilbaecher, in submitting her medical history to Rome in favor of Fr. Seelos's Cause.

In June 1986, Dr. Rufty, then working in the field of cardiology as associate professor at Wake Forest University's Bowman Gray School of

Medicine, in a letter to Angela said he had discussed her case at length with Dr. Weilbaecher at a Louisiana State University medical school reunion. Noting that both doctors had testified before the ecclesiastical board of inquiry, he added they agreed that "yours was the most amazing case we've ever been associated with."

Even Jesus found that only a small percentage of those He healed returned to give thanks. In the case of Angela Boudreaux, her gratitude to God for the cure and thanksgiving to Fr. Seelos for his prayers led her to become a tireless worker toward the Church's official recognition of the Redemptorist priest's sanctity.

Perhaps this wholehearted gratitude opened her to receive continued blessings from God through His saint. Then again, in life Fr. Seelos was a genial, compassionate man who never lost interest in those he once helped—whether they were as grateful as Angela Boudreaux or not. At any rate, in 1975 the Louisiana family felt they once again had proof of the power of Fr. Seelos's intercession. That year, twenty-year-old Angela Marie, the oldest of the family's four children, was attending the University of New Orleans. Like many students who get very good grades, she was highly stressed. Besides working her way through school playing the organ for weddings and holding down a part-time job, Angela Marie was readjusting to American life after a year as a scholarship student in France. During periods of stress, such as exam times, she had always tended to have a skin allergy that looked something like ringworm.

That allergy was acting up now, and her mom counseled her to go to the family's dermatologist, Nia Terezakis, a Catholic woman physician from India.

The same evening, Dr. Terezakis phoned Angela Marie's mother.

"Mrs. Boudreaux," the physician confided, "I'm worried. Not about the rash. But about the itty-bitty shiny black mole—a little flat thing the size of a straight pin head. I found it on your daughter's back. I cut it out deep—eleven stitches' worth—and it's being biopsied."

Neither doctor nor her family wanted to frighten Angela Marie. But they all prayed, asking the intercession of Fr. Seelos, that the dermatologist's worst fears not be realized.

At first it seemed they were. Biopsy showed a malignant melanoma, the most deadly type of skin or mole cancer. Without lumps, any sensation or pain, it quietly kills, not by the pin-size head but through the strangling, fast-growing feelers, or "roots."

Dr. Terezakis dug with her scalpel again. This time, after forty-three stitches were required to close her extensive chase after those roots, she could report that she had removed them successfully, along with the pecan-sized malignancy below the surface of the skin. The deadly feelers had almost but not quite — the difference between life and death — penetrated the young woman's lungs.

With every mole on her body removed and strict instructions to avoid the sun, Angela Marie was no worse for wear from a close brush with death.

"Mrs. Boudreaux," Dr. Terezakis said confidentially to her mother, "if your daughter hadn't come in when she did, she would have been dead in a month or two."

Pure luck? Whatever you think, the Boudreaux family, including now married and healthy Angela Marie, credit God and the intercession of family friend Francis Xavier Seelos.

In 1983, the family believes they received a fourth cure through the one-time missionary for son André, then twenty-five. Working eighteen hours a day in New Orleans' French Quarter, at about 9 p.m. on December 19, André left the restaurant where he was maître d', walking over to his second job on Bourbon Street. Suddenly two thugs cornered him, sat on him, and shot him in the face, while robbing him of the two hundred dollars in his pocket. Somehow André got to his feet and ran back to the restaurant, blood streaming from the gunshot wound, which missed his eye by half an inch. Stumbling in the door, in spite of his injured tongue and missing teeth, he managed to gasp to security men, "Call the paramedics."

By the time he was examined in a hospital, his head was swollen three times normal size, and he was in danger of suffocation. Doctors desired to do a tracheotomy, that is, to cut into the trachea, or windpipe, through the neck to permit the body air intake that way; but they wanted André's parents' permission as next of kin.

His mother took the phone call at the Boudreaux home in Gretna. She recalls that the second she put the phone down, she began at once to pray aloud for the intercession of Fr. Seelos. Immediately, she remembers, a sense of "calm came over me."

Driving toward New Orleans, she shushed her husband, Melvin, who was screaming and swearing in anger at the thieves and grief over his son, so she could focus on praying. In the middle of crossing a particular bridge, she recalled plainly four years later, Fr. Seelos, as God's messenger, seemed to say, "Tell your son when you go in [to see him], he doesn't need the operation; he'll be fine."

At the hospital the parents found their son's friends gathered, weeping. Angela calmed them with assurances that André was not going to die. Her words may have seemed a mother's need to deny reality, for another young man brought in that night who had been shot in the face with the same type of bullet died the next day.

"André should have died three times," his mother believes. But as far as she was concerned, Fr. Seelos had given her a word from God — and she believed it.

After prayer and telling her son he didn't need the tracheotomy, Angela went home and peacefully to sleep, to her husband's amazement. More typical of the parent whose child has just been shot, Melvin walked the floor.

Unable to talk or eat — he lost sixteen pounds almost overnight — and such a sight that his sister had nightmares after seeing him, André had only reassurance from his mother that, however things seemed, he was going to be fine.

She was right.

Hospitalized the night of December 19, on December 23 he was discharged. Christmas Eve he was in church with the rest of the family giving God thanks for his life.

Today there is not even a scar to show André Boudreaux was once shot in the face at close range.

⌒

Not long after the murderous attack on his son, Melvin Boudreaux developed a rare tropical skin disease that can be fatal; after more requests to the "family saint" for his prayers, Dr. Terezakis was able to control it with medication. Perhaps it was at this point God decided this family needed the mother in a particular kind of supportive environment. Perhaps Fr. Seelos had simply become especially fond of some of his "best clients." All Angela knew was she found herself unhappy in her job because of the racial injustice there. A woman of prayer, she asked God to get her out of such an un-Christian situation, as usual asking Fr. Seelos's intercession. In answer, the firm decided to discharge two of its three secretaries, Angela among them. Three days later came a call from Redemptorist Fr. Joseph Elworthy, head of the Seelos Center in the years up to the beatification. Father Elworthy wondered if Angela would take the secretary's job there.

Are ducks drawn to water?

Angela was now able to make her exuberant volunteer efforts vocational as well.

In 1999 over three decades after her original diagnosis, Angela was asked to have a final additional series of medical tests to conclude the official investigation into her cure before it became the official beatification miracle. Her liver was found to still be healthy and she in good health overall.

Fr. Seelos was beatified outdoors on the steps of St. Peter's on a soft April day not long before Easter in 2000. Angela was there as the official beatification-miracle recipient. Accompanied by her husband, Melvin, she brought up a gift from the Redemptorists on a small tray to the elderly John Paul II, Melvin carefully keeping a finger on the envelope lest some spring breeze steal it away.

She returned to her work at the Seelos Center her healthy, energy-filled self for a year of follow-up activities to the beatification. Then, as if her life's work was accomplished, Angela Boudreaux died in June 2001 of a suddenly erupting, quickly deadly colon — not liver — cancer. I immediately recalled her statement to me the first time we talked that everybody in her family dies of cancer. God's healing of her terminal liver cancer through Francis Xavier Seelos had extended her life for thirty-five healthy and energetic years of loving service to the Lord, her family, and thousands of Seelos's friends who visited the Seelos Center. To this writer, while I will always feel awe before her miracle cure, I feel even greater awe before her faith in God's healing power through His saints: I have interviewed many holy people and studied many officially recognized saints, but I have never found faith greater than Angela Boudreaux's.

Chapter 16

The Wound That Heals?

Just about everyone has heard of Padre Pio, the Italian stigmatic whose death at age eighty-one on September 23, 1968, was even reported by the *New York Times*. The biographies that sell steadily year after year, including one by the author written with help from Pio's friary, are crammed with accounts from people whose medically inexplicable healings came to them from God, they believe, through the gloved, bleeding hands of this Capuchin Franciscan priest. The next three chapters will detail some of these. This chapter takes up just one extraordinary healing: the saint's own.

The father of the boy born Francesco Forgione on May 25, 1887, was one of those Italian peasants locked in profitless farm labor on the lands of the lower Italian Peninsula. Not just a day laborer like the majority, he actually owned a few acres, but there was no way to profit to the point of educating Franci, as the future Pio was called. Heroically, Papa Forgione became one of those workers who so pulled at the heartstrings of Francesca Cabrini as they let themselves be packed like sardines — often seasick and heartsick for the families left behind — in the comfortless steerage decks of ships lurching toward an unknown fate in the United States. The hope of many like Forgione was not permanent emigration; rather, enduring years of separation, discrimination, and labor far from the beloved homeland, they sought better lives for those left behind and a decent old age for themselves. By Papa Forgione's labors in places like Mahoningtown, Pennsylvania, and the community of Jamaica, Long Island, in New York, he achieved his dream: Francesco was freed from the fields for the education that made him Pio, a Capuchin friar.

What Papa's sacrifice, the entire family's and fellow Capuchins' worries and prayers, and least of all the medical profession's efforts could not do after 1908, it appeared, was make the young Capuchin well enough to actually live in a friary. No matter to which friary his superiors assigned him—and they chose those with the most healthful climates—one foot in the door and Pio's stomach began to cramp and his temperature to rise. (He may have set the human record here, with verified levels of 120 and 125 degrees at times—107 being considered generally lethal according to medical authorities.) Each try soon resulted in a weak, emaciated, often bedridden figure vomiting, suffering "unbearable headaches," and scaring people away, if he were taken out, by tuberculosis-like symptoms, including, at times, atrocious pains in his chest.

For almost a decade this went on. After months of recuperation at home, Pio would report to a new monastery only to begin vomiting the day he arrived. A number of physicians over the years diagnosed tuberculosis. Others disagreed. Some thought the problem chronic bronchitis, but that left the stomach symptom unaccounted for. One Naples physician, without giving any name to Pio's condition, simply said it was hopeless and terminal. But whenever the stocky, reddish-haired young friar returned to his native village, he began to improve at once.

If his physical condition improved at home, his confusion, fear, and guilt did not. Counseled by letter to try again to return to a friary, he writes back very humanly, "It seems to me that I have the right and duty of not depriving myself of life at the age of twenty-four! It seems to me that God does not want this to happen." Then the young man who is already believed a saint in his hometown immediately adds in his letter to his superior, "Consider that I am more dead than alive and then do as you believe best, for I am disposed to make any sacrifice if it is a case of obedience."

Chided by return mail, in his next answer Pio eats humble pie. "With reddened eyes and trembling hand I ... beg your forgiveness ..." In effect, as he says in another letter, he is grappling with the temptation to despair. Year after year the prayers for his healing are not answered, in spite of the fact that he wants a cure so he can answer what he is sure is a genuine call from God to follow the friary life of self-denial and prayer on behalf of the wounded members of the human family.

And he can see, as can his spiritual director, a man wise in the ways of mysticism, that the root of all his life-threatening illness is not something like a TB bacillus, but something spiritual. In other words the very area that is the site of all his hopes and dreams appears to be the source of their failure. If his superiors agree that this young friar is a very rare person already capable of loving God and his fellow human beings beyond what most of us achieve in a lifetime, Pio can also be looked at as, if not a downright malingerer—no one believes that—at least as someone who may be sinning against his vocation by resisting it with every ounce of bodily strength. While they love the young mystic and try to encourage him to see God's loving hand in his strange situation, at other times his spiritual advisers become downright annoyed and badger him that it is hardly edifying for "everyone to know that a priest remains at home because of his health." Or they chide, "It is being said all over … that you are being deceived by the devil, who is taking advantage of your affection for your native soil."

Some days the confused Pio longs to die to be with God, as it seems he is going to do; on other days, he clamors to live. He broods that perhaps his illness is a punishment for his sins. He panics when it seems he may be dismissed from the Capuchin Order. Yet through all the confusion and varying emotions, he remains in love with God, whom he sees as "both the one who smites me and the one who consoles me."

Since devils, he said, were at this time appearing to Pio, buffeting and taunting him,[115] his inability to remain in a Capuchin house may be seen as just one more manifestation of their work, the Hinderer knowing the enormous good Pio would do once he could live in a friary. Others will judge Pio as a young man struggling with purely interior "devils." A third possibility is that both an inner struggle and a cosmic one were involved, as is suggested by the content of some of Pio's visions. And

---

[115] The reader who laughs at the idea of actual evil spirits should note that later when he lived in a friary many instances of attacks on Pio were witnessed, not just by the friars, but by outside guests, including a terrified bishop, Monsignor D'Agostino of Ariano Irpino. See *Padre Pio of Pietrelcina: "Everybody's Cyrenean,"* by (Padre) Alessandro of Ripabottoni, p. 65, a book recommended by Fr. Joseph Pius Martin to this author for accurate reports.

finally some will see Pio, as he himself puts it in a letter, as "toyed with by Love," God playing with the mystic, molding him, as He has done with many saints, through "senseless suffering" into one who has hoped against hope, clung to faith in despair, and continued to love God even when He seemed to treat one most unlovingly, and so become ready, in Pio's case, to be the first priest known to have borne the visible marks of the crucified Christ in his body.[116]

The war for which Pio's entire being is the battleground goes into a new phase around 1916. After years of being pressed by his miseries as well as love to go deeper and deeper into God, Pio is about to receive health in the particular way God wants Pio healthy. Shackled to his native village, Pio has been giving spiritual direction by letter to a number of people "introduced" to him by his directors. One of these whom he meets only upon her deathbed is saintly Raffaelina Cervase. She tells Pio's spiritual director to order him to a friary as soon as she dies, assuring the director this time Pio will be able to stay. Raffaelina dies March 25 in 1916, the director follows her counsel, and Pio never goes home to live again.

At first he spends much time in bed. Then like St. Paul, who prayed for healing from "a thorn in the flesh," was *not* healed, and eventually found that God willed His servant's strength be made perfect in this weakness, Pio gets well—cured of his mystics' fevers, his vomiting, and the other physical ills doctors say doom him. In fact he will enjoy quite incredible—even physically inexplicable[117]—health, in spite of some normal ups and downs until old age. There is, however, one exception to his health. In 1918 about the time his gradual healing from death's door reaches real vitality, he experiences a sudden wounding during an ecstatic vision of "a man" he is too modest to say is Christ. (He will admit that only forty-seven years later.) From this time on, the stigmata he has had intermittently, sometimes visibly, sometimes invisibly, are clearly visible and permanent.[118]

---

[116] Francis of Assisi was a brother, not a priest; other stigmatized priests, of course, may be known to God, including possibly St. Paul, who writes, "I bear the brand marks of Jesus in my body" (Gal. 6:17).

[117] See more on this topic in my book *The Sanctified Body*, misleadingly retitled in a Crossroad edition *The Mystical Body*.

[118] The wounds dried up just before his death, leaving not even a scar, something his doctor said, based on their depth, was inexplicable.

He has begged God for years, with permission of his spiritual guides, for the rarest of human vocations, that of the "victim" who participates in a mystical and/or physical way in the Passion of Christ for the salvation of the world. Now Pio has his answer. Not that Jesus needs anyone. He alone is the Redeemer. But the Lord affirms in this visible way that He will let his servant suffer redemptively. Pio, whose compassionate heart has always made him want to carry others' loads, in the rarest of vocations, will partake, by grace, in sufferings somehow joined to Christ's. In some mysterious way, allied to the Redeemer, the Franciscan priest will carry God's healing to others. With the stigmata, he will be a wounded healer in the sense of Christ's bearing our sins as Isaiah 53:5 puts it: "We were healed by his stripes." Perhaps Pio's nine-year illness, his recovery, and this ongoing wound have been necessary to together protect him from psychospiritual imbalance at such a lofty call. Perhaps, humanly, they also enrich him to become God's instrument to heal others, a wounded healer who has known what it is to be desperately ill with all the body-mind-soul ramifications of severe, even seemingly hopeless, illness. Pio is much too humble to think of himself as like his favorite saint,[119] and echo Paul: "I make up in my body what is lacking in the sufferings of Christ" (Col. 1:24). Instead the bodily sign of a much more all-encompassing suffering is, he writes a spiritual director, an "embarrassment and unbearable humiliation" to the thirty-one-year-old friar.[120] He sees himself "a wretched creature," unworthy of his burning and deeply painful, bleeding hands and feet and the deep heart wound of the Crucified One. On top of this, in divine protection from pride, the rest of his life he will be more and more unsure of his standing with the God he adores. He also, humanly, worries for some time he will bleed to death.

To his chagrin his stigmata became known locally, then nationally, and eventually, in the 1920s, internationally. Starting then and still going strong decades later, thousands of words analyzing Pio's wounds are produced by experts of various kinds and journalists. The main theory, among non-Catholic, as well as "up-to-date" Catholic writers anxious to avoid association with "medieval ideas," is that Pio is a neurotic whose fixation on Christ's Passion produced the stigmata. More

[119] With Francis of Assisi.
[120] *Letters* I, 1217-1218.

religiously inclined analysts deny neurosis but believe Pio has contemplated Christ's sufferings with such ardent love and compassion that the signs of the Passion have reproduced themselves on his flesh. To both groups, Pio, whose sense of humor is robust and who is much more a feeling person than an analytical one, snorts, "Right! Now you go meditate like that on a bull and see if you grow horns."

Surprising some, possible neurosis is looked at carefully by the Church wherever there are unusual phenomena. Causes may be set aside on this question. When Pio's Cause is opened some years after his death, the vision of Christ during which Padre Pio received the stigmata was seen not as proof the stigmata was a supernatural event—visions even in saints may have origins in the self or from devils—but acknowledged as corroborative evidence in light of factors speaking against neurosis. Perhaps the most important of these was how Pio was seen by those who knew him best, the friars who lived with him. They described a well-balanced man who was lovable, down to earth, and full of humor, including being quick to make fun of himself. All who knew him, laypeople as well as friars, testified to Pio's heroic virtue in a life spent serving others through love of God.

Too, there were the physical mysteries. The stigmata blood, even when it was old and should have putrefied, was sweetly perfumed. Any non-stigmata wounds Pio suffered healed normally; the stigmata, even when bandaged, treated, and kept under close watch in ordered studies to make sure they were not self-induced or tampered with, did not heal.

Because of the daily ongoing blood loss from the five wounds (both hands, feet, and the deep side wound like Christ's piercing by the centurion's lance), Pio's condition should have demanded careful attention to nutrition and rest. In fact his daily intake of three hundred to four hundred calories, and sometimes less, and his two to four—more often two—hours of sleep at night do not provide a physiological rationale for how for fifty years Pio carried on a most demanding all-day, everyday ministry to the huge numbers whose confessions and pleas he heard one by one in his airless wooden confessional—so many lining up that tickets had to be issued and the wait could be days. Losing blood—estimated at a cup a day—and eating primarily a few spoonfuls of vegetables or pasta, and the occasional egg, he is not even anemic. Add incidents like the time his stomach is bothering him, so he fasts eight days. Weighed at the end, he has gained weight. A visiting medical doctor's verdict: Pio is a "dead man," since living on so little while working so hard is clearly impossible for a live one.

The whole event of this extraordinary healing, encompassing an ongoing wounding, becomes explicable only if inserted into any analysis of body-mind-soul complexity, is the phrase "God acts as He wills." With that it becomes possible for me to suggest I have just put before you a bare outline of the first, and arguably the most-inexplicable miracle of God's healings associated with the adult[121] Pio.

⌒

Whether he was engaged in telling one of the simple jokes that made his friends smile, changing destinies by hearing confessions, or re-living the Passion as he said Mass before awed onlookers, one could say of Padre Pio during his life that his ministry was rich and fruitful in spite of his psychospiritual ups and downs or human foibles. These included a peasant kind of roughness and at times (perhaps feigned[122]) irritability and brusqueness. If his spiritual sensitivity to the things of God was beyond the ordinary, so was his emotional and bodily sensitivity: when each of his parents died his sureness of their spiritual destiny did not prevent great grief expressed in prolonged sobbing, fainting, and having to take to his bed for days.

He did not, however, like to be ill. In sickness Pio was always open to healing. He did not turn down a transfer to a climate that agreed better with his particular bodily makeup; he vented his frustrations when ill to his mentor and begged other friars and lay friends to pray for him—sometimes urgently. In the period of his spiritual greatness, he did not hesitate to cry out aloud, "What! You're going away without healing me?" to the Virgin Mary—and with that plea happily accepted and talked about

---

[121] As an eight-year-old child, his prayers were involved in the instantaneous healing of a "terribly deformed" little boy at the shrine of St. Pellegrino, according to Pio's reminiscences of this pilgrimage with his father, as told to Padre Raffaele, a fellow Capuchin, and reported in a publication of the friary, *Padre Pio: His Early Years* by Fr. Augustine McGregor, O.C.S.O.

[122] Some friars insist Pio feigned brusqueness, irritability, and even anger with some who came to his confessional, knowing this was the only way to bring them to change. He also did not want to pander to those who tried to idolize him.

joyously the end of an illness. (A statue of Mary from Fatima had come to the friary for veneration by helicopter, but he was too ill to go down to the church. He yelled toward the leaving helicopter.)

As said, after his stigmata God let him live in the dark about his spiritual state. "Am I pleasing to God?" he worried, even while assuring his spiritual children of God's love for them. In old age a number of conditions caused him serious breathing problems. The inability to breathe freely can trigger feelings of panic or depression. Pio experienced depression. Part of this was also normal concern about the burden he became to the other friars as his body slowly failed. With all this was interwoven a hugely compassionate heart and great human sweetness. In summation, I think it is fair to say Pio's life assures us that even "far-out" saints with rare gifts are not cardboard figures, but flesh-and-blood people with emotions and troubled times. A saint's life journey, as Pio's shows well, is a *human* journey: with its rocky patches of misery, it may at times be as clouded and frustrating to the saint as yours to you or mine to me.

In 2000 I visited Fr. Joseph Pius Martin,[123] the American-born friar at Pio's friary who had helped me in all my writings on Pio to offer only authentic material. Fr. Joseph Pius, who helped care for Pio in his last years and was present at his death, did not speak about Pio's stigmata, healings, bilocations, or other spiritual gifts. Instead he reminisced, "Pio was just a lovely person to live with." One of the other friars[124] much younger than Pio who had been a student of Pio's about the time Pio received the stigmata (he tried to hide it from them) also spoke about that sweetness and the human warmth Pio showed the student friars. He summed up Pio in a way to give us all thought—and hope. "His sanctity," the friar exclaimed, "was his humanity."

[123] This was just weeks before Fr. Joseph Pius's own death. He knew if others did not. I base this assertion on an odd remark he made during my visit: while providing me with the best sources for my Pio biography, he told me in the future I would have to apply for help to another friar whom he named.

[124] Padre Aurelio Di Iorio.

Chapter 17

A Fountain of God's Healing

Once Pio became the first known stigmatic priest—Francis of Assisi having been a brother, not a priest—people began to seek him out. Eventually, they were coming from all over the world. In the confessional, where he spent up to nineteen hours a day for the first five years after receiving the stigmata,[125] he healed lives. Georgetown theologian Monika Hellwig[126]—hardly one whose name is synonymous with pious excess in regard to saints—was living in Italy in the years just before Pio's death. During her three-year stay, what she heard convinced her that, in or out of the confessional, Pio led people to "deep conversions" as he "mediated the presence of the divine ... [leaving his visitors] inspired and assured of God's presence and care for them." Slowly, at the beginning of his world ministry, then increasingly, the gift of physical healing became an important adjunct to this primary work for God.

A verified case was that of Padre Pio's friend, construction worker Giovanni Savino. Savino was the father of eight—two of whom had been "saved" by Pio when seriously injured in separate accidents. In February 1949, the thirty-five-year-old local man was working at the friary on an addition to the building. Each morning he attended Pio's

---

[125] Between 1918, when he received the stigmata, and 1923, he heard confessions for fifteen to nineteen hours daily; then his superiors cut him back. In later years, until old age slowed him further, he was in the confessional as many as eight and as few as five hours daily, even the smaller number being a notable load with his other religious obligations.

[126] I am indebted to Ruffin's biography (see title p. 282), p. 15, for the late Dr. Hellwig's comments. She was in Italy from 1962 to 1965. Pio died in 1968.

Mass before work. From February 12 to 15, as he, as always, approached his priest benefactor for a post-Mass blessing, Pio repeated, "Courage, Giovanni, I'm praying you won't be killed." On the fifteenth a charge of dynamite blew up in the workman's face. A doctor friend of Pio's and two priests, one Franciscan, one not, rushed the man to Foggia's hospital where "numerous" fragments were removed from his left cornea. There was nothing to do for the right eye. It had been blown to a smear of jelly.

Pio's doctor friend returned to tell him Savino was blind. Pio indicated he thought some sight might be saved. And actually there was some slight hope for the left eye medically. Ten days after the accident the injured man, face and head bandaged, was awake, praying the Rosary, sometime toward one in the morning. He smelled a wonderful odor and felt three slaps on his head, understanding Pio was with him (by one of the saint's many bilocations). That morning the ophthalmologist came to see how the left eye was doing after all the fragments had been removed. It was not functioning. In fact, all sight was gone permanently. But Giovanni could see perfectly with the right eye that had been blown to a smear. Somehow it had been replaced. The doctor, an atheist, became a believer from that moment, exclaiming that he had to believe because "this happened right in front of me."

Interestingly, the new eye which functioned so well, according to Giovanni's wife Rosa "always looked a mess." There is a photograph of the healed man in the early biography *Padre Pio* by Fr. Charles Carty.

A hint of Pio's redemptive role in healings may be found in two details of Giovanni Savino's cure: Pio spent days of intense prayer, and asked many others to pray, between the accident and the eye's restoration. He also told Giovanni when, finally released from the hospital, the workman came to thank Pio, "You have no idea what this cost me." More detail of this cure will be found in a biography easier to find than Fr. Carty's, that of ordained Lutheran minister C. Bernard Ruffin.

Today many of the books on Pio by his fellow friars have been translated into English. Particularly recommended by Fr. Joseph Pius Martin is the one by Padre Alessandro (see footnote 115). However Ruffin's also recommended revised *Padre Pio: The True Story* remains one of the best from its uniquely American perspective. (This author's *Meet Padre Pio: Beloved Mystic, Miracle-Worker, and Spiritual Guide,* also recommended by the friary,[127] is for those who wish an introduction or have no time for a long, in-depth book.) According to Ruffin, the archives of Our Lady of Grace show that in Pio's lifetime "over a thousand people pronounced hopelessly ill by their doctors, were delivered of such grave maladies as cancer, heart disease, diabetes, tuberculosis, congenital birth defects and paralysis caused by spinal injuries." Following his death, a second thousand cures were attributed to Padre Pio's intercession in the first twenty years, that is 1968 to 1988. The first edition of this book appeared that year, and I have no precise figures for the healings that took place from then until 2002. That year, St. Pio of Pietrelcina's canonization took place on June 16 before at least five hundred thousand people, perhaps the largest crowd ever assembled for such an event.

Canonization ended any need to keep track of the numbers of cures attributed to Pio by those who received them, in order to *prove* God was speaking of Pio's holiness by answering prayers that invoked his intercession. Perhaps consequently there are fewer letters printed attesting cures in the friary's bimonthly magazine, *The Voice of Padre Pio*. Nevertheless, since canonization, as before, Padre Pio has continued to be a fountain of God-given health to many. Perhaps the most touching to me is a 2011 cure of advanced Parkinson's disease. The Irish sufferer from this disease had, she wrote the friars from Dublin, reached a point beyond simple acceptance of her loss of dignity, loss of mobility, and great pain — all of which, she volunteered, had taught her a lot. She was actually living in peace and gratitude to God, in spite of her condition, when she was visited by a priest from Pio's friary. The Italian visitor seemed to affirm her state as one offering her sufferings for the salvation of souls and said nothing about healing. But not long after being blessed for Pio's intercession by the visitor, she found herself grateful to God and Pio for a return to perfect health.

Here is a sampling from just one recent issue of *The Voice*:

Katherine Beck had deadly, fast-moving ovarian cancer. Surgery, she writes, "was not a success." On what should have been a last reunion with her three sisters, Katherine had a mystical experience of

---

[127] In the friary's magazine *The Voice*.

dead Padre Pio one night shared by a sister. Since there was a witness, it is fair to conclude this was no dream or fantasy. After this she returned home and her doctor, examining her, could find "no reason [for her] to visit him." She is healed.

In the same issue a man from North Ireland writes in thanksgiving for his mother's recovery from "a heart attack plus a large blood clot on her lung, also a very bad chest infection." Although she was in intensive care and had received the last rites when William O'Reilly "prayed to Padre Pio to ask Our Lord to show His divine mercy," the woman got better daily and is now back at home.

A Texas couple write of five anxious months having been told, after a routine ultrasound, their third son will likely be born with Down syndrome. The wife says, "It was a very difficult and stressful time for our family. My husband and I prayed to St. Pio day after day. During this time, we learned to trust more in God." The child was born with perfect health, no syndromes. The wife closes, "We give thanks to St. Pio for his intercession and for guiding us to trust more in God's tender mercy. Thank you, St. Pio. We love you." You note that although the mother uses that misleading term "praying to Pio," her subsequent comments make clear her excellent grasp of a saint's role vis-à-vis God.

I have dozens of other testimonies in my files, some of which will be found in my other books. There are still more in the friary archives. The only thing the recipients have in common is a willingness to ask Pio's prayers for themselves or someone else.

☙

This pertains also to the beatification and canonization miracles. With the problem of sorting out supernatural from medical intervention, in a day when every ill tends to be copiously treated whether it will do any good or not, a jokester might claim the beatification miracle was a miracle, even outside the cure: a woman hospitalized for a serious condition was healed by God, after she appealed to Pio's prayers, *before* any treatment could be started. You will find more details in my Pio biography, *Meet Padre Pio: Beloved Mystic, Miracle-Worker, and Spiritual Guide*, but a brief summary here: Mrs. Consiglia De Martino was devoted to Padre Pio, the holy priest whose heroic virtues had been recognized at this time by the title Venerable. Living in Salerno, a city not too far from Pio's friary, the Italian housewife used to make a monthly pilgrimage to the tomb of her heavenly friend and mentor.

On October 31, 1995, as she was exerting herself strenuously, she felt a frightening and painful "tearing" in her chest and around her left clavicle. She went to bed in painful discomfort. By morning, her neck had on it a protuberance the size of an orange.

Her husband away, she phoned a brother-in-law to take her to the hospital, where a scan showed her thoracic duct had ruptured. Surgery would be necessary. At that point both she and her daughter made phone calls to a friar who had been very close to Pio and was one of their family's close friends. Br. Modestino prayed for the injured woman "with confidence" since Pio had promised him that, once Pio was in Heaven, he would always get God to give positive answers to Modestino's prayers. Surgery could not be arranged the day of her admission. The next morning, nothing having yet been done for the rupture, Mrs. De Martino woke in her hospital bed to find the big swelling almost gone. November 3, that is, four days after the injury, both an x-ray and another type of scan showed every abnormality had disappeared. With these tests plus the original scan and doctor's examination for comparison, Mrs. De Martino's case proved a perfect example of a formal miracle. Certified by the Congregation for the Causes of Saints, her healing permitted Pio's beatification.

Also given in more detail in the latest printings of my Pio biography is the canonization miracle. Let me sum up for you here the cure of a dying child in a coma. It took place right in San Giovanni Rotondo, and once again humble little Br. Modestino played a role. Near death and without hope of recovery just eight months after the beatification, seven-year-old Matteo Pio Colella lay comatose in the little town's modern hospital. Called The Home for the Relief of Suffering, it was across from the friary, built by the charity of penniless Padre Pio[128] when the town had no medical facility. Matteo, whose middle name shows the family's devotion to Pio, was the younger of two sons of local doctors. The father worked at the hospital. They would later testify to the

---

[128] See my *God Will Provide* or comprehensive biographies of Padre Pio available at places like the National Centre for Padre Pio in Barto, Pennsylvania (610-845-3000), which grew out of a miracle to its foundress's young child after Pio blessed the little girl.

miracle cure and their cries for Pio's help, both as the praying parents and as physicians who had understood only too well that for Matteo in early 2000 a miracle was the only hope.

The tragic situation had begun on January 20, when their younger boy came down with "flu," feverish, headachy, and vomiting. That evening the child began breaking out in notable purple spots. More frightening to his physician parents, since it is a sign of septic shock, Matteo did not recognize his mother.

Matteo, in fact, had acute meningitis, sometimes termed "brain fever." As the next days passed, deep in a coma, his kidneys, liver, and heart weakened, as did his pulse, and he was breathing only by ventilator. Eventually, in spite of all the pediatric colleagues of his father, Antonio—a staff urologist at the hospital—could do, Matteo died. Standard efforts to revive him failed. But these doctors are men of prayer too, and one, calling on Padre Pio's prayer help, injected the dead child with a dangerously large dose of adrenaline. Matteo returned to life. This was not recovery, however: it only postponed his death in the sense of "while there is life," among believers at least, there remains hope.

Antonio had taken Matteo's mother, Maria, out of the treatment area the first night because of the boy's heartrending screams of pain as doctors tried to find a vein in a shut-down circulatory system. For the next ten days, she did not see her comatose son as he drifted toward death in a sterilized room. But she was working for Matteo every second. She spent all her time praying and seeking prayer from every convent in the area. Naturally, this doctor, wife, and mother sought prayers from Pio's confreres at his Our Lady of Grace Friary. It had been in Pio's cell, by special permission, that she had begged her friend in Heaven to watch out for the newly created family on her wedding day. Various individual friars now reached out to her, while the entire community let the distraught but praying mother join them in their evening community prayers at Pio's tomb.

Br. Modestino was one of those who reached out. Meeting with both Antonio and Maria, he counseled them on attitude and prayer. He revealed he himself was urging Pio, "Pray for Matteo; let this be the miracle for your canonization."

As stated, there are many more details in my biography, and even there I could not give all the incidents in this precisely documented series of events. Suffice to say here, after eight days in a coma, Matteo woke up—speechless and glassy-eyed but recovering from the unrecoverable. The next day he began talking—calling for Padre Pio. Seven days later, he was still covered with deep ulcers, still unable to move, but he could share with his mother that Padre Pio, angels, and a very bright light he believed to be Jesus had all been with him in the coma. Pio had told him not to worry. He would get well and do that quickly.

The eventual investigation of this cure found that ill beyond medical help—for even getting his heart to start again was no cure for the disease that was killing him—Matteo had made a medically inexplicable, complete, permanent, and relatively sudden recovery. As Br. Modestino[129]—who, after all, had been promised by God's friend Pio himself a positive answer to his prayers—had asked, Matteo's was the miracle chosen from many others to be accepted for Pio's June 2002 canonization.

Maria Colella, who had asked Padre Pio to bless her family on her wedding day, could never have dreamed how far the humble Capuchin would go to do that.[130]

---

[129] Having lived to play a role in his spiritual father's beatification and canonization, Br. Modestino died August 14, 2011, and is buried, as he desired, in his and Pio's hometown, Pietrelcina.

[130] Following the death of Fr. Joseph Pius Martin, Pio's close confrere and my mentor on Pio, details of these two miracles, more than I could actually use, were generously provided me by Charles Abercrombie of Pio's friary's English-language publication The Voice of Padre Pio along with permission for their use from the friars.

Chapter 18

"Mommy, There's an Old Man in My Room"

Like so many Irish, Ann Wilkinson of the village of Clogherhead in
County Louth, Ireland, is a natural storyteller. I give the following account only slightly condensed, basically as Ann told it to me in the
late 1980s, her lilting Irish voice at times rich with the emotions of the
Wilkinsons' experience of human suffering and God's grace. (Updates
that she and Kelly provided before this 2013 edition are in chapter 20.)

On the fifth of December 1976, my second child and second little
girl, Kelly, was born by cesarean section in the Mater Hospital in
Belfast. She was delivered by cesarean because they discovered,
before the birth, that her heart was beating very rapidly and that
she was very distressed.

While I was still under the anesthetic after the birth, I remember a nurse telling me that the little girl I had just given
birth to was very ill. They needed her name, because they were
going to baptize her. I remember thinking that if I stayed asleep
and didn't answer, maybe it was only a bad dream and when I
woke up everything would be all right. But when I woke up, I'm
afraid the reality was very, very bad. Kelly had been born with
a congenital heart defect which also caused a grossly enlarged
liver. They weren't expecting her to live through the night.

I lay in bed in the hospital and prayed that this little girl
would live. I always had great devotion to our Lady, and I said my
Rosary that night as if I was sending a message with no room for
error: it had to be from my heart, and every syllable had to be
said distinctly.

I thought about all the babies that had been aborted or given up for adoption. And I said to our Lady that I knew about the heart defect and the liver. I knew, too, that at birth the baby had been very blue and didn't breathe for a few moments so that it was suspected she might have brain damage as well. In my prayer for her intercession I told our Lady that I didn't care whether my little girl was deformed, handicapped mentally or physically, or *whatever*—I wanted her, and I'd accept her however the good Lord would give her to me. The only thing I couldn't accept was for Him to take her away.

The next morning, Dr. Muriel Fraser, who was the consultant pediatrician, visited me and told me plainly Kelly wasn't going to live. They had done a catheterization and discovered the heart hadn't developed properly: instead of the normal two ventricles, there was only one. The older Kelly got, the greater the strain it would be on the inadequate heart. Inevitably death would come from a massive heart attack. At the moment, Dr. Fraser said, they were trying to get the baby stabilized on a heart stimulant to keep the organ beating at a regular pace. If that happened, Kelly might have a future—but only for a few months. Dr. Fraser said even a heart transplant couldn't help Kelly. We just had to try to accept she wasn't going to be part of our family for very long.

While Dr. Fraser was with me, my husband, Jim, had gone to see Kelly in the special pediatric intensive care unit of another hospital. He remembers walking through this unit wearing a mask, boots, and gown and looking at all the little babies in incubators, some of them deformed and some of them who really didn't look as if they had much life left. Then he came to our baby, and he told me later this baby looked so perfect in every way that he said to the doctor who was with him how terrible it was for all the other little babies that were in the ward: they looked so ill and as if they weren't going to survive long. The doctor replied that the other children in the ward had a 30- to 50-percent chance at life, but our baby had not even a 1-percent chance of survival. There was, the doctor said, absolutely nothing anyone could do for her.

My husband couldn't accept this and continually tried to have the doctors say they had made a mistake or their equipment was faulty. But doctor after doctor told us the same: our baby wasn't going to live.

Every waking moment I spent with Kelly in the hospital. I'd be there in the morning when she woke up. I fed her, bathed her, dressed her, each time I held her in my arms knowing it was going to be that little bit harder when the time came she'd have to be given back to God. The love I had for her was so strong that I'd hold her and pray, hope and *will* her to have as strong a will to live as I had to keep her.

About three days before Christmas I was out shopping for my other daughter, Ciara (say KEE-ra), who was three. At intervals I'd ring the hospital to see how the baby was. This time I was told a doctor wanted to speak to me.

The blood seemed to drain out of me as I thought, in sheer panic, Kelly had died. But the doctor who came on the phone asked would I like to have Kelly home. I said I would *love* to have her, and he said I could have her Christmas morning. He stressed the importance of her medicine, which had to be given at frequent intervals day and night. She would have to be brought to the hospital every month for a checkup. In between, if something happened, we must call day or night.

Christmas morning, after Santa Claus had been, I went to collect Kelly. The nurses were crying, because they had gotten so attached to her. Although I was taking her home, the doctor told me, "You know, Mrs. Wilkinson, the outlook hasn't changed. Her condition is still the same."

But it didn't seem to matter that much. Having her home was one step and maybe, please God, the good Lord had heard my prayers and somehow ... Even if she could stay alive long enough for some cure or miracle to come through, I thought, that was all I needed. It was the best Christmas I'd ever had.

⌒

Christmas night, Kelly woke up at three in the morning. My mother came into the living room with some coffee as I was

feeding the baby, and we had a talk. She handed me a prayer for
the intercession of Padre Pio and said, "Say that prayer to Padre
Pio and leave it all in God's hands."

I responded I couldn't "just leave it in God's hands." I needed
a miracle, and I wasn't settling for anything less.

My mother, who is a very dear, good Catholic woman, thought
this was terrible. I think she felt I was flying in the face of God.

When she gave me the leaflet on Padre Pio with its prayer, I
was looking at it while she told me in a few words about his life.
She said he was such a holy man that he could look into your soul
and tell you what sort of a person you are. And instantly I took
a dislike to him. I smile thinking about it now, but I felt, "Well,
if he looks into *my* soul, there's no way he's going to give me the
miracle I need." Sinner that I knew I was, I decided there and
then Padre Pio wasn't for me—I would stick to asking our Lady's
intercession. Hopefully her help as a mother plus her knowing
me as a mother and the distress I was in would get her to intercede for me with her Son.

Well, month after month Kelly was taken back to the hospital for her checkup. In between times we had quite a few harrowing experiences. For at least the first nine months of her life,
she couldn't lie back. She had to sit up in a chair, or her breathing became quite erratic. Because of her condition, she wasn't
like my other little girl had been at the same age. Kelly seemed
to sleep all the time, got tired very, very easily, distressed very,
very easily, and at the least exertion whatsoever her lips would
go blue. Sometimes she became quite black from minor stresses.

I remember that each day I woke thinking, "Dear God, don't
let this be the day." And I'd lie there in utter fear listening for
her. When I could hear her laughing or moving in her room I'd
know then I could get out of bed and continue on.

During this whole time, all my friends and family were praying very hard that Kelly would be cured. I think mostly everyone
was asking our Lady's intercession. But my mother said a novena
prayer every day to Padre Pio. I still couldn't find it in my heart to
turn to him. I didn't honestly believe I was a good enough person
to get a miracle through him. I felt he had been such a good and

holy person in his life that he would accept nothing less from anyone who wanted his intercession. How wrong I was!

Yet it was just as if Padre Pio was haunting me. I'd find leaflets pertaining to him. But I was always quite quick to put any such thing out of sight or to pass it on to someone else. Still I prayed constantly. I think the most important part of my day was prayer and meditation.

When Kelly was about two and a half, I got the chance of taking her to Lourdes. At the grotto my prayer was still the same: pleading she not be taken from me. I looked around at so many other poor souls, mothers, fathers, deformed children, adults so very ill, and wondered, "My God, of all these people how are You ever going to hear my prayer for my child. I'm sure to each and every one of these people their prayers are just as important."

It was a risk just to bring Kelly to Lourdes, and I worried about putting her in the baths[131] in case she'd have an attack of some sort from the icy-cold water. But I put my trust in our Lady's intercession, and Kelly went into the water and came out without any problem. I think it took more out of me than out of her.

As I prayed in Lourdes for my miracle, it came to me to say to our Lady that if there was any way that she wanted to lead me, I was willing to go that way; but she'd have to show me. To obtain this miracle, I just lay myself at her disposal, pleading with her again as a mother that she intercede that my child not be taken from me.

We came back from Lourdes, and life seemed the same. Kelly went every month for her checkup, and every month we were told the same thing: her condition hadn't changed, and we must just take every day as it came.

---

[131] The sick may be immersed in water from the spring that was discovered by St. Bernadette in 1858, directed by the Virgin Mary during the apparitions at Lourdes. Although the water has no inherent curative properties, immediately cures began to take place, one of the earliest being a dying two-year-old who was immersed for perhaps fifteen minutes in the icy water. Although he had been extremely frail and given to serious convulsions since birth, Justin Bouhohorts recovered and became a healthy child. At seventy-seven he attended Bernadette's canonization, in Rome, dying only in 1935 at age seventy-nine or eighty.

Then one morning I received a letter telling me her doctors wanted to admit Kelly into the hospital for another catheterization to see how the heart looked now. While they were quite sure things were the same, they wanted to give her that chance. It was nearing her fourth birthday, and she really was very ill — not able to do very much. I think they felt things were becoming crucial.

I felt so desperate and lonely that I was going to have to make a decision to have this test done when any little trivial operation could kill her. But I had to give her this chance. Perhaps something would show up they could now fix. Or maybe they would see something that medicine could help so she could continue on with her life.

Kelly was due to be admitted to the hospital the next Tuesday morning, when, on Friday evening, I went into the village where I live. There I encountered a person with whom I'd had a disagreement through a misunderstanding. Because of that, I would have avoided her by preference, but she stopped me and asked about Kelly and I told her Kelly's condition was just the same and she was being admitted into the hospital.

The woman asked had I ever gotten Kelly blessed with the mitten[132] [glove] of Padre Pio? She said there was a lady in Skerries who had a mitten of Padre Pio.[133] Then she told me about a man who had had kidney problems, was blessed with the mitten, and was now doing quite well.

Considering my relationship with Padre Pio, I wasn't too sure about this, but I talked it over with my husband and we decided we would go up to Skerries on Sunday and get Kelly blessed.

When the day came and we drove into Skerries, I realized I had completely forgotten to ask the woman exactly where this lady with the mitten lived. We were seemingly getting nowhere, just going in circles, when my husband said, "Now look, Ann, I think the best thing to do is stop the car and go and ask someone

---

[132] This is the term for a glove in Ireland.

[133] Because of his embarrassment over the wounds, Padre Pio was allowed to cover his hands with fingerless soft gloves. His stigmata were hidden this way except when he was saying Mass.

if they know where this person lives; otherwise we'll be driving around here all day."

He stopped the car, and I got out and asked someone where the lady named Thornton who had the mitten of Padre Pio lived.

"Oh, sure you've stopped right outside the door" was my answer. Later I would believe our Lady had brought me to this house and to Padre Pio.

Kay Thornton, as I know her now, answered the door. In the hall there was a suitcase, and she told us that if we'd been five minutes later we'd have missed her, as she was going to San Giovanni Rotondo [where Padre Pio lived and is buried]. We brought the children in and blessed Kelly with the mitten in the name of the Father, Son, and Spirit. I also asked Kay to have a Mass said for Kelly's cure in San Giovanni and gave her money for an offering. Kay gave me magazines and prayer leaflets on the life of Padre Pio, all of which I rolled up and put in my handbag.

We left, and as it was such a nice day we decided we'd go visit friends who didn't live too far away. We were with them the rest of the day, and as we were driving home Kelly fell asleep in the back of the car.

As she was still sleeping when we reached home, I just picked her up and put her to bed. After a cup of coffee I went to bed myself. And for the first time I said a prayer asking the intercession of Padre Pio.

Barely had I finished my prayers when Kelly came into the bedroom and said there was an old man in her room.

I told her she was only dreaming.

"No, Mommy, there's an old man in my room. Come quickly so you can see."

I took her by the hand and brought her back into her room, where she pointed toward a corner and said, "Mommy, look! There he is!"

I could see absolutely nothing, so I tried to explain to her that there wasn't anyone there.

"Don't be afraid," I said.

"I'm not afraid, Mommy," she answered, "but he's there. Look!" she insisted.

By this time I was getting a bit cross. I said, "No, Kelly. Come on, you have to go to bed now and go to sleep, because we're going to Belfast in the morning. We're staying with Granny and then, the next morning, you're going to the hospital. So you need a lot of sleep."

But as I was tucking her in, she was still insisting, looking over my shoulder to see him, that there was an old man standing in the corner of her room.

I remember going back to bed and thinking, "My God, could she be sickening for something, maybe hallucinating?" I lay in bed, but I could hear her laughing and giggling in her room and somehow I fell asleep.

The next morning, I woke up and went downstairs to make breakfast. It was the usual morning, getting things organized—this time including things for my journey to Belfast—and getting my husband off to work. Kelly was up running around, and I asked her to go into the living room and get something from my handbag—I think perhaps cigarettes, as I smoked at the time. When she got in there she called, "Mommy, Daddy, come quickly!"

Well, we ran into the living room, and there she was sitting on the couch with my handbag open and a magazine that Kay Thornton had given me which pictured Padre Pio on the front.

Kelly pointed to the picture and said, "Mommy, *that's* him. That's the man that was in my room last night!"

I almost drop dead at the thought of it now, but I said, "No, Kelly, that's Padre Pio."

"But he's the man, Mommy, who was in my room last night," she insisted. She didn't say, "That's Padre Pio, who was in my room." To her it was just an old man. She had said the night before that he was an old man with a black coat. Now as I looked at the picture and saw the dark Capuchin habit, I had to accept the fact that it could have been Padre Pio that was in her room.

"If it was Padre Pio, what did he come for?" I asked myself. Was it to take her? Was this it?

Every day for four years I had wondered, "My God, will she be here next Christmas? Will she be here for her next birthday?"

After four years of waiting for her to outgrow her inadequate heart, as her last day seemed to be coming nearer and nearer I was inwardly going to pieces.

⌒

When we got to Belfast, I told my mother what had happened. She was delighted. Not only did she know a lot more about Padre Pio than I did, but she was fully convinced that Kelly was going to be all right.

But I wasn't so sure.

Tuesday Kelly was admitted, and the following day she was taken for her catheterization. I remember sitting worrying and wondering, "My God, is this it? Are they going to tell me that all my prayers have been in vain? Or are they going to tell me there's something they can do now to help her?" I remember praying for the intercession of our Lady and Padre Pio. If he had come to take her, I pleaded, let him not take her *just yet*. I wasn't prepared to give her up *just yet*. There were so many things I wanted to do with her and to show her. And again I said *I just couldn't give her up*.

Eventually they brought her back. She was lying quite still on the bed, and I was sitting beside, holding her hand when a nurse came and told me that the doctor wanted to speak with me.

During the time since Kelly's birth, Dr. Muriel Fraser had retired and another doctor in the City Hospital had taken over the case. She was a cardiologist. As I walked toward her office the long passage never seemed to end. The quicker I walked, the more it seemed that the hall lengthened. Finally I was sitting down in front of her thinking, "What is she going to say about Kelly's future?"

The cardiologist began, "Mrs. Wilkinson, I don't know how I'm going to explain this to you, but I'll try. For the past almost four years you have been coming here religiously with your daughter, and we haven't been able to give you any consolation or hope. And for that I'm very sorry. But I have in front of me Kelly's catheterization done at birth, and it clearly shows she has a single ventricle, a congenital heart defect, and a grossly enlarged liver. And then I have here the catheterization done to-day. It shows absolutely no congenital heart defect. Kelly's heart today is perfectly normal. *The piece that wasn't there is now there.* And the liver has reduced in size.

"Now last night I don't know whether Kelly told you but we were keeping a close eye on her because her heart seemed quite normal for the first time and her liver seemed to have reduced. I was quite baffled, especially when we did the catheterization, because they both look so different. My diagnosis today is that Kelly is a perfectly normal, healthy child. I can't explain it. There is no medical reason for it. Somehow you have obtained a miracle. So take Kelly home, because there's absolutely nothing wrong with her."

I burst into tears and babbled that I knew exactly what had happened, that I *had* been given a miracle, and the man through whom it came to me was Padre Pio.

Normally I would end here this account of how God used Padre Pio eight years after the Capuchin's death to make a new piece for a little girl's defective heart. But with the cooperation of Ann Wilkinson, I would like to look at another aspect of healing which I and other writ-ers on the subject usually ignore—and that is to suggest some of the very human emotions and situations that crop up after some healings, especially those as spectacular as Kelly Wilkinson's.

After all those years of worry and waiting, as mother and daughter returned home from Belfast, Kelly was the perfectly normal little girl Ann had longed for her to be. Yet odd as it may seem to those who haven't been there, the young mother found coping with the miracle "a bit of a stress in its own right."

For starters, there was a bit of "survivor's guilt." As Ann says humbly, "I couldn't understand why God had given me *my* miracle. It was some-thing I'd wanted so badly, but why did He give it to *me?*"

She was finding that a healing miracle is also a spiritual and emo-tional event, and not just for the individual cured, but for those around the person as well. Not that it confers instant spiritual—or any other kind of—maturity; but that it forces one to either run from God or deepen one's spiritual life. An atheist the author knew whose huge tumor vanished instantaneously on the day of scheduled surgery with the prayer of a friend of God's simply wouldn't acknowledge the event. In Ann's case, it is obvious that her faith was much deeper to begin with than she modestly sketches it in her story. But in the seven years between Kelly's cure and our original interviews, she acknowledged it had grown so much more that it seemed strange to her to remember that she actually worried that people might find out about the miracle when she and Kelly returned to Clogherhead. In part she was putting herself in the place of other people whose children hadn't been cured or who had even experienced losing a child. Like any sensitive person who can never forget the enormity of his or her own sufferings, she didn't wish in any way to rub salt in someone else's wounds by proclaiming, "My child had a miracle."

There was something else, too. A miracle comes to us as a dreamed-of, longed-for deliverance when we stand in such totally naked need, such obvious misery, that a good part of our acquaintances and some-times even people who are among our "nearest and dearest" may be so uncomfortable with our situation that they avoid us or lecture us like Job's comforters. We ourselves may be embarrassed that we can't "take it." After all, those mythical superheroes "other people" live through their child's death or whatever tragedy is pending and become stronger people, better Christians, while we, in our weakness, can only tremble and clamor for a miracle.

A cure, then, in spite of one's profound, ecstatic, never-to-be-erased gratitude to God, is surrounded by such raw emotions that it isn't always the easiest thing to talk about. Or as Ann says of her particular case, while she left the cardiologist's office "walking on air and couldn't wait" to tell her mother, her husband, her close friends, at the same time the cure "seemed a very personal thing" and she wasn't comfortable about sharing it with just anybody.

Another factor: she says, "I was afraid to tell anybody [outside family and friends] in case they didn't believe me."

Ann's fear of being dismissed as dishonest or perhaps a religious nut extended to anxieties for four-year-old Kelly as well. "I suppose it seems so strange" (it doesn't, only human), she says with characteristic honesty, "but I hadn't the faith to keep saying to her, 'Kelly, do you remember about Padre Pio? Do you remember seeing him in your room?'"

"I was afraid. I didn't want her going out into the street or into the village and saying she was seeing people, seeing *saints*, in her room, because people can be very hard, especially people who don't have the faith to accept something like that. And I'm sorry to say at that time I didn't have the faith to keep her memory [of Pio] going."

Even with Kelly eleven years old at the time this book's first edition appeared, Ann still had emotions to deal with. She said, "I worry a bit that because she's been cured, a lot of people now think she'll become a nun and lead a religious life. I don't know what her future's going to be. She's absolutely no different from my other girl, Ciara. And now I have a little boy, Tomas—he's four—and they're all the same. They can be good at times, and they can be bold, especially Kelly." The candid mother adds, "I'm also afraid of people thinking Kelly's got some kind of power because she's been cured. I don't think she has."

If these are some of the stresses a miracle can leave in its wake in this imperfect world, as one would expect there have been many more blessings. One of these is Ann's changed feelings for the saint she was afraid would be "too demanding" ever to intercede for someone as ordinary as Ann judged herself. Today she claims, "Padre Pio is almost a part of our family." In fact, following the cure, she developed "a sort of hunger" to know the stigmatized priest. From Kay Thornton, she learned much. And she pilgrimaged to Our Lady of Grace in San Giovanni Rotondo a number of times, particularly enjoying meeting friars who knew Pio personally.

Ann shared with me one incident at the friary that helped cement her growing friendship with the dead Capuchin.

In her words:

A lot of people obtained perfume[134] when Padre Pio was near them or [felt] some form of presence. When he was in Kelly's room that night, I didn't feel anything. I didn't smell anything. But when I went to San Giovanni the first time, I was aware that

---

[134] I have written of this mystical phenomenon associated with Padre Pio and other saints in my book *The Sanctified Body*. Known as the odor of sanctity, it may accompany certain living saints at times and signal their presence as God's messengers of healing or other graces after their death. In Pio's lifetime, the odor accompanied many of his bilocations and clung to the blood from his stigmata.

people did get this perfume, this saintly aroma. I was wondering if maybe he would let me experience it as I went into his room. But all thought of perfume, of everything, left me as I looked at the pair of sandals in the middle of the room. I was overcome with the thought of the suffering he had gone through with his bleeding feet and his other wounds. I got quite emotional, and I remember leaving the room feeling so, so sad that this poor man had gone through so much.

Then as I passed the statue of Our Lady of Fatima that stands just before you go into the corridor of cells where the friars sleep, I got this beautiful aroma of roses, and I cried uncontrollably.

There were no flowers about. There was nothing I could have obtained that perfume from. And to think that he had come to me! And given me that perfume, maybe welcoming me to San Giovanni! But I believe I had to get the perfume just there, at that statue of our Lady, because I think he was saying to me, "You know it wasn't only I that interceded for Kelly. It was our Lady that brought us together, that made all this happen."

Ann adds, "I really believe that our Lady was the intercessor who led me down the road to Padre Pio, that in God's design he had to be the one that brought healing to Kelly—and I thank God for it every day."

There is another reason Ann says things like "Oh, Padre Pio's a great man in our house, a wonderful man." At the time of Kelly's birth, the distraught mother listened to her own mother talk of Pio's sanctity and ability on occasion to see into people's hearts and immediately took a dislike to the Capuchin friar because, by her understanding of sanctity at the time, she saw Pio as, if certainly no one to confuse with God, still of a "godlike" splendor so that he must look down on his spiritual inferiors, that is, ordinary, sinful men and women. Today Ann's understanding of sanctity is much different. She says of her friend in Heaven, "I marvel that God sent someone like him to earth in our time, a person we can relate to, *just an ordinary human being* but one given so many gifts by God." It is not too much to say her relationship with the Italian Capuchin has changed her life.

"Padre Pio suffered so much," she explains. "Sometimes now when I think of the suffering he may have had to undergo or someone may have had to undergo to obtain my miracle and give me back my child, then I think of any little bit of suffering I have or trouble we have in the family or anything at all that crops up and I try to offer it up to God." Her hope, she says, is "that maybe my suffering, my unhappiness at times, can be offered up [as a prayer] to obtain happiness for someone else." Ann says earnestly, "Today I'll accept my trouble gladly so long as there's good that comes out of it somewhere."

Ann also credits Padre Pio that now, "no matter what happens, good or bad, in the family, I can always see God's hand there somewhere [and find] a meaning for everything."

The saint God sent to bless her has also opened Ann more to other members of the human family. "I feel now," she says, "that everyone, no matter who they are, whether I like them at that moment or not, is a child of God. Today I want to accept others, blemishes and all. After all, I'm not perfect ..."

She also says with emotion, "It's only when you've gone through something like that that you realize that when the chips are down, God is the only person there to help you. Material things, you see clearly, don't matter anymore. It's your love, your relationship with Him, with His saints—in my case our Lady and Padre Pio—as far as I'm concerned, that counts."

Listening to Ann, one cannot escape seeing how sharply focused this wife and mother's Christian values have become in the decade since her second child's birth with grave cardiac defects. Hearing her, a listener has no sense of either self-advertisement or that someone is mouthing the proper words. As she once resolutely said her Rosary every word "distinct and from the heart" when told her newborn was dying, Ann today says intensely, if softly, "I try to live a good life to please God. And I try to instill in the children the love for our Lady that I have because she's been so good to me and my family. I live every day trying to do good and *be* good. I'm only human and I fall sometimes—but I try very hard, and I try to teach my children to lead a good life, because at the end of the day that's all that really matters."

Chapter 19

Like the Ripples from a Stone in Water

The image of the rippling-out effect from a stone thrown into a pond is used a lot—and for good reason. It is a very good visual for something that a researcher like myself observes over and over about these miracles from God through the prayers of saints. As I keep saying, a miracle is not just for the one who receives it. In the case of an infant or child's miracle healing, since it certainly can't be claimed that a baby or tyke has been healed through self-suggestion, even more than an adult's cure it is often a wake-up call to the medical people involved. For the same reason, it may change your view of miracles and God from just reading about this sort of cure in this book.

Further still, a family living for God as the aftermath of a miracle—even if they were, as in some cases, living for God before the healing will often be profoundly affected as individuals, as a couple, and as parents. The subsequent effect on their child rearing and their children may ripple out to affect perhaps thousands of people.

Here's a quick look at that through some biographical facts on the infant Peter Smith whose miracle from destroyed eyes and pneumonia is detailed in the prologue.

Deeds sometimes must speak without words. Readying the first edition, I spoke to the miracle baby, ordained priest Peter Smith, then pastor of a Texas church, but I didn't ask the pertinent questions. In spite of the fact that I only verified he was the person who had had the miracle and he only volunteered a few quick words that showed he was certainly devoted to Mother Cabrini, I believe now-deceased Fr. Smith answered the questions I would ask today by his life. (I have also interviewed a brother.)

First a review of the basic birth facts (more details, of course, in the prologue). Peter Joseph Smith, named for his father, was blinded on the day of his birth, March 14, 1921, by a nurse's error.

Sometime before the next morning, he was given new eyes by God through the intercession of Mother Frances Xavier Cabrini. Immediately after this miracle, the baby came down with pneumonia but was healed again after another night of prayer for her intercession by Cabrini's daughters.

The Smiths had lost their first baby as an infant. Now the Catholic father and mother—she in the hospital but shielded from all this, not that hard in an era when birth was regarded as requiring a good rest by the mother after delivery—were told that their second child and first son was a miracle.

Peter's parents were devout even before his birth. The miracle magnified that, so he grew up in a very devout family indeed.

It helped that he was born during an era between World War I and the first post–WW II decade when Catholics in the United States were still more or less ghettoized for ill and for good. Secular culture having less impact than later, the triumvirate of Catholic home-church-school generally stamped its children strongly.

In the Smiths' case, Peter was the first of three boys. Raymond was born two years after Peter's 1921 birth, and twelve years after Raymond, Margaret Reilly Smith gave birth in 1935 to John. Because of the family's love for Mother Cabrini, this last child's middle name honored her. "I was the first child," Msgr. John Smith claims, "to be named for her. She was not yet even beatified." Today Raymond has a family and Msgr. John serves a New York State parish.

Peter's life unfolded as many people in that era probably imagined it would for someone who had a great miracle and a family deeply touched by the event. The Smiths stayed close to Mother Cabrini as Peter grew up. And Cabrini's daughters, the Missionary Sisters of the Sacred Heart, who had prayed their hearts out invoking her intercession, stayed close to the Smiths as well. The widowed mother—Peter Senior died in 1937—and her miracle child, then in his late teens, were present by invitation at the 1938 exhumation of Mother Cabrini's remains and, that same year, at her beatification in Rome. Peter, after serving in World War II's armed forces and living to tell the tale of participating in eleven

Pacific invasions, entered the seminary. It was one of the Missionary Daughters who financed his education. And it was at Mother Cabrini's eastern shrine that he was ordained June 2, 1951.

Nine years later, Fr. Peter answered a bishop's plea for priests for Texas. It was 1960, and with nearly a decade of priestly experience, he was immediately made pastor of St. Joseph's parish in Alamo. Then from 1964 he served faithfully as pastor of Immaculate Conception Church in Edinburg, Texas, until retirement twenty-eight years later in 1992. But all thirty-two years of his Texas service, he was also on call for Mother Cabrini. Msgr. John Smith recalls his older brother traveling widely, preaching and speaking about her. Naturally, he told about the miracle he had received as an infant in order that he might promote faith that "the age of miracles has not passed" and introduce others to Mother Cabrini's intercession. While he became nearsighted with the passing of the years, he could assure questioners that his eyes, unusually beautiful and expressive in his photos, had always been, and remained, healthy.

In 1980 the Missionary Sisters of the Sacred Heart honored Fr. Smith for all he had done to make their foundress known.

In 1992 at age seventy, Fr. Peter Smith retired to his home state, New York, to be near his family. Although retired, he never stopped serving in one priestly capacity or another during the next ten years. He died of an aneurysm around midnight during the night of February 11-12, 2002, a death not that different from Mother Cabrini's. In a last act of service, he had anointed forty people that day.

The stone of his infant miracle had made a big splash. And since you are reading this, it is still rippling out.

Chapter 20

Miracle Kids

"I live every day trying to do good and *be* good," Ann Wilkinson said eleven years after her child had a miracle (ch. 18). Twenty years later, speaking to Ann for this new edition, those commitments appear stronger than ever and seem to be bearing a lot of fruit for others.[135] Of course, Ann's story, from the day she began to pray her heart out for her just-born child doctors said must die, was clearly that of a good person of real faith. Observing the still-unquenchable fire to serve God that the miracle lit in Ann, in her husband in a less extroverted way, and in other parents of miracle kids, I began to wonder what kind of people children who had miracles very young grew into *raised by such people*. Was the life of miracle infant Peter Smith just a fluke?

For those of you who may find this of interest too, this chapter is the fruit of interviews with Ann's daughter Kelly and, separately, with another miracle child with an equally remarkable mother and faith-filled father.

Both adult miracle kids insist they are just ordinary people. Suggesting they might be different brings laughter or annoyance. Understandably from their perspective. Certainly a miracle child develops in most ways like any normal child. Kelly Wilkinson, for instance, looks back in her thirties on a typical relationship with her three-years-older sister:

---

[135] For instance, the man who tells Ann he has always thought things like Kelly's healing, which she has described the previous day, happened only to rich and special people. Tied up in his life duties, he has never made time for religion. "But you're just like me," he says. "I figured maybe I better be part of this." That morning he has made his first confession in twenty years.

childhood fights and bickering, then, in her teens, the closeness they enjoy in adulthood putting out its first shoots.

Like her mom, Kelly sees herself as no different from her siblings.

Similar in her attitude to Irish Kelly is the other miracle child, an American (you'll see why no name ahead). Her cure as a tyke was accepted for a saint's beatification. Today a grandmother, the American insists, "Life for us [miracle kids] is like everybody else's." And one of the American's siblings [of several children in that family] volunteers, "I was about ten or eleven at the beatification. My sister [the beatification miracle recipient] was just my sister. Perfectly irritating at times—like any of my other siblings—as irritating as no doubt her siblings were to her."

Since each feels so strongly she is not different, I'll start with the ways they *are* like everyone else. Yes, miracle kids like all people—saints included—come into the world with personal good points and with weaknesses that require work not to do damage to self and others.

Nor do they get a free pass through life. Kelly notes with irritation, "A common misconception of many people who hear my story is that because you were cured by Padre Pio, you must live a charmed and very easy life." Then she reels off things that disprove this has been the case: Kelly's first love when she was just out of her teens was killed in an automobile accident. Years later, happily married, she had the sorrow and grief of two miscarriages before a successful pregnancy. She hemorrhaged dangerously with the birth of her second child, experiencing terror she would die and leave her children. At the time we talked, not long after that, her infant had been hospitalized and required surgery before reaching its sixth month, giving her and her husband a small frightening taste of her parents' experience with her. "Scary," Kelly emphasizes.

⁓

The American miracle child, having lived longer, has been through more and worse trials, most horrible the injuries in an accident and subsequent death of one of her children. Marital problems ended in permanent separation. Enough said. Admittedly, the lives of each of these living women show being a miracle child comes with no passport to Easy Street.

Fearful situations, deaths, and other losses intensify for anyone the struggle to become or remain spiritually healthy human beings. As you read on, you can judge whether these women have, as I find, succeeded at that.

If they have, it is in spite of the fact that each carries one or more burdens precisely from having been a miracle recipient. Recall the American's sibling's humorous appraisal that, miracle child or no, her sister could be just as irritating as the family's other children. The same sibling describes seriously and sympathetically how the miracle child came under pressure from the sisters running her high school. These women belonged to the order of the saint God had beatified through their student's miracle cure as a tiny child. As the living, breathing, walking testimony to their foundress's sanctity, "my sister's feet weren't supposed to touch the ground," her sibling laughs ruefully; "and visible graces were supposed to be shooting out of her body; yet she was just so normal, a regular teenager."

Happily, until the American miracle child's presence in Rome as an older teen for the saint's beatification, and, again years later, for the canonization, as a married woman with children of her own, she avoided the additional pressure of the public eye. With each of those events that healthy anonymity was breached. At times to this day, there has been periodic intrusion from the press, writers like this one, or people drawn to the saint.

At the time of the saint's canonization in Rome, for example, one of the American's sisters remembers that she herself was at the saint's American shrine for the celebration taking place there. With her were the children of her miracle sister, who was attending the ceremonies at the Vatican with her husband and parents. To the babysitting sister's chagrin, it proved impossible to attend the reception following the Mass of thanksgiving because "everyone wanted to touch the children." They even wanted to touch the aunt!

Once at least, real darkness reached a sinister hand toward the American miracle child. A telephone caller told her—she was now a young mother—that her child, thankfully sick on the sofa before her eyes rather than at school, had been kidnapped and she must meet the creepy caller in a secluded place to avoid dire consequences. This change in recent years in attitude toward those blessed with a miracle[136] is one reason I feel I simply can't give this American's name or the name of the saint of her miracle, both ways to find her.

Kelly was spared the particular burden of media or more deadly intrusion. Although her cure met all seven criteria for an official miracle, Padre Pio's poverty-vowed Capuchins decided they would present for the beatification miracle a local cure (pp. 194-195) (that is, one near Pio's friary) that required minimal medical documentation.

That made it possible for the Wilkinsons to see their child did not show up in some American supermarket tabloid. Because they also saw Kelly kept a low profile locally—and brought her up without any sense of "specialness"—they could also spare her the pressure of heavy or impossible expectations. This even though, in the Ireland of that time, her mother, Ann, feared some who knew about the miracle would expect Kelly to become a nun. Today the particular burden as a miracle child Kelly describes is the collection of feelings, also experienced by her mother, known as survivor's guilt. Kelly looks at a parent with a sick child visiting her mother for Ann's prayers and squirms, "There I am blatantly right out in front of them healthy and happy." In her mid-teens, seeing the dead father of four young children, she says that guilt made her wish she could take his place. She sums up, "So while being cured has obviously saved my life, it has raised some questions and, at times, caused me a lot of confusing and guilt-ridden thoughts."

⌒

At this point some readers may be convinced a miracle is tough luck for a child. You miss out on waltzing into Heaven before you've had a chance to screw up. God does not rear you with a little halo over your trike. Instead He lets you, like everyone else, have traits and issues as child and adult you'll have to struggle with, and—throwing in a few

---

[136] This American's experiences show another thing about authenticated miracle recipients that was rare when I wrote the first edition of this book but is common today: media wring dry the private life of anyone noteworthy for any reason for easy copy for readers equally eager to breach others' privacy. The problem is forcing some Causes to keep the identity of beatification and canonization miracle recipients undisclosed. This limits the person's witness and is a cross when the individuals and their families are so grateful and wish, in most cases, to give glory and honor to God and God's saint by speaking openly of what God has done.

extra ones precisely related to your wondrous healing—He says nix to effortless "happily ever after."

~

Time to turn to the blessings, the ways miracle kids—these two women and others I know—I contend are *not* ordinary adults. After my decades of saint and miracle watching, here are special attributes I see. No matter that neither they nor their close relatives—who share the traits—see them. Didn't St. Padre Pio wonder if he was pleasing to God? Wasn't St. André Bessette blind to his role in the God-given healings that flowed through him? Why shouldn't miracle kids and the families they grew up in also fail to see themselves with perfect clarity?

A child's miracle may begin with a grandparent or one of those persons of faith God uses to link those in need to a praying saint. But in every case I know—definitely including the American's mother and father—these children had parents who didn't reject God's direct help when medical science came up short. The Wilkinsons, for instance, got in their car and went looking for the woman Ann had been told blessed those seeking healing with a relic[137] of Padre Pio. Kelly was blessed in the name of the Trinity by laywoman Kay Thornton, and Pio appeared, carrying God's healing, in Kelly's room that night. Receiving a miracle (and who does is a mystery: an asking saint may not [2 Cor. 12:8] and an atheist may [pp. 153-154]), the miracle child and his or her siblings are raised by people who *know by experience* of the most tangible kind, the healed child in their arms, that God is real.

Without claiming perfection in any way—that would be silly—these are not ordinary parents. Their children all, so far as I can see, imbibe

---

[137] If this is a new word or idea, relax: it's biblical. If you're nonreligious, think of it as something you treasure from someone not there visibly. For me, a good analogy is the hair of my mother, who died very young. When I look at the wavy honey-blonde locks, I feel connected to her love and even experience, in a completely nonmystical way, her presence. Similar is the relic of a saint—some part of the person, like hair or, given lesser honor, something belonging to the person, like a handkerchief. No magic object but, rather, like the handkerchiefs, work aprons, or other objects of the Apostles that carried healing [see Acts 19:12 and Acts 5:15], a relic is simply a link or a sign, if you prefer, pointing to the prayer of the holy person for the individual seeking help for self or others.

a not-that-common mind set and values. A miracle kid may get mad at God, may doubt, but would be unlikely to decide there is no God. In a society that pushes self-promotion, these miracle kids as adults tell me on purpose information that could make someone think less of them. (It has the opposite effect.)

For instance, Kelly, who works four days a week with a long commute and two very young children—one of whom had just had the frightening health problem when she and I talked—*volunteers* that she does not get to Mass as often as she would like. She is also quick to talk about the times she has had, so to speak, a tiff with God about tragic or potentially tragic events in her life, such as her boyfriend's death or the miscarriages.

The same desire to expose what may be considered faults or, at least, ordinary human weaknesses, is very strong in the American miracle child.

Talking to the American, my notes are studded with her comments like these:

"I feel privileged and honored" to have God's help "to get through my disposition."

"I could get caught up in the material world—[in that sense] I'm worldly and yet I love Jesus too, so I have that battle."

"The way I sin because I'm human I need Confession and Communion so I can grow in Him."

"We all need deliverance: it doesn't stop until we take our last breath."

"Prayer is so necessary. [In this life] you're always on your knees."

The farthest from trumpeting her ordinary human weakness the American miracle recipient will move is to admit—in what is clearly a huge understatement: "I kind of cooperate [with God's grace] a little bit."

Then she goes right back to making statements with genuine fervor such as, "We all [I think while she believes this with all her heart, she also hopes I will see *she* certainly does] have to work out our salvation. We all have to pray and work through our struggles."

Both the Irish woman and the American offer no information about grace-filled moments or either spiritual or material achievements. It seems to me in each humility is probably long ingrained. I also suspect, talking to me, each is consciously concerned to give me no chance to think too well of her. Neither speaks of her miracle. To get Kelly, for instance, to speak of memories she has of Padre Pio's appearance to her at age four, I have to ask. Putting it down not to anything supernatural but to "a good memory," she does recall the old man—who with his beard reminded her of one of her grandfathers—in her room. Although her parents did nothing to keep up the memory so Kelly would not be thought odd, she even recalls the disagreement back and forth with her mother, who insisted the man Kelly saw wasn't there. Kelly remembers too, the tyke she was, wondering why the old man was wearing a brown dress and had a piece of rope around his waist.

Years later, a teacher of her older sister, Ciara, had told the class the story. Ciara told Kelly, who asked her mom, "Why are they talking about me?" Only then did Kelly get a low-key presentation on the miracle. Apparently deeply affected by the miracle, the teacher continued to tell the story each year. When she was old enough to be in that class, Kelly recalls humorously some "delightful attention," for a day or two from her classmates before, she says, their minds flitted to other topics. In secondary school with nuns, Kelly says she was even less remarked. That she keeps it light, even poking a little fun at herself, reminds of St. Pio, who once self-mockingly said, after a bomb scare, that he wasn't scared as he had a Pio relic with him!

And that brings me to another observation: these miracle kids, as adults, tend to have characteristics similar to the saint whose prayers brought them God's healing. Hang on a moment before you dismiss this. Consider that their parents understandably became devoted to the saint of the miracle that gave them back their child.

St. Paul counseled, "Be imitators of me as I am of Christ" (1 Cor. 11:1). But zealous Paul is not the contemplative apostle John. Following Jesus by living the particular spirituality of "their" saint, parents naturally bring their children up in it too.

In the case of the American miracle child, she has spoken of the purpose of everyone's life as being "to work out our salvation." This was a preoccupation of the saint of her miracle. The American doesn't talk about her personal life, but one of her sisters tells me of the adult miracle child's devotion to her children and grandchildren. "She lives for them," the sister says.

Family devotion, with deep seriousness about each one's salvation, is another core trait of the American's saint. Also reminiscent of the saint whose warm geniality made her beloved by many beyond her family is the American's geniality. Like her saint, who helped many women and girls, the American also has a special ministry, one could say, to women. Hairdressers have been dubbed the secular person's confessor or psychiatrist. Perhaps in part because she loves beauty,[138] the American became a hairstylist. From her deep life in God, so obvious as she talks, I can see how she might be used not just to make other women look more attractive but to make their souls more beautiful as well. The American has spoken humbly of her temperament as a burden she struggles with. That may be true—since it seems to be to some degree for anyone with self-awareness, even the holy. But, again, a sibling sees it differently. Noting how well her sister has coped with the various burdens of miracle-child status, she says, "It helps that she can find the humor in anything," adding, "it is very hard to offend her." The miracle woman obliquely mentions another trait that is part of some people's geniality and definitely useful in helping others find God: "You can't judge anyone," the American insists "because you don't know what has hardened them.

Padre Pio was used by God in a huge healing ministry. Kelly has grown up watching her outgoing mother with her gift of easy speech set aside Ann's personal dislike of dredging up the time when she had a toddler on the verge of death, in order to serve others desperate for healing as she was. She even gives talks at times, and Kelly sees how they help people. Kelly has also seen her shy, quiet, very private father go out, when her mother can't, to visit the sick and pray for healing. The Wilkinsons are accompanied by a Pio glove—like the one Kelly was blessed with the day her miracle took place. The glove was given for the purpose by Pio's spiritual son and sometimes caregiver, American-born Capuchin Fr. Joseph Pius Martin.[139] He became Ann's spiritual direc-

---

[138] Today it is spiritual beauty she mentions as attracting her, saying, "As you grow older, you need the peace of beauty. You get to see it in the beauty and peace of those who have achieved spiritually or given their lives like a Mother Teresa. You see the beauty of God coming through them."

[139] Fr. Joseph Pius, helping me, the author, with authentic materials for my Pio writings, introduced me to the Wilkinsons.

tor, when she voyaged to San Giovanni, seven-year-old Kelly in tow, to report the cure in gratitude to God and Pio and their emissary, Kay Thornton. Fr. Joseph Pius had Ann start a Padre Pio Prayer group and lead pilgrimages to Pio's friary and, today, shrine.

When the time comes, Kelly knows she will carry on this effort to meet others' needs, setting aside her own discomfort and reluctance to meet parents with terminally ill children. When they ask if she thinks they will receive a miracle, she will, no doubt, repeat what her mother says (learned from Fr. Joseph Pius): "I don't know if you will receive a miracle; God doesn't always give us what we ask for but I know He always gives us what we need."

Of course every Catholic saint's spirituality models charity to a heroic degree, love for God often poured out in some kind of service to neighbor. I'm not canonizing anyone, but I think this chapter shows these women, reared by people with a faith that sparks deeds of charity, have grown up, as the American's refusal to judge others clearly shows, to be more than usually charitable and empathetic. (Even what Kelly ascribes to survivor's guilt (p. 208) can also be seen as empathetic compassion like that of Pio, who was always wanting to take on someone's sufferings to spare the person.)

The final thing I find "un-ordinary" about miracle children and their families is how they see suffering.

As I now consider typical of her, Kelly in her later thirties does not start with her view of suffering today—or *just* give me that more spiritually mature response. She wants to share that when she was younger, her reaction to personal suffering was "not always to be happy with God." The Irish woman remembers aloud moments, such as her miscarriages, when, as Kelly puts it, "Padre Pio, I would say, had his fingers in his ears ... I was devastated and aimed my anger at him." Still Kelly adds, "Even in tough times, I always knew Padre Pio wasn't too far away, even if he didn't answer my prayers exactly as I had wanted him to ... I know he is always there for me and these things happen for a reason."

When Kelly talks about the loss of her boyfriend when she was twenty, she makes no effort almost twenty years later to sugarcoat the emotions she had for publication. She has not stuffed away but instead shares feelings one could expect of someone at twenty: "My life fell apart ... This really made me question my faith. Padre Pio was not my favorite person at the time ... I felt God was punishing me. I believed in God, but if God and Padre Pio weren't going to help me out, I had no time for God." Angry in her grief, she still never doubted God's existence. Nor did her attitude freeze into implacable resentment of God or Padre Pio for not preventing the accident. Instead, having as a teen both wanted to be like her friends and yet still focused on "what [does] Pio want of me?" she says she asked God (this is the period when she thinks she wasn't talking to Him) whether He had "put me here to help his [the dead youth's] parents." Years later she still saw easing their suffering as important: those parents brought up the gifts at Kelly's wedding, and she was a bridesmaid to the dead youth's sister. Yet she knows now that her life has other tasks, too—in other words, she believes she was spared for a purpose or more than one even if she can't yet precisely name to herself what her life is for.

Fifteen years after the accident and other hard patches like the miscarriages, she has grown into a different view of suffering. She says, "It's life; [it's] not God or Padre Pio punishing you. They [God and the saints] give you the strength to cope and get up the next day and get on with it and be the kind of person you ought to be."

⌒

The American miracle child, now a grandmother, also thinks about suffering. She experiences, too, "as you get older your view changes." For her: "suffering is scary but when you know what suffering is all about, it's not so scary. Something in suffering," she muses, "brings you closer to God."

Then from the vantage point of a life nearly twice as long as Kelly's, the American offers her understanding of miracles in general: "Healings [happen to] promote God's glory." Having been given life by one, she fully appreciates that "the physical healings are wonderful." Still she immediately puts them in a larger perspective, "[But] we've all got to die. [So] the material is not as important as our spiritual [health]. The spiritual healings are the [greatest] thing because they go on forever, even into the next life."

Such remarks, to this writer, place miracle kids in a wider world than most folks, one in which, as the American puts it without realizing not everyone does, people "keep on growing every minute" toward God.

Chapter 21

"A Witch Doctor Greater Than Any Other"

Jaw thrust forward menacingly, the stocky native in the loincloth pointed to his wounded child: "You bullet removing, we you helping. You not saving, we you killing." To punctuate their chief's pidgin Spanish, eighty-odd men made ominous gestures with rifles, blow pipes, or arrows.

Sr. Maria Troncatti blanched as all eyes turned to the forty-one-year-old nun, whose medical education had begun and ended with a wartime Red Cross nursing course.

For days she and two young sisters, with a small escort, had sunk deeper and deeper into the steaming green of the densely packed jungle where Ecuador abuts Peru. Climbing and descending, the heels of their shoes long gouged off by stones or sucked away by the ever-present slimy mud, they pressed wearily forward under trees so laced together by vines that the sky seemed lost forever. In this endless green tunnel of huge cedar, giant bamboo, and tall palm, attacked by clouds of nipping, puncturing insects, the nuns alternately dripped hot rain or suffocated under the heavy, humid air, while their civilized noses gagged in certain places from the stench of rotting fruits, decaying flowers, and leaves blackening in the mud. With the fervent prayer of intense anxiety, the party plunged into a bridgeless, waist-high river, then were entombed again in the jungle, with its unnerving rustlings of poisonous reptiles, cries of unseen wild animals, and the strident squawks and screeches of the birds.

Once Maria had simply fainted.

"Take heart," one of the accompanying party cajoled as she came to.

"Take heart! What kind of heart have *you* to bury three of us alive in this jungle which has no beginning and no end!" she exploded, her sensitive face, swollen with bites, collapsing into sobs.

Normally so soft-spoken and gentle, serving others with a sunny smile and forgetfulness of self, according to those who had been her companions for years, Sr. Maria was half hysterical as every step into this fearsome land drew her that much farther from civilization or, it seemed, from life itself, at least as she could conceive it. In this state of terror, anxiety, and exhaustion, she arrived at her destination, where perhaps some twenty whites lived, and confronted her welcoming committee: a fierce warrior band armed to the teeth who would kill her, the two young nuns in her charge, and the traveling party unless she operated successfully on the chief's child.

"But I'm no doctor. And anyway there's nothing to operate with! No instruments!" she babbled. But there was no way out; it was literally do or die.

Caught four days earlier in a crossfire between her Jivaro tribe and another band of Indians, the chief's thirteen- or fourteen-year-old daughter had a bullet lodged in her chest. At sight of those dark, fever-bright eyes and flushed cheeks, Sr. Maria felt that compassion which made her such a gifted nurse rising in spite of her own turmoil. She put a gentle hand on the burning forehead.

Then, with a deep sigh and a murmured prayer, she asked someone to fetch water, someone else to start a fire for boiling it, and began digging in the nuns' bags for clean linen. After that, she looked for a tool that could dig out a bullet without introducing infection. In a short time her scrubbed hands were sterilizing a tiny penknife. After washing the girl's chest, she applied hot towels over the abscessed area. Then to the Indians' wonderment, she painted the flesh with iodine while she said a slow, thoughtful Hail Mary. Finally, she cut into the abscess. Immediately and wonderfully, the bullet popped out. The chief and his band roared approval.

That night, the girl, her wound cleaned out and bandaged, lay next to Sr. Maria, who gave her frequent sips of liquid. In spite of the exhausting journey, the nun could not have slept. The warriors were celebrating. Sr. Maria shivered at the sound of their fierce, throbbing drums. She did not know they were sending a message into the green darkness: "A witch doctor greater than any other witch doctor has come among us. Free passage must be given to her forever and to all those who are with her."

Born into an exceptionally close-knit family of goat herders in the Italian Alps, Maria Troncatti knew only mountain pastures and villages until, at twenty-one, she left her grieving parents, sisters, and brother to enter a new universe of trains, cities, and educated people as a Salesian postulant. The emotional parting from her family, so reluctant to let her go (her father collapsed in a faint, unable to say goodbye, while her oldest sister insisted, "But why can't you do good *here?*") and the alien surroundings brought on such depression and fits of weeping that for six months it was touch and go whether to simply send the goat girl home. That overcome, before her permanent vows, ill health threatened her vocation until a last-ditch novena to Don Bosco put a stop to a succession of ailments.

Ten years after joining the Salesians, now stable and happy in her vocation, Maria was swept away by a flash flood that inundated the convent, drowning another nun. She was saved in an inexplicable manner after agreeing to an unspoken voice that urged, "But you have to be a missionary." Even then the family-lover added to the bargain the life of her brother serving in World War I. At the war's end, the thirty-nine-year-old nun, who had gained invaluable experience nursing victims of the conflict, was accepted with those half her age as a missionary to South America.

To say goodbye to her family, Maria made her first visit home in her seventeen years as a nun. Two of her four sisters were dead. Old, her parents were still as inconsolable. And nuns sent to South America, they knew as well as she, could look forward to no home furloughs in the 1920s. To end her own and their distress, she cut short her week's stay, only begging they would always write her.

Two years learning Spanish while, in effect, practicing medicine in a doctorless little town on the road to Quito, and Maria was sent to the fearsome jungle, where her life had been immediately put on the line.

Thanks to everyone's prayers more than medical skill, she believed, they were alive for the moment. But the new "witch doctor" trembled with terror and wept continually the next few days as she contemplated being "buried alive," as she put it, in this deadly green dungeon with no road for escape and only five households of colonists to furnish protection from natives so fierce their name meant either "savage" (Kivaro /Jivaro) or simply "enemy" (Shuar).

The morning those who had led them in prepared to leave the three nuns, Maria's silent tears erupted into sobs and she fled to a small clearing. There her anguish boiled over in cries and weeping as if her heart would break, recalls the young sister who followed her and stood silently by. This witness also says Maria's "veritable agony," like Jesus in Gethsemane, ended in a peaceful whispered, "Oh, Jesus, if You're content to remain in loneliness … why shouldn't I be?"

⌒

Forty-five years later, eighty-six years old and still in the jungle, Mother Maria was killed in a plane crash in 1969 shortly after making a private prayer offering of her life to bring peace between feuding white settlers and the natives. Salesian Fr. Angelo Botta, who knew her, explained in 2012, "When she was about to take that last flight, she did so with the great pain of leaving behind Sucúa town torn apart by the threat of some unknown and hidden 'whites' who wanted to set fire to what remained of the Salesian mission; and the many Shuar [natives] who openly threatened bloody revenge … A few hours later, around her coffin, bathed in tears and prayers … pardon and peace broke out."

Fr. Botta calls this "her first great miracle." This happened because if few remembered her in her native Italy, in the jungle of Ecuador she was a legend. When news of her death hit the various settlements, colonists, soldiers, natives, and her fellow Salesians, all wept together for their "*abuelita*,"[140] their doctor, consoler, helper, sometimes conscience, and above all their mother. Other nuns' bodies had been flown out for burial: Mother Maria's had to be left in the jungle that had so terrified her on arrival and yet had become for her a beloved homeland, because armed men would have fought to keep her remains.

Humble and unpretentious, lovable in her tender love for God and the whole human family, bubbling with cheer and good humor, Mother Maria's was the sanctity that comes from a timid soul's saying yes to God even when He seemed to ask of her more than she could bear. From that

---

[140] Little grandmother.

heroic yes, made in agony and tears, Mother Maria's sensitive heart was enlarged and transformed to meld the courageous, protective strength of a patriarch with the tenderest compassion and love of a mother. From such a heart flowed healing.

Many of her cures came from a genius for makeshift medicine. But others are medically inexplicable. Consider this one:

In 1929, only four years after making peace with the place God had sent her, the nun was making a now almost routine several days' journey on foot. Stopping at another Salesian mission camp, Mother Maria found Augustus Zuñiga, an eighteen- or nineteen-year-old boy who worked on bridge construction for the remote area with one of the Salesian priests. A partially completed span had collapsed. Climbing up to inspect a girder, Augustus slipped and hurtled onto rocks far below. He was very badly hurt: "Six or seven ribs were broken on the left side of the thorax from his chest as far down as his floating ribs. The last two cervical vertebrae of his spinal column were cracked and his intestines hardened in his abdomen." In the fifteen or twenty days since the accident, his only treatment had been saline compresses and chicha (used like coffee,[141] the usually root- or grain-based drink, I'm told, is rich in nutrients).

Begged to treat the boy, Sr. Maria could only join the pleader's tears with her own. Then she asked to go into the chapel.

"Mary Help of Christians will tell me what to do," she explained.

Although she had been on foot in rough terrain all day, the nun took no time for sleep but remained in the chapel in fervent prayer for hours. Finally another nun insisted she come out and have at least a hot drink. She obeyed but was at early Mass the next morning praying again.

"Now, Mother Maria," they asked after the liturgy, "will you please treat Augustus?"

"I'll give him a laxative," she said almost offhandedly, a remark and tone which appeared highly inappropriate, even flippant, considering the seriousness of the boy's condition.

She went to him carrying a tray. On it were a glass and a prayer book, while under her arm was a roll of bandage. She shut the door, then turned to the patient.

---

[141] A stronger version is made for celebrating.

"Augustus, all I can give you for your stomach is a laxative, so drink it up." She raised him and he drank.

"Now the rest of your treatment," she said, her countenance seeming to Augustus to radiate light. "Take off your shirt." Painfully, he did.

From the prayer book she drew a picture of Mary Help of Christians surrounded by apostles, evangelists, and angels.

"Kiss it, Augustus. This is your medicine," she said serenely. Running her sensitive fingers compassionately over the broken ribs, she placed the picture over them, then firmly bandaged the whole area. As she worked, she prayed aloud the Hail Mary, Augustus joining in.

"Now the medicine for the top of the spinal column," she went on, this time pulling a picture of the newly beatified John Bosco from the prayer book.

"Kiss it," she said again. Then she had Augustus roll over, and bandaged Don Bosco's picture over the cracked cervical vertebrae.

"Now you must not move until I give permission," she told him. For the next four days she waited on him, as he remained immobile. Then, on the fifth day, she ordered, "Try to sit up without help." Effortlessly he raised himself.

"Now try to get out of bed."

Up with the same ease, he walked.

"How do you feel?"

"Fine, Mother Maria."

"Good. Now back to bed." By the sixth day, even his abdominal pains were gone, and he felt compelled to get up and run. But permission was refused.

The seventh day, however, she removed his bandages. After he kissed the two pictures once more, she replaced them in her prayer book. She made him walk, raise his arms, bend over. Nothing caused even a twinge. That afternoon he was swimming in the river, diving, and cavorting like any other splendid young specimen of manhood.

The next morning Mother Maria resumed her journey.

During Mother Maria's ten years at a mission station at Macas, with only the most primitive medical equipment but armed with the healing love of sanctity, she performed many other extraordinary cures. Fingers almost completely severed by machete were restored, men wounded dreadfully in jungle battles or farm mishaps recovered, a baby whose eye appeared lost in an accident sees perfectly (Mother Maria recommended that case to the intercession of St. Maria Mazzarello, foundress of her order), and a child swollen like a melon from some jungle disorder was cured with the help of a relic of Don Bosco.

In 1936, while stationed at Guayaquil, she healed a young nun, Angela Forestan, who had been unsuccessfully treated by surgery for a problem in her thighbone. Decalcifying, the bone would no longer support her weight. Moreover, it caused the nun such pain, it appeared she would have to give up missionary work and return to Italy. Worse even than the pain was her depression. When the doctors could do no more, Mother Maria asked permission to try. That granted, she procured the long bone from a cow's leg, crushed it, and dried the powder. Adding a few other, unknown ingredients, she made up some pills.

To Sr. Angela, she said, "Here! Take two of these every day, and on January 31 [the feast day of their order's cofounder, St. John Bosco, canonized in 1934] we'll go to the Salesian sanctuary for a mass of thanksgiving. Meantime keep quiet and trust Don Bosco."

January 31, Sr. Angela walked on her "useless" leg to the Salesian sanctuary to give thanks for what she considered a miracle recovery. Mother Maria was with her, sharing the joy and giving every ounce of credit to the prayers of Don Bosco and the Blessed Virgin Mary.

Although still disparaged by some physicians, bone meal for years has been sold as both a preventative and a cure for calcium loss, so the pills Mother Maria made were not a placebo. Moreover, a doctor I discussed this case with points out that if a young person begins using a weight-bearing decalcifying bone — and it may be decalcifying, he adds, simply for lack of use because of pain — while ingesting an adequate calcium supply, the bone can remineralize, as it will not do in an older person.

Sr. Angela was young. I find no evidence that Mother Maria made her walk, but I would not want, years later, to insist she didn't. Let us not claim, then, anything like a miracle occurred; but, on the other hand, it is clearly appropriate to applaud Mother Maria for having, by whatever means, succeeded where professional medical men had failed.

Another testimony is that of a Salesian missionary priest whose continual vomiting doctors, again, had failed to cure. Says Fr. Lova:

I suffered with severe liver trouble for three years. She looked after me like a mother. No sacrifice was too great. She was ready for
anything day or night. I could have died a thousand times had it
not been for her. The worst time of all was when I got sunstroke
… Sister Maria was sent for, but she declared she could do nothing for me. However she said, "Bring him to Sevilla,[142] and I will
look after him." They improvised a stretcher, and I was carried to
Sevilla. Slowly but surely she cured me.

Asked in 1969 what medicines she used, he could recall none. "I
don't know how she did it. I can't explain it," he admitted. "But cure
me she certainly did."

Another testimony that the holy nun may have had a healing
charism is given by Daniel Gonzalez, who was knocked by a mule into
a vat full of boiling cane syrup. It was hours before Mother Maria could
make her way through the jungle on foot to the horribly swollen and
blistered figure, continually writhing and fainting from the pain. The
nun could only apply ointment and bind him up like a swaddled babe,
saying, "Mary Help of Christians!" at every turn of the bandage.

In the case of Sr. Angela, Mother Maria's use of bone meal could be
considered evidence she got cures where others failed simply because
she was medically ahead of her time. Without discrediting her natural
medical aptitude, which could even be considered marked by genius,
the case of Mr. Gonzalez discredits any general theory of this kind. I
have discussed proper treatment of serious burns with medical men, and
the consensus from plastic surgeons to family physicians is that Mother
Maria used exactly the opposite of today's idea of proper treatment. In
fact her primitive handling of the case could have killed the patient,
and if he had lived, the scars would have been terrible. But Mr. Gonzalez not only lived; he had not even a scar from his hideous experience.
He also testified that Mother Maria treated him another time when, in
his estimation, the situation called for the last sacraments. With a tone
of assurance, she insisted, "No, Mr. Daniel, God will cure you," and he
recovered.

Poisoned by a hostile native in 1949, Ft. Albino Gomezcoello was
carried to Mother Maria more dead than alive. For many days, he recalls,

---

[142] Another jungle "town."

"I was aware of nothing." Yet occasionally he had a lucid moment. At such times, "day or night I saw her at my bedside, rosary in hand." Fr. Albino also recovered against all expectations.

A servant girl in a colonist's family says: "I had a bad hand and could not use it. The doctor prescribed expensive injections I could not afford, so I went to consult Mother Maria. She said to me, 'Do not worry, my child. Take this ointment and use it every night. I will pray for you, and I am sure you will get better.' The hand did heal in spite of the fact that the doctor had told me I should never be able to use it."

A woman named Juana De Lara tells how she arrived with her third son, who was very frail, for one of those consultations. Sadly she told Mother Maria how nothing could be done for the child, who was skin and bones.

"Leave him with me, Juanita," Mother Maria offered. After three months he returned home completely cured.

Similar tales, some detailed, some as brief as Juana De Lara's, stud the first biography of the Italian missionary to Ecuador, *Beloved Jungle*, by Maria Domenica Grassiano—which has been my source for this sampling of cures during Mother Maria's lifetime.

After her death the elderly missionary's memory did not gradually fade away; instead, her old friends and new ones talk of a desire to help that seems as alive as ever and a prayer power undiminished by death. On September 7, 1986, Maria Troncatti's Cause was officially opened in the cathedral of the town of Macas in Ecuador. In 2008 her heroic virtue was recognized with the title Venerable, that is, one worthy of veneration. Among the virtues noted were her great faith, patience, and loving kindness. The Salesian report cited her work of "evangelization in the midst of all kinds of dangers" as "an exceptional catechist" while also "working for the jungle's peoples as 'nurse, surgeon, orthopedist, dentist, and anesthetist' and effectively promoting "the emancipation of the ... [tribal] women."

The healings that since her death people attribute to Maria's prayers are regularly reported in two sources: the Spanish-language *Boletin Informativo*, which supports her Cause, and the Italian publication *Conosci?*, which gives testimonies of graces received through the intercession of six members of her order whose holiness makes them candidates for eventual canonization. Samples from the one copy of each publication I was sent by the Secretary General of the Daughters of Mary Help of Christians:

A father in Ecuador has a daughter "who for a long time was gravely ill." The family consults both medical doctors and local healers. Finally the child is hospitalized for a month; still no treatments bring improvement, and physicians cannot agree as to whether surgery should be attempted. Brought home no better, for the child, as her father puts it, "death begins to look like the only way out." While the heartsick parents ponder what to do next, the father appeals to Mother Maria's prayers. Unexpectedly, the girl is immediately restored to normal health.

A mother in Florence, Italy, has similar grateful feelings to God and Mother Maria's prayers in the case of her son. Two specialists had said surgery was necessary but would pose grave risks to the child. Trying to weigh the two perilous courses, the mother sees a leaflet on Maria Troncatti, is struck by the expression of goodness in the nun's photograph, and implores her intercession that a third specialist she and her husband are going to consult will guide the parents as to God's will for their son. The third doctor's verdict: without any risky surgery, this condition will correct itself in time.

A man from the jungle town of Macas in Ecuador loses the sight in his left eye. He travels to Cuenca for fifty days of treatment, which, he says, "was absolutely useless. After that," he writes, "I was successively at Ambato, Los Sapos, and Guayaquil in search of other medical care, but I found no help and, what's worse, was robbed of my money." Discouraged, he returns home only to hear of a Shuar Indian who also had lost his sight and been treated in Guayaquil to no avail, then recovered his vision after putting on the glasses of Mother Troncatti with a prayer for her intercession.

"What you have done for my brother, do for me," he prays. Expressing his faith in God and in Mother's prayer power, he, his wife, and their children all promise to make a good confession so the cure might encompass his whole person and the family. Suddenly his sight returns, enabling him to work although there is still some dysfunction of the eye. When he writes his testimony, in June, however, this is gone, having gradually cleared up, so that the eye has been perfect for two months.

A man hit over the head while working in the mountains believes he is dying and is rushed by plane to a hospital. He calls on Mother Maria's prayers and recuperates without incident.

A Salesian nun who works in the Ecuador jungle dislocates her ankle when she falls. A woman skilled in massage attempts to put the bone back into position but fails. In spite of salve and being wrapped, the swollen ankle causes Sr. Lutgarda Nieto intense pain. Awake in the night, she thinks "of Sister Troncatti, who during her life had given me so many proofs of her affection."

To the dead nun, the living one says, "Now you've got to show you wish me well and get God to cure me; I need to stand on this foot and work."

The result: "She heard me at once," Sr. Lutgarda reports. The next day, Sunday, April 5, 1981, without either pain or swelling in her ankle, she is racing about hard at work at a church fiesta.

Andréa Pellegrini, an Italian mother, offers her testimony:

This past June the doctor diagnosed that my three-year-old daughter had a massive tumor near her right kidney. The pediatric center in Brescia defined it as malignant. A risky surgery was necessary since its position was so close to the nerve bundles that could impair the lower joints.

The night before the operation, while in the play room of the hospital, I casually picked up the leaflet *Conosci?*[143] and I read about the people who had benefited from Sister Troncatti's help.

One case struck me, for it was so similar to ours, for it dealt with removing a tumor that had grown on a vein. Then and there I turned with great faith to Sister Troncatti, extending my prayers right through the operation on the next morning. After two hours the doctor came out to reassure me that the massive tumor was removed without any damage to the tissues or the nearby organs. Further tests proved that the tumor was benign. Now, six months later, my child is perfectly well, thanks to the assistance of Sister Maria Troncatti.

---

[143] "Do You Know?"

A final sample of cures being attributed to Mother Maria's prayer intercession since her death is reported by another nun from Guayaquil, Ecuador. The nun has a married sister who has had rheumatic fever for a long time and has been at this point hospitalized for more than three months with heart complications. Permitted to go home, almost at once she must return to the Pasteur Clinic in Quito because of "grave cardiac insufficiency with obstruction of two heart valves." She has already had heart surgery; now she must have another operation, but just the catheterization tests cause her situation to deteriorate so seriously that the surgery must be postponed for fifteen days.

After the six-and-a-half-hour surgery, the married woman's condition only becomes more critical day by day. "Each morning," the nun writes, "as I arrived to visit her, I found new and painful surprises." When loss of consciousness, at first hoped to be only a transitory effect of the anesthesia, proves persistent, the nun and other sisters begin a novena to Mother Maria Troncatti, asking her prayers.

But her sister's condition seems only to worsen. She begins to have attacks of a type of epilepsy and then goes completely blind. At this point her sister says: "I put a relic of Sister Maria near the bedside of the patient praying with new insistence, 'I trust you, Sister Maria. You who in this world never spared yourself to do good, pray my sister gets back her vision and is cured.'"

The next morning the sick woman can see light. Gradually her sight returns until it is once more normal, but she is still not out of the woods. Not only is her entire right side paralyzed, but a grave hemorrhage re-opens the surgical incision and almost proves fatal. Still the ill woman's sister writes, "Our prayers continued, constant and faith-filled." And finally the failing body begins to stabilize and convalesce.

When she is ultimately discharged, the bill is stupendous after so many days in such critical condition. But a benefactor comes forward and pays everything, to the nun's joy in God's beneficence. She ends her account: "Two years passed and my sister was truly well. A last surprise we attribute to Sister Maria's prayers, a gift of joy for the whole family: my sister had a daughter, healthy and strong. This gift of God is the more precious because the doctors had forbidden any thought of pregnancy after the last heart surgery and also told my sister later that her anti-coagulant medication must make the prohibition permanent."

More testimonies could be given, but these must do so there is room for the cure accepted as the official beatification miracle when Mother Troncatti became Bl. Maria Troncatti on November 23, 2012. Fittingly, since in life she had given herself for the men, women, and children of Ecuador, the cure obtained from God went to an Ecuadorean wife and mother of five young children. Josefa Yolanda Solórzano Pisco lay dying in 2002 from one of the most dangerous forms of malaria. Plasmodium falciparum—its medical title—is the most deadly of the five forms of malaria, the one from which almost all deaths result. In Josefa the disease quickly led to an irreversible degenerative process. In other words everything in Josefa Pisco's body was failing.

When Salesian priest Fr. Edgar Ivan Segarra was called in to give the last rites, the patient had at worst a few hours, at best a few days, to live. Fr. Edgar, had a typical Salesian compassionate heart for children. He thought of those five little ones about to lose their mom. He gave the rites but also proposed a novena for the prayer intercession of Venerable Mother Troncatti. As you probably know, a novena [from the Latin word for nine] is nine consecutive days of prayer for a particular intention. Josefa likely didn't even have nine *hours*, but the novena was started. Hours, then days went by, and rather than dying, the young mother got better until she had, against every expectation, recovered. The recovery having been the fruit of prayer, not medical treatment, was affirmed by first Ecuadorian diocesan authorities, then by the Medical Consultative Committee of the Congregation for the Causes of Saints in Rome.

More numerous than her many cures in life and death, however, are the memories and testimonies, among those who knew her, of Maria Troncatti's courage in the face of hardship and danger, her resourcefulness in doing good with seemingly nothing at her disposal, and above all her charity, which finds a way to give when there is literally nothing left to give. Typical is her friends' memory, recounted in *Beloved Jungle*, of the time when the nuns and their charges were facing starvation at Sevilla and a man led a three-year-old girl up to Mother Maria.

"My wife left and I'm sick," he said. "You take her." Eagerly Mother Maria reached for the child, exclaiming, "Anther blessing from heaven!"

"Another mouth to feed, you mean," snorted another nun behind her.

"Goodness gracious!" Mother Maria turned her pitifully thin frame to the equally gaunt worrier. "Let us have a little more faith, Sister!"

In every need, that was her answer: turn trustingly to God. Like every saint, she would insist of any cures attributed to her, "They are all the work of His hands."

Chapter 22

Nothing Is Beyond God's Power to Heal —
AIDS, Death, Dying, Loss . . .

Miracles of healing are going on all the time and all around us wherever on the globe we live. Some are so extraordinary they are hard to believe. But, hopefully, at this point, you can make that leap of faith — even when it is a stretch — to belief in God's miracles through His saints, not simplistically, but in cases verified by the Church's stringent examination and / or attested by reliable, first-person witnesses. Just as every saint highlights some attribute of God, a miracle may offer a particular aspect of God not previously considered. This is just one way in which a miracle is not just for the recipient and that individual's life circle. Like those healings done by Jesus during His life which still speak powerfully through the Scripture reports, every miracle is for the rest of us too. This chapter and the next three offer a sampling of events of our time, each of which may have some message for you whether it is simply the reality of unseen miracles in our midst, the power of the compassion of God's saints, the truth that God's miracles through saints, if asked for, may go to individuals whose culture and spiritual traditions are far from the Judeo-Christian, and over all these events the compassion of God Himself. Finally, there is the reminder even believers need: that no condition is impossible for God to cure. As Venerable Solanus Casey said to a woman struggling to believe healing from a serious disease like hers was possible, "Don't you know God can cure cancer just as easily as the common cold?" May the smorgasbord of these last chapters, along with the entire book, feed your soul, reader, and — through you — others!

The young, terribly emaciated AIDS patient lies listlessly in bed. He has returned home — a tough trip — to his native country from another

African nation. (I am regretfully removing many details, even changing his name because of his anxiety to protect his privacy.) His doctors at the hospital where he was being treated have counseled terminally ill Phillip to make the trip back to his homeland so he can die among his family. Br. Phillip had been studying for the priesthood with a religious order, when the disease, which has an incubation period of eight or nine years, manifested itself. The young man is now not that far from the end. He can barely lift his legs from peripheral neuritis, for one thing. Like anyone dying of AIDS, he needs a lot of care, which his family members are doing their best to provide.

Phillip's country, like most of Africa, is very poor. Like many, young Phillip not that many years earlier had set out for another nation that was poor too, but less poor, and known as having jobs. Terribly home-sick, he had run out of funds before reaching the city where he hoped to find work. A Catholic, he went to the main church in the place where he happened to find himself. Staffed by the religious order he would later join, Phillip was given shelter and offered the money to go home in exchange for a few days' labor. Back at home, he kept in touch with his benefactors by the occasional letter or phone call. He felt God calling him to become a priest himself. Accepted by this community, he re-turned to them, settled in, and quickly learned the local language even as he progressed in his priestly studies. Then came the disease, most likely the fruit — charitably none of his religious community asked — of some long-ago teenage sexual act.

AIDS was a main cause of death in his native country in 1996, as in so many African nations at that time. But his home parish was not will-ing to let this promising young member die with only prayers for not too torturous a death. Phillip's favorite saint, "the one with whose charism he identified most" was an obscure Italian, Bl. Luigi Scrosoppi. Parish-ioners began to seek the prayer intercession of Bl. Luigi. The religious community of the young sufferer joined in, also praying that Bl. Luigi would go to God on behalf of the young man. Let God heal Phillip of AIDS in honor of God's friend Scrosoppi.

Few people had heard of Luigi Scrosoppi. Nor have many heard of him today. He was in the modern era but not a recent figure, having died at eighty in 1884. Besides founding the Sisters of Providence of St. Ca-jetan of Thiene to shelter orphaned girls, he was like many priest saints, known for humble, self-giving charity that showed itself in heroic service to the poor, the sick, and other needy. It was an anti-priest area and era. Yet even a virulently anti-Catholic paper, detailing his undertakings, exclaimed, "As impossible as it appears this philanthropist is a priest!" and unknowingly pierced the heart of Scrosoppi's life when they described his motive: "zeal, as God's minister, to do good to his neighbor."

So far then, Luigi Scrosoppi is like his contemporary Don Bosco and many other nineteenth-century saints. But he had his unique qualities too. In an era when men in general looked down on women as incompetent to do anything without a man's direction—as humble as he was wise—Luigi made one of the Providence Sisters his spiritual director. On his deathbed, this master of humility wanted to say goodbye, not just to the priests in his community or to them and the sisters but to the gardener and the other lowly members of the sisters' establishment too.

Bl. Luigi and Phillip, in the timelessness of God's eternal present, were brothers in their concern for these lowliest members of God's human family. Still Scrosoppi was a late nineteenth-century Italian who lived long before AIDS existed—or the nation Phillip lived in for that matter. As many people prayed for the dead priest's prayer intercession, Phillip one night dreamed of Bl. Luigi. The compassionate Italian priest assured the dying African seminarian of Phillip's healing. The next morning, after what may be called a simple dream, or may be seen as a dream in the directive biblical sense experienced by Jesus' foster father, Joseph, Phillip woke feeling well. With no impediment from the polyneuritis that hours before had disabled his lower limbs, he leapt out of bed. Emaciated, yes, but his whole being felt as it had before AIDS. Medical examination exposed the simple reason for that: Phillip didn't have AIDS anymore. Soon he was back at his priestly studies.

Perhaps you find believing in an AIDS miracle tough. It may help that, not just local medical men, but the medical investigators of the Vatican as well, agreed that Phillip no longer had AIDS and "miracle" was the only answer to the sudden total cure. Passing all seven tests, it became the miracle for Scrosoppi's canonization.

As this is written in 2010 another priest, who knows him, described Phillip, now Fr. Phillip, as "a very pastoral priest," thus following in the footsteps of St. Luigi. He did not remain with the religious community, however. Discernment either showed that this was not his priestly call or that he and the community would never be able to get on with the works of a priest if he remained where he could easily be identified as the world's first verified AIDS miracle. The author has spoken with Fr. Phillip and can say from this first-hand knowledge that he is alive and well and works somewhere in Africa, as a good, celibate priest.

He was not the only one affected by his cure. A group of priests who knew about it began to study this St. Luigi. "The miracle is continuing in our community," one told me. He said before they studied St. Luigi they lived comfortable lives in a nice house, serving middle-class people like themselves. Today they live among the very needy, housed along with their soup kitchen and various other ministries—including to street children and juvenile delinquents—in a derelict factory.

Another outgrowth of the miracle: the saint's order of women, which had no members in that country, was drawn to work with these priests too. Five sisters—one each from Italy, Rumania, and Togo and two from India—plus a first local vocation, make up the six-woman team that is improving life for an entire community. Phillip was saved from AIDS for a life of service and to remind others with AIDS that God is with them, not against them; but his miracle has become, as the priest I spoke to puts it, "a continuing miracle" for countless others.

Nothing is impossible for God to heal. This is wonderful, but there is more. Even those of us who receive miracles will be birthed out of this life into the next at some point.

You have most likely already read the chapter of this book devoted to a sampling of the numerous graces relating to health continuing at the shrine of St. John Neumann, even after his canonization. But there is one area I referred to only briefly in that chapter—the final healing of death.

St. John Neumann, who had a heart attack and died on the sidewalk age forty-eight while returning from an errand of charity, died comparatively young. He had assisted plenty of his multinational flock in their dying during his lifetime, with his God-given gift for speaking roughly a dozen languages not his own. And he continues, with many other saints to assist the dying in the present day. My long-time neighbor Judith Hodgins of Calabasas, California, is from Philadelphia originally, having met her husband, Bob, when he was attending Villanova University and she, as Judith Phillips, was a student at Rosemont College there.

When Judy was still in high school, her maternal grandfather, Ferenz (Frank) Hoch-Olbricht of Bayville, New Jersey, then in his mid-seventies, was diagnosed with stomach cancer. Judy recalls this "very gentle and kind—probably too much so—grandfather" as "a very devout Catholic." The granddaughter of this immigrant from Czechoslovakia remembers he "had desperately wanted to be a priest but there was no money for him to go [to the seminary]." Instead his income as a finish carpenter was needed to help support his family in the old country. Sacrificing his own dream, with some of the money he sent home from America, a sister was enabled to become a nun. When he retired to Bayville, Frank had been a founding member of a new parish where he did a lot of free finish work in the church he helped get built.

His diagnosis left his relatives deeply distressed—and not just because he was terminally ill. They understood people get old and die. But this disease as the *means* of death ran in the family, and Frank's sister, daughter, and others feared that, like their other kin who had died of it, he faced a particularly *painful* death. A devout Catholic like her father, Judith's mother, with her curious teenage daughter in tow, time and again during the year-long period of the family patriarch's illness, roughly mid-1964 to his death in mid-1965, took the train into downtown Philadelphia. She would walk over to the shrine connected to St. Peter's Church and there—filled with hope—ask then Bl. John Neumann's intercession that Judy's grandpa suffer no pain. And he never did. The extended family were joyfully astounded. But no one began thinking of it as a miracle until after the devout Czech-American's death. Then his hospital nurses shared their amazement: they confirmed the family's experience that death from this type of cancer was in the mid-1960s accompanied by great pain and suffering. Yet they had seen with their own eyes that this patient had been pain free all the way to death.

Although Judy is now a grandmother herself, she has never forgotten this family event in which she was a more curious than expectant prayer participant at age seventeen—a family "miracle" representative of so many graces through a saint that are known only to the life circle of the recipient. Following the death and the nurse's amazement, the mother-daughter twosome went back to Neumann's shrine with great joy to say prayers of thanksgiving. "We were overwhelmed with gratitude," says Judy. She also continues to remember that, even as a high school senior, with her mind on all the things young girls think about, the shrine touched her. She recalls a place of peaceful serenity and "spiritual emanations" that left her "full of spiritual contentment. We always felt," she concludes "more peaceful when we left and blessed that we had the shrine there for us to visit."

The late Fr. Charles Fehrenbach of St. John Neumann's shrine told me of Brian Baker, a tiny child with terminal cancer, who received a wonderful cure through Neumann. Three years later cancer returned in a different form and the little boy died. A man of remarkable faith himself, Fr. Charles was awed by the serenity of the parents. "We could not have dealt with our child dying" at the earlier time, they explained to Fr. Fehrenbach. They felt in some mysterious way, certainly not the simplistic one that he changed God's mind but perhaps, expressing a profound idea crudely, that drawing on some spiritual treasury related to the sacrificial life John Neumann lived for others, God had honored Neumann by giving their family those three years with their son, time needed to move into a larger view of life and death. Perhaps they now knew, as Neumann's good friend and fellow holy man Fr. Seelos once assured grieving parents: "Your child is not lost to you; your child is saved for you for all eternity" (p. 161). Or to put it another way, perhaps they now saw that the purpose of this life is preparation for something much bigger, much more wonderful. Some of us take decades and even then will need further growth or throwing away of excess baggage in an antechamber to Heaven. Others, right down to the very young (see p. 72 for one child like this), seem to do their "studies" in a flash and, unburdened, move right on.

I hope these stories from the dozens in my files regarding St. John Neumann will give you, Catholics and non, some perhaps new thoughts on death and some idea of why a lot of people love to visit shrines,[144] places made holy, as young Judith Phillips experienced, by their association with men and women who lived for God and remain at work as His instruments after death.

---

[144] There are many saints' shrines in North America. Not so many as in Europe which has six thousand Church-approved shrines, according to Vatican-approved Florida healer Francis McNutt, yet shrines still dot the United States, Mexico, and Canada. One may also "visit" through the web, through the bulletins put out by many of them, or by writing to them for prayer.

Chapter 23

Miracles Here, There, and Everywhere
—Across Time and Space Too

Zbigniew Chojnowski is a well-educated economist and director of the public bus system in the largest city of his part of Poland. A nice-looking married man, he has a smile that leaps from a photo to make the viewer smile too. Zbig is also a great friend, in God, of a priest named Stanislaus Papczynski, who died in 1701. Stanislaus lived basically in the seventeenth century, so two centuries before St. Luigi Scrosoppi. He has been dead then *a long time.* The pair met through Zbig's reading about the other's life and the many favors,[145] including medical, he is still obtaining for people from God.

The reader at this point will not need a long explanation of how spiritual friendships, special affinities, can link those far separated in earthly time. But it will not hurt to say two things. First, that these friendships have many spiritual benefits for the living partner. Zbig, for instance, says, "I don't have any mystical experiences, [but] I have my inner experiences with Fr. Stanislaus." Then he adds wisely, "It's nothing that others don't experience. I consider him my patron, my intercessor. That's it." Under "inner experiences," I think it's reasonable to assume lots of God's work in Zbig. Second, these relationships may be used by God, beyond those personal spiritual benefits, to fulfill other wonderful purposes of God.

Here is an example from Zbigniew Chojnowski's relationship with Stanislaus:

---

[145] These may also be found as a regular feature of the magazine from the United States Divine Mercy shrine.

Zbig has a cousin who is also his goddaughter. In March 2001, the young married woman was two months pregnant. The previous year she had been pregnant too and lost that baby in a miscarriage. At the end of March, Zbig learned that his cousin was in the hospital, her pregnancy threatened. Immediately he turned to his heavenly friend for prayer. He asked other friends, his charismatic prayer group, and family members to do the same. The prayer group, especially, had had a number of striking instances where they had asked Fr. Stanislaus's prayers for people—with problems from cancers to alcohol addiction—and healing had followed. Zbig never doubted the connection with Fr. Stanislaus because the cures usually came as a novena ended or immediately after. (Remember, a novena is just praying for something nine days straight, either addressing God directly or asking a saint in Heaven to pray with you or intercede for you, however you like to think of it.) Zbig says sincerely, "I have seen many miracles through the intercession of ... Stanislaus—some small, some big."

In this instance, two days after Zbig and others began appealing to the dead priest for prayers, his cousin was released from the hospital, her pregnancy intact. Everyone breathed a sigh of relief. But two days later, a Sunday, she was hospitalized again with severe abdominal pain. This time the news could not have been worse: the amniotic sac had shrunk. Due to a tear, almost all the amniotic fluid had leaked away. The baby, it was now discovered, had not been growing normally due to an inadequate blood flow through the umbilical cord. In-utero testing verifying there was no heartbeat just confirmed the obvious. The baby, a boy, was dead. With that formal declaration by the doctor, the only thing left was to hope miscarriage would be spontaneous.

Zbig heard the sad news but he didn't stop the novena or change his prayer request to Stanislaus on behalf of his cousin and her child.

On Wednesday, April 4, 2001, there had still been no spontaneous miscarriage. The doctor decided to remove the dead infant. But just before the surgery, an ultrasound showed a heartbeat. Excitedly, more tests were done. Not only was the baby alive, but the tear in the sac had mended and the blood was flowing as it ought to through the umbilical cord.

It was the eighth day of Zbig's novena.

Baby Sebastian was born in perfect health October 17, 2001.

Because no medical explanation could be found for what had taken place, Zbig's friendship with the dead priest ended up doing even more than bringing his cousin God's help. On the basis of that healing, Venerable Fr. Stanislaus—whose heroic virtues had been recognized some time earlier—became *Blessed* Stanislaus Papczynski on September 16, 2007, beatified by Pope Benedict XVI in Lichen, Poland.

An almost-six-year-old Sebastian—very spiffy in his pinstripe suit—with the help of his parents, brought his dead benefactor's relic to the altar .Wisely, his parents have saved the story of his miracle birth to tell him when he can better understand it. It is to help them do this that the beginning of this story does not give the name of the city where Zbig carries on his friendship with God and Bl. Stanislaus or name Sebastian's parents.

There is no reason, however, not to quote Zbig one more time: "We live in a world," he says, "where there are many miracles around [us]. Usually we don't see them, and even if we do, we usually don't offer thanks for them."

Those who do offer thanks often report favors through Bl. Stanislaus to the Marians of the Immaculate Conception's shrine to Divine Mercy in Stockbridge, Massachusetts. This men's thriving religious order regards Stanislaus Papczynski as their founder and has a regular column of these letters in their quarterly magazine, *The Marian Helper*. A sample comes from a woman living in Baden, Pennsylvania. Her letter shows a saint not only not bound by time but not bound by space either. Bl. Stanislaus certainly never visited the area later called Pennsylvania. Referring to Bl. Stanislaus's reputation for helping troubled pregnancies and babies, this grandmother reported she requested the saint's prayers for her granddaughter then in utero. Doctors offered the parents abortion as, they said, the child had Dandy-Walker syndrome with hydrocephalus. They also said the baby was deficient in brain matter due to the fluid that accompanies this syndrome in the ventricles leading to the brain. Physically and mentally, the medical verdict: if the pregnancy was not "terminated," the baby would have a short lifespan, severely handicapped both physically and mentally. The parents refused the abortion. Baby Kamryn was born June 14, 2008, her grandmother reports, having neither hydrocephalus nor fluid-filled ventricles. Praising

God and thanking the saint for his prayers, her grandmother rejoices that the newborn "was perfect physically."

Yes, Bl. Stanislaus is one of many saints dead a long time, as we imagine death, but alive and active in God.

Chapter 24

The Saint Who Won an Emmy
—Talking about God

God has friends in places little connected with Him in the public mind. Would you believe an American proposed for official sainthood whose prime time television show brought him an Emmy[146]—for talking about God yet!

TV star Fulton John Sheen's heroic virtue was recognized with the title Venerable in June 2012. You know well by now that it is God's approval through a miracle that permits a beatification. In this Cause miracles seem in good supply. So beatification could come soon. When it does Archbishop Fulton J. Sheen may have the distinction of ending up with not just one shrine but two.

This is because Sheen died in a diocese with lots of other holy to push toward official sainthood, and he did not belong to a religious order that might have spurred a Cause. Proponents of one went to Bishop Daniel Jenky, C.S.C., head of the Diocese of Peoria, Illinois. A Cause could be opened in that diocese because Sheen—the oldest of his Illinois family's four sons—was born and raised within its boundaries and ordained for the diocese, where some of his family still live. Sheen, however, lent by his Illinois bishop to teach for the benefit of the larger Church, spent his adult life in other places, a good swath of the latter part of it in New York, first (1951-1965) as an auxiliary bishop of New York, then (1966-1969) as Bishop of Rochester. Praying at the celebrity archbishop's grave in the crypt under the high altar of New York City's

---

[146] The industry's highest accolade. His in 1952 was as Most Outstanding Television Personality.

St. Patrick's Cathedral has been limited to special occasions, such as the Mass said by Cardinal Timothy Dolan a few months after he took over the diocese in 2009. That commemorated the thirtieth anniversary of Sheen's death. The inaccessibility of the burial place could change with beatification as well, as the grave[147] becomes a New York shrine to Fulton Sheen, in addition to one, no doubt, in Peoria.[148]

When it does, a religious-order priest may lead the parade of those rejoicing. No one is more enthusiastic about the holiness of Archbishop Sheen—he was given the title in his last years as a sort of "well done"—than vice-postulator for the Peoria-run Cause, New York–state priest Andrew Apostoli, C.F.R. Fr. Apostoli, a communicator himself, on Catholic television among other places, was ordained by Sheen and loves to tell stories that highlight Sheen's virtue and achievements.

Not only a widely read author, the native of El Paso, Illinois, was famous for *Life Is Worth Living*, his television show seen by millions when there were only three networks (ABC, NBC, and CBS) in the United States and the whole country seemed to park itself before "the tube" nightly. Although one of television's biggest stars, full of personal charisma, with a sense of the dramatic that could make viewers weep, as well as wit and a sense of comedy that evoked bubbles of laughter, Sheen was also revered among those, like Apostoli, who looked past the show for his spiritual attributes: primarily his deep love of Christ exemplified, among other ways, by his unfailingly spending an hour a day—he called it a Holy Hour—in prayer before the eucharistic Christ. Apostoli says that when he saw Sheen, he wanted to be like him—not the celebrity aspect but "the man of God."

Sheen was also known, too, in an unecumenical era for turning from enemies to friends the other three big-name religious figures in the United States: "the nation's pastor," proponent of "positive thinking" Presbyterian Norman Vincent Peale of famous Riverside Drive Church in New York; world-traveling evangelist Billy Graham; and evangelical

---

[147] There is some possibility of the body's being moved to Peoria, but even if that occurs, a New York shrine is likely.

[148] Inside the Museums of the Catholic Diocese of Peoria in that city is the Archbishop Sheen Museum, which, after beatification, could be given shrine status; in El Paso, Illinois, Sheen's birthplace, is another non-profit, the volunteer-staffed Fulton Sheen Illinois Museum and Spiritual Centre. Both are run by people with great devotion to Sheen.

mega-church pioneer Robert Schuller of California. Graham for years in his crusades tried to "rescue" Catholics, and Peale and Schuller, too, were from anti-Catholic denominations. If many Protestants believed Catholics doomed, many Catholics, as well, cheerfully consigned "the other side" to Hell. Sheen's unusual take was that all Protestant-Catholic fights "were lovers' quarrels" and he maintained, practically alone during the era, "The closer we come to the heart of the One we love, the closer we come to each other." His personal charm did the rest, and these three outstanding Protestant Christians became his comrades in Christ. Sheen was also known for his stand against racism when that form of non-love, too, was accepted by most people.

It was Billy Graham—no slouch himself at communicating Christ —who said, "Sheen was the greatest communicator of the twentieth century." Looking at Sheen's background, this is surprising. When he started his educational path to the priesthood, the successful business-man's[149] son's potential for scholarship, not for communicating to huge groups of ordinary people, was what drew attention. Sent to be educated at some of the world's foremost schools, the University of Louvain in Belgium, the Sorbonne in Paris, and the Angelicum in Rome, he was the first American at Louvain to win the prestigious Cardinal Mercier Prize for International Philosophy.

He came back to America and, after three years in his home diocese,[150] began to teach theology and philosophy at Washington DC's Catholic University as an educationally sophisticated intellectual of proven brilliance. Yet he would become known for the ability—often by coining witty and pithy sayings—"to explain spirituality and the Catholic faith in ways that everyone could understand." And he did it first on radio—so it wasn't his striking good looks that had people hanging on his words. That was as early as 1930, when he began a Sunday-night broadcast called *The Catholic Hour*. Sponsored by the Church, for twenty years he taught Catholicism that way. From 1951 he "starred" on

---

[149] Because he owned two farms and sent his sons to work on them summers, it is sometimes said in error, Fulton was "a farmer's son."

[150] Before giving him to the larger Church, Sheen's bishop first tested him on humility and obedience by sending him as an assistant to the pastor of a poor, struggling parish. Sheen not only went without a murmur, but, under the pastor, revitalized the congregation.

television. On TV he taught Life and why it is worth living—a subject which led to God through every topic imaginable. In that anti-Catholic era, 1951 to 1957, there he was before millions, mostly non-Catholics, in full—some would say exaggerated—Catholic regalia: black clerical garb, a large crucifix on his chest, and a big magenta cape flowing behind him. In down-to-earth, humorous talks about life's basics, aimed at people of every faith or none, his soft-sell approach won friends for Christ and the Church, his converts too many to detail. And he won the prime-time-ratings battle as well over stars on at the same time, such as funnyman Milton Berle, who quipped, "He's not bad for a guy using old material [referring to the Scriptures]."

All his life Fulton Sheen had outshone everyone around him with intellectual brilliance, charm, looks, and success. He grappled at times with vanity and attraction to "the good life" of the celebrity, succeeding, according to the judgment of observers, in conquering those only too human tendencies to live for Christ, not self. Then at the height of the TV celebrity's fame, when he was achieving remarkable things for Christ on and off the screen, God permitted that through no fault of Sheen's, he was stripped of everything he had achieved through the work of a powerful enemy. *Treasure in Clay*, Sheen's autobiography, written some years later, reports many things this individual did *for* Sheen over the years. About the painful betrayal, there is not even a hint. Shorn of even his beloved Society for the Propagation of the Faith—for which he had raised millions, donating all his TV income—he was shuffled off to lead a diocese.

Trying to serve as a diocesan bishop either did not suit his gifts or others did not appreciate them. Either way, his last years were difficult ones, as if Christ were polishing this gem via tribulation to shine even more brightly. Happily both Paul VI and John Paul II showed their appreciation, Paul by making him an archbishop when he left the diocese to return to being a roving ambassador for Christ and John Paul with an embrace and words of commendation from one brilliant communicator to another on the pope's trip to the United States just months before Sheen's death.

Twenty-four years after his death and burial at St. Patrick's Cathedral as a bishop of New York, his Cause was opened in September 2003 by the Peoria Diocese. His case is a good example of two things I mentioned in the introduction: first, that someone with no observable healing gifts during his/her lifetime, when God wants the individual to receive the honors of beatification and, perhaps, canonization, will be the focus of cures after death; secondly, among the many healings going on at all times, seemingly invisibly to the world in general, are cures through the intercession of those whose Causes are under way, such cures sent to Rome in the early stages of a Cause as signs that God is interested in this individual's being held up to others as a role model (p. xxiii).

Already in the summer of 2006, when the Cause for this Servant of God was only open three years, there were two cures of a magnitude to potentially qualify as official miracles—and definitely, in any case, worth sending to Rome. Following ceremonies in Peoria and in Pittsburgh, for each of the healings respectively, the Cause's Rome-based postulator, Andréa Ambrosi, present at both, hand carried them to the Congregation for the Causes of Saints.

The first healing recipient was Therese Kearney of Champaign, Illinois, then in her early seventies. During a surgery in 1999, Mrs. Kearney suffered a tear in her pulmonary artery. Told his wife would probably not make it, Frank Kearney, a long-time admirer of the media star priest, sought Sheen's prayer intercession. (Sheen at this time had been dead twenty years.) His wife lived, and this was considered something beyond what medicine could have done. The couple died in 2006, seven years later, he in February and she, at age 79, in September. But the healing had already survived the diocesan-level vetting. Details of her cure—over five hundred pages of medical data and testimonies by the witnesses, who included the doctors involved, a nurse, a priest, and family members—had been assembled under Msgr. Richard Soseman, as delegate of the bishop of Peoria. Packed and sealed in a witnessed ceremony, just five days after Therese Kearney's death, the records were officially turned over to the postulator for transport to Rome.

Postulator Ambrosi made a second stop for similar ceremonies in Pittsburgh. There he picked up a thousand pages of meticulous testimony and medical records on the cure of a seriously ill infant boy whose family belong to the Ukrainian Diocese of St. Josaphat in Parma, Ohio. The Catholic Ukrainian diocese is small and without either the personnel or financial resources to conduct the necessary investigation of a cure. The Pittsburgh diocese took over for them. While details of the infant's cure were withheld, Fr. Ambrosi said only that the baby was "gravely ill" when his parents sought Archbishop Sheen's prayer intercession. Vice-postulator Fr. Andrew Apostoli has said the infant had three life-threatening conditions, one of which was the worst form of sepsis. The fact of this being a cure from God, not from medical means, was supported by the main doctors involved in the case. "All of them," Ambrosi concluded, "recognized that a force superior to their medical science intervened for his [the infant's] recovery."

About four years later, in 2010, another infant is also said to have received a miracle, this one in Peoria. The facts actually made public, with the cooperation of the family, when Sheen was named Venerable in 2012 show the devotion Sheen can inspire.

Bonnie Engstrom and her family live in a small central-Illinois town not that far from El Paso, Illinois, the little town where Sheen was born. Bonnie had a special feeling for then Servant of God Sheen, she explains, precisely because he was "born in this small insignificant town, El Paso, followed God's will in his life, and became a great instrument of the Lord." To Bonnie, this showed "it doesn't matter where you're from." She and her husband, Travis, agreed that the child of her current pregnancy would be James Fulton, the middle name honoring Sheen. Throughout this pregnancy, as she went about her daily chores as wife and mother, Bonnie also sought the prayer support of the dead TV-star evangelist.

But during James Fulton's birth at the family home that September (2010), Fulton Sheen did not actually seem to be proving much of a friend: a previously undetected knot in the umbilical cord became so tight during delivery that the baby was born blue, without pulse or breath. Mother and the stillborn baby were rushed by ambulance to St. Francis Medical Center in Peoria.

Engstrom remembers chanting Fulton Sheen's name over and over as a team of doctors and nurses worked on the baby. It seemed fruitless, and the ER group prepared to pronounce the Engstrom infant dead when suddenly his heart began to beat.

Today, apparently no worse for his harrowing birth because he is developing normally, James — along with his mother — is now a kind of star himself since mother and child are playing a role in their heavenly friend's ascent to official sainthood. On the other hand, the small-town tyke is also, to his family's joy, just like his older siblings.

As for Bonnie Engstrom, she finds her faith affirmed that God does work miracles. "Every milestone [in development] he has crossed was a milestone we thought he wouldn't achieve," she says with a kind of awe. The miracle of her stillborn baby's not only returning to life but being undamaged has touched her in other ways too. One is that the mother of what today is considered a large family appreciates her vocation "a lot more." She says when she sees her children do something, such as James, who should be dead, shaking toys at her, trying to be cute, she is able "to appreciate all those little moments more."

Time will tell which of the cures being studied in Rome, this one, the two others, or one yet to come, proves the beatification miracle. There are other cures not chosen for Rome, apparently. Vice-postulator Fr. Andrew Apostoli notes that an extraordinary number of cases where people report the archbishop's intercession involve infants.

Thinking about these and the elderly woman's or the Ohio infant's cures, if neither of the latter becomes the beatification miracle, two physician-proclaimed miracles that took place in our time and maybe not that far away from where you live may just fade away. Will the day ever come, for instance, in this new climate in which miracle recipients often have to be or choose to be protected, when you and I learn the details that caused more than one doctor to credit something beyond what medical skill can do for saving the seriously ill Ohio baby? Even James's survival — in spite of being in the news — could one day soon be remembered by those close to him alone. Only one thing is sure: each of these events is an example of the miracles most of us will never be aware of and yet, as miracle "middleman" Zbig Chojnowski puts it, are going on all around us.

Chapter 25

Mother and Intercessor for *All*

Holy people known, loved, and *seen* 'round the world — international figures you watch on the news who sometimes turn up in person in the country where you live until they seem almost as familiar as your friends — were new in the twentieth century. Like her admiring friend John Paul II, Mother Teresa of Calcutta was a household name.

"Mother! Mother!" people cried when her smiling face and familiar figure in its white sari edged with bands of blue — topped if it were cold by the shapeless, drab old sweater — emerged from a vehicle or perhaps from some unimpressive building housing a group of her spiritual children. Those children might be dressed like her, members of the Missionaries of Charity, or they might be members of one of her two men's congregations, her cloistered women's order, the organization of ill and disabled laypeople who backed her works up with prayer support, or other Catholic groups who considered her their leader. These all were made up of individuals striving for holiness by serving, either directly or through prayer, all those (p. 25) John Paul II so loved, the littlest and the least among us. Although she probably never thought of it, these vibrant followers of Jesus out to slake His thirst for souls through loving service to any in need, were, in God, Mother Teresa's huge gift to the Church.

But, on a scale not seen before the twentieth century, Mother Teresa was also a huge gift to the world outside the Church, a Catholic saint nurturing large numbers of non-Catholic spiritual children too.

In a supranatural way, the Albanian-born citizen of India can be seen as a mother to all. First in India, then later to countries all over the globe, favoring the neediest ones or those where war or other crises left a flotsam of misery, she brought her smile, which was not dependent on how she felt but her gift to God and her trust in God's providence. Like a loving mother, she tended the family—not just the Catholic family but, it often seemed, the whole human family.

When this writer watched her on TV somehow—much later I read it was done completely by prayer[151]—get civil-war combatants in West Beirut to cease shelling and bombing long enough for her to rush into a building caught in the battle zone to comfort and rescue (via Red Cross ambulances) thirty-eight mentally and physically disabled Muslim youths, ages seven to twenty-one, and those of their equally terrified caregivers who had not abandoned them, I sighed with the kind of relief people feel when things in life look black and Mom turns up to help.

The best mothers turn toward, not away from, the child in big trouble. In 1985 Mother received a plea from an American doctor for help. At that time in the United States, AIDS sufferers—even children or adults who got the virus from blood transfusions—were as feared and rejected, Mother found, as her leper children in India. She wasted no time. In what was called "the miracle of Manhattan" she opened a hostel, staffed by five of her Missionaries of Charity sisters, so men dying of AIDS, who were pariahs to their own families, had somewhere to die receiving loving care. Typically, officials who had been deaf to all previous pleas, on hers released three young dying men from their prison cells so she could do the same for them. Mother was not approving any actions or lifestyles; nor, she said, did she have any call to establish blame or guilt. Her aim: succoring Jesus in another of His many distressing disguises. As so often, her unconditional love changed people. Healthy people were in some cases inspired to take up ministry to AIDS sufferers (although she and the work received opposition too).

As for the patients, for those who wanted it, there was periodic religious instruction and the sisters had Mass and the Rosary for themselves each day in the chapel with its crucifix and placard of Jesus' words: "I thirst." The men could join in any part of this they desired—or not. In every situation where people faced death, Mother's charge to her followers was to give the love that will enable individuals to make their

---

[151] Kathryn Spink, *Mother Teresa: A Complete Authorized Biography* (San Francisco: Harper, 1997), 189. John Paul II, who requested she go to Lebanon in solidarity with all its sufferers, was perhaps praying too.

peace with God. Mother later joyfully shared being with one of the men who recognized her as his friend and confided joining each of his sufferings to Christ's. She was with him in the chapel as he spoke tenderly aloud to Jesus with love. Such moments were balm to her soul. What she did not share, because it would have been self-promotion, anathema to her, was that AIDS patients the Missionaries cared for who came to their deaths having undergone a complete turnaround in their relationship with God, most often did so because, through Mother and her daughters, they had experienced God's love.[152]

Dramatic rescue missions and thousands of quieter ones got her eventually tapped by a bunch of non-Catholic Swedes in that generally nonreligious country for the Nobel Peace Prize. Her works of love for her "spouse," as she called Jesus, also put her on the cover of the American magazine *Time* and other publications in the western world by editors usually practicing no religion. Books on her always found buyers.

How did one obscure woman arrive at this point? Originally an Albanian citizen and twenty-year-member of an Irish teaching order working in India, Teresa received permission, after much struggle — interior[153] and exterior — to leave the Sisters of Loreto, a congregation in which she was loved and very happy. She founded the Missionaries of Charity, answering a call given her first in 1946 during a profound spiritual experience on a train and continuing over several years of ongoing encounters with Jesus. Throughout her life, she tried and managed well to keep these experiences quiet,[154] lest they deflect attention from Jesus to Teresa. Today we know in those mystical dialogues Jesus asked Teresa to slake His thirst on the Cross for souls, millions not loving Him, He sorrowed, because they didn't know Him.

Yet He took her out of her Catholic institution where she longed to stay and placed her in a basically Hindu slum[155] to somehow live this out. (Many American Catholics today feel beleaguered and would like

[152] Spink, *Mother Teresa: A Complete Authorized Biography*, 203-210. These pages also report both the expansion of and opposition to this work.

[153] See the full account in *Mother Teresa: Come Be My Light*, edited by postulator Brian Kolodiejchuk, or a briefer one in my *God Will Provide*.

[154] See Kolodiejchuck's book.

[155] Calcutta is an almost 80-percent-Hindu city with 20 percent Muslims, less than 1 percent Christians, and a number of other minority faiths.

to huddle in Catholic enclaves the way Teresa longed to remain in the security of Loreto. What God asked of her might evoke pondering if one has a call, instead, to let God's love work through him or her in places as seemingly unlikely as the Hindu slum in which Mother Teresa was plunked down.)

Primarily Hindu, with Muslims as the second major group, India is not always religiously tolerant. Going back to the post–WW II religion-based slaughterings that partitioned the country into Muslim Pakistan and Hindu India, India is still a place where people killing each other for having the "wrong" religion can erupt. Christians nationwide make up only 2 percent of the whole country's population, and Catholics are a minority among Christians. Occasionally in America there are news reports of attacks on or murders of those seen as trying to convert Hindus or Muslims to Christianity.

Jesus' call to Mother was not to evangelization in the overt sense. Jesus wanted Mother to slake His thirst for souls to love Him by first getting some elementary medical training, then bringing that kind of help to the nearest slum. She was also to make herself available to little groups of children to teach them to write, modeling letters with a stick in the mud outside their huts, and to just spend time visiting—being with—people. It was a quiet kind of one-person, one-family, or few-kids-at-a-time service of love. There she saw Jesus "in the distressing disguise," as she put it, of half-starved people, some actually dying of hunger, struggling to survive hour by hour, day by day. Those she visited made her welcome, one mother of a family in a squalid shack begging Teresa to come again, saying the visitor's smile lit up their home. Soon joined by former pupils and then other young women, Mother's simple work grew rapidly into help for many of the needs of these "poorest of the poor" and other desperately poor around India.

From the beginning, and later to people admiring the Missionaries of Charity homes in India for the dying, for lepers, for orphans, for deformed children, for castaway aged, for all the forms of care for the poorest, she insisted not argumentatively but insisted nevertheless, "We are not social workers; we do this for Jesus."

In what can only be called one of God's mysteries—never ceasing to affirm noncombatively with a smile it was all for Jesus—over the long years of her work Mother Teresa became a national treasure in

Hindu-Muslim India, winning not just popularity but awards, including a major national one, honored even with her likeness on postage stamps.

Mahatma Gandhi, revered by millions of his countrymen as a statesman and holy man (Teresa was in India during his lifetime, but he was dead, assassinated, before she embarked on works he would have noticed), famously remarked that he was drawn to the Christian ideal; he just never saw any Christian live it. Perhaps what served Teresa of Calcutta among Indians was that they (as later the world) saw the selflessness ideal lived in her when it got about that here was one who did not hesitate to tenderly pull from the trash with her bare hands some human discard whose shriveled, stinking flesh was being eaten by maggots. Moreover, as a woman in Britain who saw her on TV in that post-Christian society once said, something—maybe Someone—in Mother Teresa spoke to people, sometimes spoke, people said, beyond anyone the observer had ever seen or heard before. India has a tradition that just being in the presence of the holy confers great spiritual blessings. God's mysteries are not easily unraveled, but it can be suggested that the people of India, as those elsewhere, found something healing and enticingly beautiful for their beings in Mother Teresa because she managed in the most unlikely environments to live Jesus, emit Jesus; to, in words attributed to St. Francis of Assisi, "preach the gospel in all places and at all times, and—if absolutely necessary—use words."

Spending most of her life in non-Christian environments, she somehow gave Jesus what He asked by becoming more and more a mother figure to India and the world. (Already in 1935, still a Loreto teacher, poor children she taught dubbed her "Ma," Indian for Mother.) And she did it while God permitted Teresa herself to live in spiritual darkness after that great early period of intimacy with Jesus, in order that she might mystically participate in the suffering of His longing for souls. Because she smiled and met so many needs, the world simply did not notice, as children with an ill mother who manages to feed and care for them may not notice that Mom had her human struggles.

In another facet of the mystery, besides all her Roman Catholic children and people of every kind outside India who took her for a spiritual mentor, Teresa was a mother to large numbers of Indian volunteers in her varied institutions. They were largely Hindus, but there were also

Muslims, Jews, Protestants, Buddhists, and among the short-termers, Western-born seekers and others from all over with no affiliation. What she was spoke so profoundly to some of them that they did become Catholic. (There were non-Indian converts, too, outside India. They included the occasional well-known person. And she had visits from famous seekers like Princess Diana, the troubled wife of England's heir to the throne.) But the majority of the faithful volunteers in India remained Hindus or Muslims who loved their spiritual mother deeply. If they did not become Christian, they were deeply favorable to this one Christian, whom they saw living in a way many tried to follow.

Saints are never spared critics. Because Teresa kept her mandates from the Lord so quiet, she got much criticism for not using her fame to tackle social issues. When she did tackle a social issue, abortion, her stand that it is a terrible kind of poverty in a society and individuals that kills unborn children, brought criticism from VIPs, as well as acclaim from others (typically, she offered "Bring them to me," and opened homes for unwanted children from which she sent many to adoptive parents).

One of many controversies surrounding her regarded baptism. Some Indian critics and other critics disapprovingly dismissed all her work as mere grabs for people to baptize who were too sick, too illiterate, or too disabled to protest. Some fervent Catholics approvingly trumpeted that Mother Teresa baptized everyone she could. Others equally fervent approvingly trumpeted Mother as the great example of God's love that falls on all because she respected people's religious freedom.

It seems both Catholic groups were correct. Enter Fr. Tony Chacko, who joined her men's congregation at the age of sixteen and knew her for thirty-four years,[156] to clear away the confusion regarding who was baptized and who not. About claims that those who entered the famous House for the Dying left, dead or alive, baptized, Fr. Tony shares as one who was there: if an individual brought there in terrible shape recovered and was able to leave, there was absolutely no coercion for that person to adopt the religion of the Missionaries of Charity before leaving. Remember, of course (pp. 261-262), that the love of the Missionar-

---

[156] Fr. Chacko is currently serving as a priest in a California diocese after somehow surviving being shot three times for too effectively getting Brazilian youth away from their drug lord.

ies, it was hoped, would—without coercion—open all to God. But, Fr. Tony explains, if someone were dying, as was often the case when brought in or shortly thereafter, without ability from weakness or being comatose to state a religious preference, these individuals, Fr. Tony says, were given "conditional baptism." This basically means, he goes on, "we assumed"—again, he is speaking as one who was there—that, without being able to express it, the individuals may have in their mind or deep in their heart what is called baptism of desire, that longing for "God," who, if they but knew it, is Christ. If this is the case, the baptism honors that desire. If this is not the case, since it is conditional upon that desire, the baptism does not override the individuals' freedom of choice.

As to coercing people "not too ill to resist" to become Catholic, from purely practical reasons Mother could hardly have insisted those who came to volunteer for a day, a month, or long term meet any religious test before they spooned food into an orphan or washed bedding at the home for the dying (by stomping it with their feet; Mother not wanting her institutions to have washing machines when the poor did not). From the volunteers who helped her for years, and loved their tiny[157] fellow Indian citizen, come no claims, to this writer's best knowledge, of coercion. Fr. Tony confirms the sometimes misunderstood reports are true that she said to her Hindu helpers and Muslim helpers she wanted them to become "better Hindus" or "better Muslims." He explains while she would have been filled with joy to see everyone know and love Jesus, in the many cases where that grace was not given, she and the spiritual children listening to her, understood she was urging they come closer to God, not pushing non-Catholic religion.

Long before her death her little band in the slums of Calcutta, grown into a spiritual army, had attracted so many members they were working among the very poor not just in India and other Third World countries, but in over a hundred countries, including the United States and Canada.[158] The West's many lonely, isolated individuals unwanted by kin were, to her, as needy as any slum dweller.

---

[157] Five feet, four inches; osteoporosis gradually shrank her to about five feet.

[158] Mother Teresa visited North America many times, and her active orders, the Missionaries of Charity women's and men's branches were established among the very poor in such North American spots as the Bronx, New York; Skid Row in Los Angeles; pockets of poverty at opposite ends of Canada, in Toronto and Vancouver; and Mexico–U.S. border

With this worldwide outreach, at her death on September 5, 1997, Mother left thousands of bettered lives and dozens of tangible institutions dotting the globe. With her daughters' and sons' help, she had tended people wherever God called her like the best of mothers, and her loving prayers had gone up to God for all the children He had given her. That many of them were not Catholic can be seen only as a mystery of His will.

Mother was home when she died, in the building where the work for Jesus had begun. It had long become the motherhouse—sold to them by a Muslim decades earlier below cost, for God's sake, the seller said. India gave her a state funeral attended by dignitaries from around the world. Her body was borne through the streets of Calcutta on the same gun carriage that had transported India's greatest, including Mahatma Gandhi, as tens of thousands of Indians lined the route for a final glimpse of the Mother of the Poor. Earlier her body had been carried from the motherhouse's chapel to a church accessible to the poor, who crammed in to file past and speak a last word. That first trip was made in a Missionary of Charity ambulance. On the windshield someone stuck one word: Mother.

Mother Teresa's friend John Paul was still alive when she died. He waived three years of the five-year waiting period to start a Cause for a woman much of the world had already canonized in their hearts. Still, like every other candidate for formal sainthood, her life would have to be studied to see if her virtues were truly heroic. Assuming heroic virtue were found, then would come the need for a miracle meeting the seven criteria if the Cause were to proceed past "Venerable."

This book has spoken about miracles through Catholic saints going to Protestants, Jews, Muslims, and people of no particular religious persuasion — when they or someone asked for them. Servant of God Teresa of Calcutta, as she was now called, would take that visible love

---

towns San Ysidro, California, and Tijuana, Mexico. For some years her seminarians lived and were taught in Tijuana. She also had a house of her contemplative sisters in what is called Holy Row in Alhambra, a Los Angeles suburb home to cloistered Carmelites, active Carmelites, and a diocesan parish.

of God for the entire human family through the Catholic Church to an even broader place in her beatification miracle.

One year had passed after Mother's death when the following events took place in Mother Teresa's adopted homeland:

Monika Besra was a thirty-year-old native of India from a very poor rural area of West Bengal. Married to a somewhat older farmer, she, her husband, and their five children were low-caste people living in a dirt-floored hut in a remote area. Like many in the Third World, their god was local, a deity living in a little shrine in their village. There offerings were made to propitiate the god in hopes he would let things go well. Also like many in the Third World, Monika became ill with TB. She received various medications, not too consistently because they had to be paid for. The disease progressed until she was said in 1997 — experiencing fever, headache, and vomiting — to be suffering from TB meningitis.

Then there was the big lump — whatever you called it: a gynecological specialist, after an ultrasound, dubbed it a "large cystic lesion in the lower abdomen and pelvis, suggestive of an ovarian cyst"; other doctors called it a tumor on the ovary. Whether this was part of, or separate from, the TB was disputed. There was no dispute — two unconnected doctors agreed — that her distended abdomen gave her the appearance of a woman six months pregnant. Monika confirms that and that she was in terrible pain.

She ended up in May 1998 at Navajivan, the Missionaries of Charity home for the sick and the dying in Patiram, also in Bengal. She was one of about 150 patients cared for by the sisters. People are taken in based on need not religion. They are charged nothing.

Due to Monika's serious condition, the sisters took her twice to Balurghat District Hospital and in August to North Bengal Hospital for more specialized care than they could provide. They hoped surgery could be done for the "tumor." But the medical verdict was that Monika was too ill and weak to withstand the anesthesia needed to investigate the mass surgically. The Missionaries were advised to try to "feed her up" for three months. The hope was that she would gain strength and could be brought back for the operation.

Monika herself had no illusions: she would tell a reporter later that she went back to the home sure she was dying. Medication had helped the fevers and headache, but she continued vomiting — even water and medicine — making it impossible for her to eat. So how was she to be built up? And, as she says: "The tumor kept getting bigger. The pain made me almost senseless."

Six days after her return from North Bengal Medical College was the first anniversary of Mother Teresa's death, September 5, 1998. At the home there were special events, including Adoration of Jesus in the Eucharist in the residence's chapel and healing prayer. Monika was invited at 8 a.m. to participate, thought she was too weak, and then decided to go. It took two attendants to get her into the chapel, she later recalled. She says, "As soon as I entered I felt a ray of light from Mother's photo coming to me. It came out from that photograph and into my heart. I became nervous. I became hot, and I didn't feel well." She told the attendants to just let her sit so she could rest. She says, "I did not tell them what had happened." When she eventually was taken back to her bed, she says, "I was feeling different. I felt my mind had changed."

Sr. Bartholomea, the home superior, recounts: "At 5 p.m. we ended the Exposition [Jesus exposed for adoration in a eucharistic Host], and I called Sr. Ann [Sevika] and said, 'Let's pray over Monika. Mother [Teresa] may heal her.' This day was for me a very special day. So with that faith we went to Monika.

"We laid our hands on her, and another patient was there [praying with us]. I prayed silently in my heart: 'Mother, today is your death anniversary. You love all the people in our homes. Now Monika is sick; please heal her.' Then we prayed out loud nine times the Memorarae because Mother loved this prayer very much." As a sign of their call for Mother Teresa's prayers, they placed on Monika's stomach a Marian medal that had been touched to Mother's body. With Monika's permission at some point they secured the medal to Monika's waist, near the young mother's swollen abdomen. Sr. Bartholomea concludes: "I looked at Monika's face. It was looking relaxed, and she was sleeping. We kept silence for a while and [then] moved out to the convent."

Monika says: "At night, around one o'clock, I woke up as usual, and I was feeling lighter and with no pain. I touched my abdomen. I could not find the tumor. I told my bedside neighbor [Samira Tudu], 'See, I am feeling lighter and there is no pain [because] the tumor is gone.'"

Next morning, September 6, she told various sisters about her experience in the chapel. Not only they but Samira, and Handsa, one of the laypeople who helped care for the patients, would confirm what the whole place was talking about: Monika's stomach was flat without any lumps; the great pain was gone, as were all her symptoms. She was in good shape!

Jubilant sisters took Monika to various doctors to confirm she no longer had either tumor or TB. Doctors at the municipal hospital in the Communist-run area and others acknowledged the tumor and the TB were gone. They insisted she had been cured through the TB medicine, re-diagnosing the tumor as a tubercular mass. When told the tumor disappeared in eight hours, one of these doctors said this was "impossible. She is lying . . . It is not possible to believe in miracles." But another doctor at private Woodland Hospital in Calcutta admitted, "To say this is a miracle is technically difficult for us [as doctors] but I will say that, to the best of my knowledge as a doctor, this case is inexplicable."

The sisters reported all this to the officials of Mother Teresa's Cause in Calcutta. It went through the usual gamut of diocesan inquiry under Archbishop Henry D'Souza and then was sent on to the Congregation for the Causes of Saints.

The medical committee of the Congregation for the Causes of Saints conducted a several-month inquiry under Prof. Raffaele Cortesini of Rome University Medical School. He has, according to English journalist Mike Brown, investigated seven hundred proposed miracles, including three hundred that proved to meet all seven requirements. Dr. Cortesini noted first, in his interview by Brown, that Monika was very near death if she could not tolerate even exploratory surgery, satisfying the requirement that an illness be serious. That the tumor/cyst was real had been verified by ultrasound and various doctors. Had it been a cyst that burst, the abdominal cavity would have been filled with the distending fluid. It was not. Above all, the TB and the mass, whatever it was, had vanished suddenly and completely. No drug could do that. The cure was accepted for Mother Teresa's beatification.

Bengal is an area about equally divided between Hindus and Muslims with a Catholic minority. Monika is a member of an indigenous tribe long resident in this part of India. As mentioned, her god was a little enshrined object in her village. Thus, she is described as an animist. God's friend, Mother Teresa, loved and served everybody in God's name. Monika's healing is a reminder that God, too, cares for everybody.

Following the cure, Monika's life changed. The illiterate low-caste woman from a poor farmer's family went on a train for the first time in her life in June 1999, traveling to Calcutta "to give thanks" to Mother Teresa at her burial place. When her cure was accepted as God's vote for Mother Teresa's beatification, it was made possible for Monika to be in Rome to attend those ceremonies. She was, after all, the one whom God favored to make the event possible.

Some of India's newspapers suggested she had been coerced to become a Christian by the Missionaries of Charity. Journalist Mike Brown of England's *Telegraph Magazine*, to whom I am indebted for his outstanding article (the portion pertaining to this miracle sent me by the Postulator of Mother Teresa's Cause and the Missionaries of Charity sisters in San Ysidro, California, as a reliable account of the miracle and matters pertaining to it), told Monika what was being claimed. The miracle recipient, whom Brown has described as "graceful and composed with an air of palpable serenity," took this in. Then she not only replied, "Nobody can tell me what to believe," but added, "or stop me." But in Rome she made a decision. She says, "I was not Christian before, but I thought Mother has done this [obtained the healing from God] … and after returning home, I would take Christianity and obey Mother as next to God."

Brown also asked the Indian woman why she thought she had received the miracle. After long thought, she said simply she didn't know.

In that, she joined every healing recipient in these pages. What they do know is that, through one of His friends, God's tender mercy touched them. Faced with eternal mysteries, understanding this — that it all goes back to God — is enough.

Where to Request Prayers
or Report Prayer Answers
Regarding the Saints of This Book

The organizations listed below are not out to make a profit; usually run by volunteers devoted to the saint or by individuals who have taken lifelong vows of poverty, with as few paid helpers as possible, they exist as little islands of spiritual and psychological support for our human family. Books and other materials they produce, for instance, are usually sold for just what it costs—or even less—to print them. Unfortunately this kind of service to God's children does not exempt them from utility bills, postage fees, printing expenses, and all the other costs of keeping doors open day after day, year after year.

Please keep this in mind when you ask for their prayers and/or services, and, if possible, see that the human exchange you are engaged in is not one-sided, but includes your donation and prayer for them as well.

BESSETTE, Bl. André

St. Joseph's Oratory
3800 Queen Mary Road, Montreal, Canada H3V 1116
514-733-2811
http://www.saint-joseph.org/

BOSCO, St. John

Mary Help of Christians Basilica
Casa Madre Opere Don Bosco
Via Maria Ausiliatrice, 33, Torino, Italy 10152

Provincial Office
148 Main Street, New Rochelle, NY 10802
914-636-4225
http://www.salesians.org/

Provincial Office
1100 Franklin Street, San Francisco, CA 94109
415-441-7144
http://www.donboscowest.org/

BOJAXHIU (born Gonxha Agnes), Bl. (Mother) Teresa of Calcutta

Prayer requests may be sent to the Missionaries of Charity at the addresses below, but reports of healings or other favors sent to either address should be marked: "Attention: Postulator Brian Kolodiejchuk, M.C."

The Director, Mother Teresa Center
524 West Calle Primera, Suite 1005N
San Ysidro, CA 92173
Phone/fax 0052664 621 3763 (Tijuana, Mexico)

Mother Teresa Centre
Piazza S. Gregorio al Celio, 2, 00184 Roma, Italy
Phone: +39 06 772-60230; fax: +39 06 700-1668
E-mail: mtc@motherteresa.org

CABRINI, St. Frances Xavier

Mother Cabrini League
434 W. Deming Place, Chicago, IL 60614

The United States has three Cabrini shrines.
In the East: the saint's tomb:

Mother Cabrini Shrine (site of the saint's tomb)
701 Fort Washington Avenue, New York, NY 10040
212-923-3536
http://www.mothercabrini.org/ministries/shrine_ny.asp

In the Midwest: the National Shrine of St. Frances Xavier Cabrini (reopened in 2012 following a period of remodeling after demolition of Columbus Hospital, in which it was previously housed). The original room in which Cabrini died in 1917 is still there, as are exhibits of memorabilia and the original hospital chapel. If you are looking for directions don't use the old Columbus Hospital Chapel designation.

National Shrine of St. Frances Xavier Cabrini
2520 N. Lakeview Avenue, Chicago, IL 60614
773-360-5115
http://cabrinishrinechicago.com/mother-cabrini/
http://cabrinishrinechicago.com/calendar-of-events/

In the West, a shrine is situated at a site sold to the saint for a pittance because all effort to find water there proved fruitless. After prayer Cabrini marked a spot, directed, "Dig here," and water was discovered. It is accessible to ordinary vehicles in all seasons:

Cabrini Shrine
20189 Cabrini Boulevard, Golden, CO 80401
303-526-0758
http://www.mothercabrinishrine.org/

CASEY, Venerable Solanus

Father Solanus Guild
1718 Mt. Elliott, Detroit, MI 48207
313-579-2100
http://www.solanuscasey.org/index.shtml

FORGIONE, St. (Padre) Pio

In the United States and Canada, the Capuchins have authorized a center for reporting cures and requesting prayers. These intentions are prayed for by people devoted to Padre Pio, and then prayer requests and reported cures are forwarded to Padre Pio's Italian friary.

National Centre for Padre Pio, Inc.
R.D. 1, Box 134, Barto, PA 19504
215-845-3000
http://www.padrepio.org/

Individuals may also send prayer requests or report cures directly to the Italian friary where Padre Pio lived:

Our Lady of Grace Friary
San Giovanni Rotondo FG, 71013 Italy

The Voice of Padre Pio magazine
http://www.vocedipadrepio.com/eng/

JOHN PAUL II: see WOJTYLA, Karol

NEUMANN, St. John

National Shrine of St. John Neumann
St. Peter's Church
1019 North Fifth Street, Philadelphia, PA 19123
215-627-3080; 215-627-2386
http://www.stjohnneumann.org/

PADRE PIO: see FORGIONE, St. (Padre) Pio

PAPCZYNSKI, Bl. Stanislaus

Br. Andrew Mączyński, M.I.C.
Vice-Postulator of the Marian Causes of Canonization
Marians of the Immaculate Conception
Eden Hill, Stockbridge, MA 01263
E-mail: graces@marian.org
For prayer cards: 1-800-462-7426

SCROSOPPI, St. Luigi

Catholic Church of St. Aloysius
Oxford Oratory
25 Woodstock Road, Oxford OX2 6HA
England
Phone: 01865 315 800
http://www.oxfordoratory.org.uk/

SEELOS, Bl. Francis Xavier

Seelos Welcome Center
919 Josephine Street, New Orleans, LA 70130
504-525-2495
http://www.seelos.org/

SETON, St. Elizabeth

National Shrine of St. Elizabeth Ann Seton
339 S. Seton Avenue, Emmitsburg, MD 21717
301-447-6606
http://www.setonheritage.org/

SHEEN, Venerable Fulton J.

To request information and/or prayers, contact either of the Sheen Museums. To report medical-healing favors, anything sent to either address should be marked: "Attention: Vice-Postulator Andrew Apostoli." Material may also be sent to the Diocesan Representative for the Cause, who works under Bishop Daniel Jenky.

The Archbishop Sheen Museum
419 NE Madison Avenue, Peoria, IL 61603
309-671-1550
E-mail: sr_lea@cdop.org
http://www.cdopmuseums.org/p/the-archbishop-fulton-j-sheen-museum.html/

Fulton Sheen Illinois Museum and Spiritual Centre
17 E. Main Street, El Paso, IL 61738
309-527-4062
E-mail: fjsheen@elpaso.net
http://www.archbishopfultonsheencentre.com/

FR. SOLANUS: see CASEY, Venerable Solanus

TERESA OF CALCUTTA: see BOJAXHIU (born Gonxha Agnes), Bl. (Mother) Teresa of Calcutta

TRONCATTI, Bl. Maria

To request prayer support or report cures or favors received through the intercession of this member of the Daughters of Mary Help of Christians branch of the Salesian family, write in English or Italian:

> Postulator of Sister Maria Troncatti's Cause
> Figlie di Maria Ausiliatrice
> Via Dell'Ateneo Salesiano, 81
> 00129 ROMA, Italy

Spanish-fluent readers may also report cures or request prayer support from:

> *Boletin Informativo*
> Rvdo. P. Alfredo Germani, Vice-Postulador de la Causa
> Immaculata Concezione
> Mendez, Ecuador

WOJTYLA, Karol (Bl. Pope John Paul II)

Visit his grave at St. Peter's, Rome.

Check online for a shrine or a museum. Depending on where you live, there may be one nearby.

If you have information on a cure received by you or someone in whose case you have pertinent material to provide, until he is canonized, contact:

> Msgr. Slawomir Oder
> Vicariato di Roma
> Piazza S. Giovanni in Laterano, 6/a, 00184 Roma, Italy

Biographical and Other Sources

BESSETTE, Bl. André

The most important of the materials supplied by Vice-Postulator Bernard Lafrenière, C.S.C., are: *Le Frère André (1845-1937) et l'Oratoire Saint-Joseph du Mont Royal*, by Étienne Catta (Montreal et Paris: Fides, 1965); the out-of-print French work includes testimonies from the beatification process and other official data pertaining to the saint's Cause and life; and *Brother André, C.S.C: The Wonder Man of Mount Royal* (rev. ed.), by Henri-Paul Bergeron, D.S.C., translated from the French by Réal Boudreau, C.S.C. (Montreal: Fides, 1958); three recollections by the saint's former superior, Albert Cousineau, C.S.C.: "Man of Faith Undaunted," "Brother André, as I Knew Him," and "Brother André and the Power of Prayer," all published by St. Joseph's Oratory, 1960; and a discussion of the problems cures often run into with the medical establishment and others: "La Guérison de Martin Hannon" in *Annales de Saint Joseph*, 13ième année, no. 3, Mars 1924.

Consulted works not supplied by the vice-postulator are: *The Miracle of the Mountain*, by Alden Hatch (New York: Hawthorn Books, Inc., 1959); *Brother André of Saint Joseph's Oratory*, by William H. Gregory (New York: William J. Hirten Co., Inc., 1925); and *Brother André of Mount Royal*, by Katherine Burton (Notre Dame: Ave Maria Press, 1943).

BOJAXHIU (born Gonxha Agnes), Bl. (Mother) Teresa of Calcutta

One of the very best biographies is Kathryn Spink's *Mother Teresa: A Complete Authorized Biography* (San Francisco: Harper, 1997). See also her book *I Need Souls Like You: Sharing in the Work of Mother Teresa through Prayer and Suffering*. San Francisco: HarperCollins, 1984. Kathryn Spink was a writer, not an intimate of Mother Teresa but a close friend of the woman who, close to Mother, founded with her the Sick and Suffering Co-Workers. This organization, no longer an official one, provides prayer support to the Missionaries. Its prominence in Mother Teresa's overall community helps us understand her spirituality and thinking. One may also understand her better by reading the saint's book *Love: A Fruit Always in Season: Daily Meditations by Mother Teresa*, edited by Dorothy S. Hunt (San Francisco: Ignatius Press, 1987).

In *Mother Teresa: Come Be My Light: The Private Writings of the Saint of Calcutta*, edited and with commentary by Brian Kolodiejchuk (New York: Doubleday, 2007) we see her soul in her own words with an intimate's commentary. Fr. Edward Le Joly wrote *Servant of Love: Mother Teresa and Her Missionaries of Charity* (New York: Harper and Row, 1977) at her request early on to explain who the Missionaries were. He was part of their spiritual formation. The late Fr. Joseph Langford was very close to Mother and founded her second men's order. See his book *Mother Teresa's Secret Fire: The Encounter That Changed Her Life and How It Can Transform Your Own* (Huntington, Indiana: Our Sunday Visitor, 2008). See also *Love Without Boundaries: Mother Teresa of Calcutta*, by Georges Gorée and Jean Barbier and translated by Paula Speakman (Dublin: Veritas, 1974).

Also consulted for this book was the June 21, 2003, *Telegraph Magazine* article "The Making of a Saint: Did Mother Teresa Cure This Woman with a Miracle? Mick Brown on a Question of Faith," 35-39.

BOSCO, St. John

All material on the beatification and canonization miracles was supplied by Editor-in-Chief Diego Borgatello, S.D.B., from both testimonies and the official materials of the Cause being quoted in at that time unedited portions of volume 19 of the twenty-volume *Biographical Memoirs* then in process of translation from the original Italian.

Other healings and biographical information are from published volumes of the American edition of *The Biographical Memoirs of Saint John Bosco*, by Giovanni Battista Lemoyne, S.D.B., Eugenio Ceria, S.D.B., or Angelo Amadei, S.D.B. (New Rochelle, New York: Salesiana Publishers, Inc., various years); *Don Bosco: A Spiritual Portrait*, by Edna Beyer

Phelan (Garden City, New York: Doubleday & Company, Inc., 1963); *Saint John Bosco*, by A. Auffray, S.D. (Blaisdon, England: Salesian Publications, 1930); *Father Alfonso*, by Peter M. Rinaldi, S.D.B. (New Rochelle, New York: Salesiana Publishers, Inc., n.d.); and the author's own work in progress on this saint based on the above and other materials.

CABRINI, St. Frances Xavier

Beatification process and other testimonies by doctors, nurses, and others involved in the healing miracles were supplied by Sister Ursula, M.S.C., the archivist of the Missionary Sisters of the Sacred Heart, from materials kept at Cabrini College, Radnor, Pennsylvania.

Biographical information is taken primarily from the account of the saint's associate Mother Saverio De Maria, M.S.C., *Mother Frances Xavier Cabrini*, English version edited and translated Rose Basile Green, Ph.D. (Chicago: Missionary Sisters of the Sacred Heart, 1984).

Other materials were supplied by Sr. Consolata, M.S.C., of Mother Cabrini (formerly Columbus) Hospital, Seattle; Christine Conrath of the Cabrini League, Chicago; Mother Annunciata, M.S.C., of Golden, Colorado; and Sr. Alberta Surico, M.S.C., of New York City. For this edition, additional material is from miracle recipient Fr. Peter Smith's brother (see acknowledgments).

CASEY, Venerable Solanus

Materials furnished by the vice-postulator, the late Br. Leo Wollenweber, O.F.M. Cap., and for this edition by the present vice-postulator Br. Richard Merling, include: first-person accounts of cures in bulletins and other publications of the Father Solanus Guild; portions of the saint's log book entries and other first-person testimonies of cures reported in the earliest sanctioned biography, *The Porter of Saint Bonaventure's*, by James Patrick Derum (Detroit: The Fidelity Press, 1968); and *Thank God Ahead of Time: The Life and Spirituality of Solanus Casey*, by Michael H. Crosby, O.F.M., Cap. (Chicago: Franciscan Herald Press, 1985). A more intellectual look at Fr. Solanus, a popular version of two volumes of the three-volume Posito or official summary of Father Solanus's life submitted to the Congregation for the Causes of Saints, is edited by Fr. Crosby as well. This is: *Solanus Casey: The Official Account of a Virtuous American Life* (New York: Crossroad, 2000). Writings of the saint consulted are primarily letters and the attestation (in the original German and in the English translation) the saint, signed in 1901.

FORGIONE, St. (Padre) Pio

Information on several of the major cures attributed to Padre Pio since his death and verification of cures such as that of Giovanni Savino, which occurred during Padre Pio's lifetime, comes from American Joseph Pius Martin, O.F.M. Cap., of Our Lady of Grace Friary, San Giovanni Rotondo, and since his death in 2000, with permission of the friars, Charles Abercrombie of the Friary's English-language publication.

Tape and letter exchanges between Ann Wilkinson and the author are the source for the healing of Kelly Wilkinson. Updates with both by phone and e-mail.

The first cure associated with Padre Pio during his lifetime I report from *Pio of Pietrelcina: Infancy and Adolescence*, by Alessandro Da Ripabottoni, O.F.M. Cap. (San Giovanni Rotondo, Italy: Edizioni Padre Pio da Pietrelcina, 1969); and *Padre Pio: His Early Years*, by Augustine McGregor, O.C.S.O. (San Giovanni Rotondo, Italy: Edizioni Padre Pio da Pietrelcina, 1985).

Major sources on Pio's health and stigmata include (of eight biographies and several booklets consulted): *Padre Pio: The Stigmatist*, by Rev. Charles Mortimer Carty (Rockford, Illinois: TAN Books and Publishers, Inc., 1971); *A City on a Mountain: Padre Pio of Pietrelcina, O.F.M. Cap.*, by Rev. Pascal P. Parente (Washington, New Jersey: Ave Maria Institute, n.d.); *Padre Pio: The True Story*, by C. Bernard Ruffin (Huntington, Indiana: Our Sunday Visitor, Inc., 1982); and *The Stigmata and Modern Science*, by Charles M. Carty (Rockford, Illinois: TAN Books and Publishers, Inc., 1971).

Due to their lack of access to many important materials, Fr. Martin warns that most books on Padre Pio (he makes an exception for Ruffin's work, particularly the revised edition, completed after the saint's death) contain errors and should not be quoted without further verification.

JOHN PAUL II: see WOJTYLA, Karol

NEUMANN, St. John

The late Fr. Charles Fehrenbach, C.SS.R., on the staff at the shrine was a source of many healings, including making it possible for me to interview a recipient. Materials furnished by the Redemptorists staffing Neumann's shrine include facsimiles of portions of the log of cures kept by Fr. Charles; accounts of early cures compiled by Postulator Joseph Wissel, C.SS.R., late in the nineteenth century under the title *Sex miracula exponuntur intercession Venerabilis Episcopi obtenta*; and accounts of cures in various publications of the shrine, including the quarterly bulletins.

The account of a cure in the new edition can be found in *Saint John Neumann: Wonder-Worker of Philadelphia: Recent Miracles, 1961-1991*, by Fr. Timothy E. Byerley (Philadelphia: National Shrine of St. John Neumann, 1992). Biographical information is taken primarily from *Bishop John Neumann C.SS.R.: Fourth Bishop of Philadelphia*, by Michael J. Curley, C.SS.R. (Philadelphia: Bishop Neumann Center, 1952); and *Saint John Neumann: Bishop of Philadelphia*, by James J. Galvin, C.SS.R. (Baltimore: Helicon Press, Inc., 1964).

PADRE PIO: see FORGIONE, St. (Padre) Pio

PAPCZYNSKI, Bl. Stanislaus

My sources are online accounts of his life and the monthly columns regarding graces attributed to his intercession in *Marian Helper*, a magazine put out by his order (http://marian.org/marianhelper/index.php). A cure from this column will be found in the book. For privacy considerations, I do not give the precise source of the beatification miracle. Both are used with permission.

SCROSOPPI, St. Luigi

I have used biographical material online which I was directed to by Stratford Caldecott, then at Sophia Institute Press, and materials there on the AIDS cure, which has since been removed. I also interviewed priests in Africa by phone and e-mail who knew the miracle recipient, spoke to the pertinent African diocesan archivist, and spoke to the recipient as well. While the material I used is no longer available, using the saint's name, you may access biographical information on him from well-known Catholic sites that should have reliable information.

FR. SOLANUS: see CASEY, Venerable Solanus

SEELOS, Bl. Francis Xavier

Information on the Boudreaux family cures was obtained by the author's interviews via phone, in person, and by letter with Angela Boudreaux. Mrs. Boudreaux and Seelos Center director Joseph Elworthy, C.SS.R., supplied written materials on cures and Fr. Seelos's life: *Father Francis X. Seelos, C.SS.R.*, by Thomas Artz, C.SS.R. (New Orleans: The Seelos Center, 1979), and *Meet Father Seelos*, by former vice-postulator John Vaughn, C.SS.R. (New Orleans: The Seelos Center, n.d.); *Cheerful Ascetic*, by Michael J. Curley, C.SS.R. (New Orleans: The Redemptorist Fathers, 1969); *Times-Picayune* article dated October 6, 1986; and various issues of *Father Seelos and Sanctity*, published monthly by the Redemptorists. From present director Byron Miller, C.SS.R.: new cures, a 2012 *Times-Picayune* article, and help and referrals on the saint-making process.

SETON, St. Elizabeth Ann Bayley

Testimonies and medical attestations by those involved in the Sr. Gertrude Korzendorfer and Anne O'Neill cures were originally supplied by the late Sylvester A. Taggart, C.M., director of the now defunct Mother Seton Guild; additional details came from Daughters of Charity archivist Sr. Aloysia of St. Joseph's Provincial House, Emmitsburg, Maryland; pertinent to the O'Neill cure, see also "Dr. Coley's Toxins" in *Science* (April 1984): 68-73; details of the James Porter cure, obtained through the Seton Causeway, were elaborated on by Sister Patricia Newhouse, S.C., and Mrs. Mary T. Porter through phone interviews and letters; Sr. Anne Courtney, archivist at Mount St. Vincent, Bronx, New York, supplied other important material. In the latest edition additional updates on this miracle come from Jim's sister Sharon Porter Boardman. Updates on the Anne O'Neill cure come from her and her family. Updated medical information for the chapters is from Kathy Sheahan, R.N., and Walter Urba, M.D.

Principal biographical sources are *Mrs. Seton: Foundress of the American Sisters of Charity*, by Joseph I. Dirvin, C.M. (New York: Farrar, Straus and Giroux, Inc., 1962); *Mother Seton: Mother of Many Daughters* by Rev. Charles I. White, revised and edited by the Sisters of Charity of Mount St. Vincent-on-Hudson, New York (Garden City, New York:

Doubleday & Company, Inc., 1949); and *Elizabeth Bayley Seton*, by Dr. Annabelle Melville (New York: Berkley Publishing Group, Inc., 1985).

SHEEN, Venerable Fulton J.

Materials on cures are from individuals who have authenticated reports, from news sources (reports of the two miracles collected by Postulator Ambrosi), and the stillborn miracle is from the mother's report in Internet interviews. I have also used an interview with Vice-Postulator Andrew Apostoli. See also *Treasure in Clay: The Autobiography of Fulton J. Sheen* (New York: Image Books/Doubleday, 1982).

TERESA OF CALCUTTA: see BOJAXHIU (born Gonxha Agnes), Bl. (Mother) Teresa of Calcutta

TRONCATTI, Bl. Maria

All biographical material and cures that occurred during Maria Troncatti's lifetime are from *Beloved Jungle: Sister Maria Troncatti, Daughter of Mary Help of Christians, the Kivaros Sister Missionary*, by Maria Domenica Grassiano (Rome: Daughters of Mary Help of Christians, 1971). Another source is *The Wild Forest: My Terror, My Glory*, by A. Magnabosco (Rome: Daughters of Mary, Help of Christians, 1989).

After-death cures attributed to her intercession, supplied by Sr. Emilia Anzani, F.M.A., secretary general of the order's headquarters in Rome, are from *Boletin Informativo*, published in Spanish in Macas, Ecuador, under the direction of the vice-postulator of Troncatti's Cause, Alfredo Germani, S.D.B., or from the Italian-language bulletin *Conosci?* Cures for the update not from those sources are from Salesian Sisters, Daughters of Mary, Help of Christians Sr. Rachel Racrotti, Sr. Lucy M. Roces, and Sr. Brittany Harrison, and from online material. At various sites under "Troncatti beatification" will be found as of July 2013 interviews with three individuals who knew her and details of the miracle.

WOJTYLA, Karol (Pope St. John Paul II)

There are many excellent biographies and books authored by the pope on my shelves, but the books I quoted from and most consulted for this work are George Weigel's *Witness to Hope: The Biography of Pope John Paul II* (New York: Cliff Street Books, 1999); Pawel Zuchniewicz's

Miracles of John Paul I: Santo Subito (Toronto: Catholic Youth Studio-KSM, Inc., 2006); and *Let Me Go to the Father's House: John Paul II's Strength in Weakness*, by Stanislaw Dziwisz; Czeslaw Drazek, S.J.; Renato Buzzonetti; Angelo Comastri (Boston: Pauline Books and Media, 2006).

Carroll, Felix. "The Story of a Miracle." *Marian Helper* (Summer 2012): 12-13.

Catholic News Agency. "Healing of Colombian Man Could Pave Way for John Paul II Canonization." July 17, 2012. http://www.catholic-newsagency.com/news/healing-of-colombian-man-could-pave-way-for-john-paul-ii-canonization/.

Catholic News Service. "French Nun Says Life Has Changed Since She Was Healed Thanks to JPII." March 30, 2007. http://www.catholicnews.com/.

Connor, Tanya. "Nuns Who Experienced JPII Miracle Bring Message of Hope." *Tidings*, May 11, 2012, 5, 15.

Cordoba, Javier / Associated Press. "Costa Rican Woman Weeps As She Describes John Paul II Miracle." *Portland Press Herald*, July 5, 2013. http://www.pressherald.com/news/Costa-Rican-woman-weeps-as-she-describes-John-Paul-II-miracle-.html.

Donadio, Rachel. "Pope Propels John Paul II and John XXIII to Sainthood." *New York Times*, July 5, 2013. http://www.nytimes.com/2013/07/06/world/europe/papal-encyclical-gets-2-authors-for-first-time.html.

Doyle, Fr. T. "12 Miracles a Week!" *101 Times* 19, no. 1 (Spring 2007).

Fabré, Sr. Marie Thomas. "Witness to a Medical Miracle." Talk given at the Medicine, Bioethics, and Spirituality Conference, Worcester, Massachusetts, May 1, 2013.

Manila Times. "'John Paul II Has Cured Me,' French Nun Recounts." March 4, 2007. http://www.manilatimes.net/.

National Catholic Register. "Miracle Could Lead to John Paul II's Canonization." July 17, 2012. http://www.ncregister.com/daily-news/miracle-could-lead-to-john-paul-iis-canonization#ixzz2ZW5DbhK8.

Normand, Sr. Marie Simon-Pierre. "My Miraculous Cure." Talk given at the Medicine, Bioethics, and Spirituality Conference, Worcester, Massachusetts, May 1, 2013.

Orange County Register, June 29, 2005, 2.

"Pope Blessed John Paul II". http://saints.sqpn.com/.

Redzioch, Wlodzimierz. "Looking for a Miracle: Postulator Awaits John Paul's Canonization (Part 2)." *Zenit*, May 8, 2012. http://www.zenit.org/en/articles/looking-for-a-miracle-postulator-awaits-john-paul-s-canonization-part-2.

Times-Picayune. "Miracle Under Scrutiny in John Paul II Beatification." March 29, 2010. http://www.nola.com/.

Tornielli, Andrea. "The Vatican Doctors Approve the Miracle to Make Wojtyla a Saint." *Vatican Insider*, April 22, 2013. http://vaticaninsider.lastampa.it/en/the-vatican/detail/articolo/wojtyla-wojtyla-wojtyla-24259/.

Wooden, Cindy. 2007. "Pope: John Paul's Ministry, Agony Showed His Love of Christ." *Tidings*, April 6, 23.

Zenit. "John Paul II Closer to Canonization." December 20, 2009. http://www.zenit.org/en.

ADDITIONAL PUBLICATIONS REFERRED TO

Bosco, St. John. *The Life of St. Joseph Cafasso: A Brief Account of the Life of St. Joseph Cafasso Given by St. John Bosco in His Two Panegyrics on the Saint Preached on the 10th of July and the 30th of August, 1860*. Former title: *A Saint Speaks for Another Saint*. Translated from the Italian by Rev. Patrick O'Connell, B.D. Rockford, Illinois: TAN Books, 1983.

Cade, C. Maxwell and Nona Coxhead. *The Awakened Mind: Biofeedback and the Development of Higher States of Awareness*. New York: Delacorte Press/Eleanor Friede, 1979.

Claret, St. Antonio Maria. *Autobiography*. Edited by Jose Maria Vinas, C.M.F. Chicago: Claretian Publications, 1976.

Groeneveld, Fr. Albertus, O.Carm. *A Heart on Fire: An Outline of the Saintly Life and Heroic Death of Father Titus Brandsma, Carmelite.* Faversham, Kent, England: no publisher named, 1954.

Kolbe, St. Maximilian. *Gli Scritti di Massimiliano Kolbe eroe di Oswiecim e Beato della Chiesa.* Translated from the original Polish by Cristoforo Zambelli. 3 vols. Firenze: Edizioni Citta di Vita, 1975.

Krieger, Dolores. *Therapeutic Touch.* Englewood Cliffs, New Jersey: Prentice-Hall, 1979.

MacNutt, Francis. *The Power to Heal.* Notre Dame, Indiana: Ave Maria Press, 1977.

Martin, St. Thérèse (of Lisieux). *Autobiography.* Translated by John Beevers. Garden City, New York: Doubleday and Co., 1957.

Treece, Patricia. *A Man for Others.* San Francisco: Harper and Row, 1982; Libertyville, Illinois: Marytown Press, 2013.

———. "Even Disabled, the Christian Is Never Useless." Pecos, New Mexico: Dove Publications, n.d.

Acknowledgments

For the 1987 edition

My hope that this book will be useful to our human family lies above all in the fact that it has received so much prayer; for that vital content I particularly thank Alice Williams, Eva Engholm, Judith Hodgins, and my daughter, Katherine.

After thanking my editor Patricia A. Kossmann and her excellent staff at Doubleday Image, there is too much research involved in a book like this to name all who assisted me. I can only wholeheartedly thank each of you who shared with me your experience of God's healing through His saints and each of you who assisted me over the past decade with materials and information: archivists, librarians, medical men, researchers on healing and related matters, biographers, vice-postulators, administrators of religious orders, and the staffs of the numerous organizations and publications where lives intertwine with the saints of this book.

I acknowledge my special debt to the following, upon whom I made unusually heavy demands: Sr. Ursula, M.S.C., of Cabrini College, Radnor, Pennsylvania; Rev. Bernard Lafreniere, C.S.C., of St. Joseph's Oratory, Montreal; Mary Maloney and the late Fr. Ralph Lavigne S.S.S., of the Eymard League, New York City; Fr. Maurice Prefontaine, S.S.S., of Salt Lake City; Br. Leo Wollenweber, O.F.M. Cap., of Detroit; Fr. Charles Fehrenbach, C.SS.R., of Philadelphia; Sr. Patricia Newhouse, S.C., of Lansing, Michigan; Conventual Franciscans Br. Charles Madden and Br. Francis Mary Kalvelage, of Marytown Friary, Libertyville, Illinois; Sr. Emilia Anzani, F.M.A., of Rome; Fr. Diego Borgatello, S.D.B., of New Rochelle, New York; Mrs. Angela Boudreaux and Fr. Joseph

Elworthy, C.SS.R., of the Seelos Center, New Orleans; the late Fr. Sylvester A. Taggart, C.M., of Emmitsburg, Maryland; Fr. James McCurry, O.F.M. Conv., of Granby, Massachusetts; Fr. Valerian Czywil, O.F.M. Conv., of Peabody, Massachusetts; and Fr. Joseph Pius Martin, O.F.M. Cap., of San Giovanni Rotondo, Italy.

For sharing both published and unpublished research on healers and recipients of healing and physiological aspects of prayer and meditation — all of which helped me better understand the healing charisms of sanctity and how saints' bodies may compensate by prayer and their relationship with God for lack of normal sleep and nutritional requirements — I thank Geoffrey Blundell, Isabel Cade, and the late C. Maxwell Cade and associates of the Institute for Psychobiological Research, and Elizabeth St. John — all of London — and Edgar Chase of Derby.

For their information on cure rates, treatments, and publications on the various cancers mentioned in this book, my gratitude to the National Cancer Institute, of Bethesda, Maryland, for instituting the national toll-free phone number 1-800-4CANCER and for the Institute's Cancer Information Service in the Jonsson Comprehensive Cancer Center at UCLA.

My thanks to Michael Herbst, M.D., of Malibu, for his help in turning medical terminology into intelligible English.

Finally my gratitude to my friend Franca Aschenbrenner for writing my Italian research letters and checking many of my translations from that language.

I have tried to leave no stone unturned, no clue unfollowed over the past decade to ensure an accurate and neither overblown nor inappropriately minimized sampling of God's dealings in our midst through His saints. For errors, however, including any in my translations of materials otherwise unavailable in English, mine must be the sole responsibility.

For the 2013 edition

First let me thank two men: 2008-2009 Sophia editor Stratford Caldecott, who brought the book to founding publisher John Barger, and John, who accepted the book for Sophia Institute Press before financial difficulties forced Sophia's hiatus. I thank Sophia's current president, Charlie McKinney, for his genuine interest in a book leftover from someone else's watch and the time he has put into it. Thanks also, Charlie, for a brilliant suggestion. A heart full of gratitude to Nora Malone, the kindest editor in the world, who has been a joy and blessing to work with on many fronts and helped me clean up my grammar, and amazing Sheila Perry, also a joy, in the production department of Sophia under the old regime and the new. Sheila has heroically helped me from Sophia's office in New Hampshire—and done it cheerfully—with technical issues that threatened to swamp the entire project. Or at least swamp me. For technical help—equally cheerfully given—including letting his printer live at my house for extended periods—on this end, I am hugely in the debt of Michael Sheahan, as I am to his wife, Kathy, for putting on her nurse's cap and helping research various medical conditions. I thank both the Sheahans for many other practical personal helps and for prayer. I also would like to thank the following, who have either taken over positions in Causes or shrines since the first edition or who have let me condense a report they wrote of a miracle, interview them about a new miracle that they or a friend or loved one received, or let me interview them to update their present condition after my writing about their miracle in the first edition. The list of those to whom I am truly grateful also includes experts in theology, in medical matters, in the changed process for making saints—all the other areas this sort of project of necessity wanders into.

My gratitude to: Msgr. John F. Smith of Our Lady of Mt. Carmel, Tuxedo, New York; Father James McCurry, O.F.M. Conv., who taught me it's always right to pray for healing during my child's cancer and all those who have taught me the many ways healing can occur; Capuchin co-vice-postulators of Fr. Solanus's Cause: Father Solanus Guild head and editor of its quarterly publication Br. Richard Merling and Father Solanus Center Director Fr. Larry Webber; assistants Mary Comfort and Dennis Till; Polish journalist Pawel Zuchniewicz for giving the world an entire book of healings through John Paul II, *Miracles of John Paul II: Santo Subito*, and for the miracle cure of a child I have condensed from its pages; UK journalist Mike Brown for his carefully researched June 21, 2003, article "The Making of a Saint" in England's *Telegraph Magazine*, parts of which were sent me by the Missionaries of Charity as a detailed, accurate account of Teresa of Calcutta's beatification cure.(I regret that to date efforts to contact Mr. Brown have been fruitless.) My gratitude to Fr. Jerome Bevilacqua, O.S.A. (now retired, but one-time teacher for the seminarians of Mother Teresa's men's branch) for getting me in contact with the San Ysidro, California, group of the women Missionaries of Charity. In turn I thank them — Sr. M. Annaleah, M.C., Sr. Callisita, M.C., Sr. Ozana, M.C. — who have all answered questions or in some way helped me regarding the beatification miracle for Teresa, especially for arranging an interview with the postulator of her Cause, Fr. Brian Kolodiejchuk, M.C. Thanks to Fr. Brian for giving me and the world the information in his fine book presenting and commenting on Mother Teresa's private writings. Thanks to Father Tony Chacko, who worked with Mother Teresa for thirty-four years, for information on her interfaith relations.

Gratitude to:

Personal friend Judith Hodgins for letting me share the story of her grandfather's painless death through St. John Neumann. The Redemptorists who have staffed St. John Neumann's shrine since Fr. Fehrenbach's time, above all those serving 2009-2013, especially Fr. Kevin Moley, C.SS.R, director from 2009 to 2010 and present provincial of the order's Baltimore Province.

Nancy Costello, whose hats include director of communications for the Missionary Sisters of the Sacred Heart of Jesus (Cabrini sisters), and Missionary Sister Bridget Zanin of the National Cabrini shrine, Chicago. Special thanks for finding me a new copy of the bio by Cabrini's companion I wore to shreds.

Frère Donald Nadeau, C.S.C., of the Bureau de la Cause at the Oratoire Saint-Joseph in Montreal in 2009; Fr. Mario Lachapelle, C.S.C., of Rome, vice-postulator of the Cause for St. André Bessette and the order's assistant general that same year; and also in 2009 Jean-Francois Rioux, archivist for the order in Montreal; and Fr. Bob Antonelli, C.S.C., of the University of Portland in Oregon, who was instrumental in putting me in touch with this newer generation of Holy Cross.

Sr. Patricia Newhouse, once again, for facilitating interviews with those healed through Mother Seton and/or their family members, including Anne O'Neill, mother Felixina and siblings Jeanne, Margaret Mary, and Celine; James Porter and his sister Sharon Porter Boardman. Regarding Coley's toxins and other medical efforts to help childhood leukemia and other cancer victims, my thanks to Walter Urba, M.D., Ph.D, an immunology specialist and head of cancer research (largely focused on immunotherapy), at the Robert W. Franz Cancer Research Center in the Earle A. Chiles Research Institute of the Providence (Portland) Medical Center in Oregon.

Thanks to Ashley Treece, M.D., and Sandy Toner, R.N., for input regarding aneurysms.

Seelos Center Director Byron Miller, C.SS.R.; Joyce Bourgeois of the Center, Mary Staehle and the Boudreaux family; Mary Ellen Heibel, her husband, John, and Rose Love; Michael K. Gibson, M.D., Ph.D. of the University of Pittsburgh Cancer Institute and Brooke Kubiak, Dr. Gibson's administrative assistant.

Besides Charles Abercrombie, thanked below, I wish to express deep gratitude to Ann Wilkinson, who has once again let me interview her on the continuing effects on her family, and many others through her, of the miracle for her child through Padre Pio's intercession. Equal thanks to daughter Kelly for her honest sharing of what it is like to be a miracle child. Thanks also to the unnamed American and her family for sharing on the same topic.

Gratitude to editor Dave Came of the Divine Mercy Shrine in Stockbridge, Massachusetts, for putting out the always inspirational *Marian Helper* magazine from the shrine. I am indebted to both Dave and to shrine director Marian Fr. Michael Gaitley for the basic material that let me refer to Fr. Gaitley's dad's miracle and summarize healings through the Marians' founder, now Bl. Stanislaus Papczynski, especially the one that led to the Polish priest's beatification. Thanks also to Megan Carlotta there. Also gratitude to the Marians and the healthcare professionals for making available to me and others (see sources) detailed first-person accounts of John Paul II's beatification miracle.

Salesian Sisters, Daughters of Mary, Help of Christians Sr. Rachel Racrotti, Sr. Lucy M. Roces, and Sr. Brittany Harrison. For their memories of Mother Troncatti, thanks also to the Salesian Bulletin U.S.A's and online testimonies by still-living Br. Cosimo Cossu, Fr. John Vigna, and Fr. Angelo Botta.

Although I won't name them—that privacy thing again!—my thanks first to Stratford Caldecott, who, as my Sophia editor, asked me to include St. Luigi Scrosoppi in this book, and to the congregation in England who provided the material on the first AIDS miracle to play a role in raising a saint to the altars. Also thanks to the order of "Father

Phillip" and all those in the African nation where he studied for and was ordained to the priesthood for their assistance in getting all the facts, even if I answered the miracle recipient's plea for protection by dropping all the particulars that might have made locating him possible.

For her enthusiastic help regarding miracles through Fulton Sheen, my thanks to Karen Fulte of El Paso, Illinois, who sent me Sheen's autobiography and to Paul Funfsinn, who put her in touch with me. Thanks to the director of the Archbishop Sheen Foundation, who also gave me needed information on the Sheen Peoria diocesan museum and the Cause there, and vice-postulator of Sheen's Cause Fr. Andrew Apostoli, C.F.R.

Theologian Tom Nash has helped me again for this book, this time regarding comments on Padre Pio by theologian Monika Hellwig. Also lending me her knowledge and talent again is my friend Barbara Crowe, whose reading of the manuscript and comments, as always, proved so useful for clarity and style. Similarly I am grateful to my daughter, Katherine Wilson, for reading portions of the manuscript in her busy schedule and her always helpful comments. I thank friends Francis X. Levy and wife Mary, he for technically backing up my work and both for prayer backup. Also for prayer, thanks to Katherine, Barbara, and many others, including the late Fr. Jerome Young, O.S.B., of Mt. Angel Abbey, Oregon, and Alice Williams, who must also be thanked for sharing what God did for her through "soaking prayer." Charles Abercrombie of *The Voice of Padre Pio*, Pio's friary's English-language publication, must be thanked again for prior materials (condensed here) provided along with permission by the friars for their use. And once again I am in the debt of my friend, fellow author, and outstanding researcher, Trappist Fr. Martinus Cawley of Our Lady of Guadalupe Abbey, Oregon. Regarding some of the changes in requirements for miracles in the Causes of saints, my thanks to the vice-postulators for Fr. Seelos, Fr. Solanus, and Br. André for materials and to expert Matthew Bunson, author of several encyclopedias or other reference books on saints, for sharing some of his knowledge.

Thanks are theirs! Any mistakes are mine!

An Invitation

Reader, the book that you hold in your hands was published by Sophia Institute Press. Sophia Institute seeks to nurture the spiritual, moral, and cultural life of souls and to spread the Gospel of Christ in conformity with the authentic teachings of the Roman Catholic Church.

Our press fulfills this mission by offering translations, reprints, and new publications that afford readers a rich source of the enduring wisdom of mankind.

We also operate two popular online Catholic resources: CrisisMagazine.com and CatholicExchange.com.

Crisis Magazine provides insightful cultural analysis that arms readers with the arguments necessary for navigating the ideological and theological minefields of the day. *Catholic Exchange* provides world news from a Catholic perspective as well as daily devotionals and articles that will help you to grow in holiness and live a life consistent with the teachings of the Church.

Sophia Institute Press also serves as the publisher for the Thomas More College of Liberal Arts and Holy Spirit College. Both colleges provide university-level education under the guiding light of Catholic teaching. If you know a young person seeking a college that takes seriously the adventure of learning and the quest for truth, please bring these institutions to his attention.

www.SophiaInstitute.com
www.CatholicExchange.com
www.CrisisMagazine.com

Sophia Institute Press® is a registered trademark of Sophia Institute.
Sophia Institute is a tax-exempt institution as defined by the
Internal Revenue Code, Section 501(c)(3). Tax I.D. 22-2548708.